STO

9-30-68

The Future of Small Business

PRAEGER SPECIAL STUDIES IN
U.S. ECONOMIC AND SOCIAL DEVELOPMENT

The Future of Small Business

Edward D. Hollander and others

Prepared by
Robert R. Nathan Associates, Inc.

FREDERICK A. PRAEGER, Publishers
New York · Washington · London

The purpose of the Praeger Special Studies is to make specialized research monographs in U.S. and international economics and politics available to the academic, business, and government communities. For further information, write to the Special Projects Division, Frederick A. Praeger, Publishers, 111 Fourth Avenue, New York, N.Y. 10003.

FREDERICK A. PRAEGER, PUBLISHERS
111 Fourth Avenue, New York, N.Y. 10003, U.S.A.
5, Cromwell Place, London S.W. 7, England

Published in the United States of America in 1967
by Frederick A. Praeger, Inc., Publishers

Second printing, 1968

Library of Congress Catalog Card Number: 66-26563

Printed in the United States of America

1480920

ACKNOWLEDGMENTS

This study is the work of many staff members of Robert R. Nathan Associates in addition to the principal author. Chief among the contributors were Mrs. Mary Lou Munts, whose painstaking analysis of the anatomy of small business appears in Chapters 3, 4, and 5 and who edited the entire manuscript in the absence of the principal author from the country; Dr. Malcolm D. Rivkin, who is responsible for Chapter 9; Mrs. Eleanor F. Silverman, who prepared the section on "Small Business and Labor"; Mrs. Ruth V. Lyons, who assembled the basic statistics, including Appendixes A and B; David L. Chewning and Gary L. Damkoehler, who contributed the section on "Small Business Organization and Management"; and Jeremy C. Ulin, who contributed to several sections of Chapter 8.

Robert R. Nathan and Dr. Franz B. Wolf participated in the design of the analyses and, with Jerome Jacobson, reviewed and greatly improved the manuscript. Dr. Peter Newman probed the theoretical literature and contributed significantly to the framework of analysis.

Miss Betty C. Churchill served as a consultant, bringing to the study her expertise as an analyst of the business population.

Miss Patricia Dobrosky prepared the Bibliography.

Mrs. Pauline K. Lloyd prepared the manuscript for publication with uncommon patience and skill.

Dr. Padraic Frucht of the Small Business Administration and his staff reviewed the preliminary draft, and the study is much the better for their insights and criticisms. However, the analyses and conclusions are the responsibility of the authors. The authors gratefully acknowledge the courtesy of the Small Business Administration in releasing the study for publication, with the explicit understanding that it in no way represents the policies or views of the Small Business Administration or its officials.

Edward D. Hollander

Washington, D.C.

CONTENTS

LIST OF TEXT TABLES

LIST OF CHARTS

INTRODUCTION

This study was undertaken in 1964-65 by Robert R. Nathan Associates, Inc. under contract with the Small Business Administration to analyze the principal economic factors affecting the freedom of entry, the viability and the prospects for small business as such, and to project these factors forward to the early 1970's in order to appraise the outlook for small business.

Specifically, the undertaking was to examine small business in an economic context. This is somewhat different from an examination in a political context (e.g., small business in terms of Jeffersonian ideology) or in a social context (e.g., small business as a breeder of the middle class), although both political and social conditions enter into economic considerations, as will be seen. In this study we have attempted to approach the subject of small business through an analysis of the factors and institutions of the market—the market for goods and services primarily, but also the capital market and the labor market—which have a significant effect on the viability of small business.

It should be noted that by its terms of reference and framework of analysis this is a study of the impact of economic forces on small business, not of the impact of small business on the economy. Hence, it is not concerned primarily with such questions as the role of small business as innovator and competitor in the economy but rather with the reverse: the effect of innovation and competition on small business. Again, the two aspects cannot be entirely disentangled; but they are not the same, and the focus and emphasis here are on the latter aspect.

Neither is the present study mainly concerned with the effects of bigness and concentration. That is a subject of critical importance, and most of the past analyses of business scale and of size distribution have been addressed to it. Obviously, bigness and concentration—separately and in combination—impinge on small business as supplier, customer, or competitor, and these relationships are considered in the analysis of the terms of coexistence of small business with big. But beyond these relationships lies an area of inquiry into the factors shaping the future of small business which are not merely the obverse of the factors making big business big.

In short, this study is focused on small business as such: its anatomy, its behavior, its place in the American economy, its strengths and disabilities, and the forces at work in the American community which affect it differentially and will principally determine its future.

The analysis falls into three phases. The first is concerned with the characteristics (apart from size, per se) which differentiate small business from large, in terms of viability, growth, profitability, etc., as well as age and industrial and market characteristics.

The second is concerned with the forces at work and their differential impact on small business. The forces to be identified may be purely economic (e.g., the rates and directions of economic growth and structural changes in demand and markets). Or they may be primarily technological (e.g., the effects of innovation) or social (e.g., the trends in growth and urbanization of population). Or they may arise from decisions of public policy (e.g., the effects of general or selective Government procurement policies or Federal monetary and tax policies). In each case, an effort has been made to focus as specifically as possible on the economic consequences of these forces as they affect small business, favorably or unfavorably.

Third, the study attempts to forecast or project the significant factors into the future and to infer their effects on the outlook for small business for the next five to ten years.

One observer has summed up the trend by saying, "The large firms have grown larger and the small firms more numerous."

The fact that the existence and persistence of small business is compatible with the existence and growth of big business does not account for the size distribution of American business at any given time. A number of factors have been shown to have a bearing on the size distribution.

First, our mass economy, with its advanced technology, generates wide variations among industries and markets in the size of business required for optimum efficiency. To some extent, therefore, the size distribution of business is a function of the distribution by industry and by markets.

Second, the very high rates of births and infant deaths and the rising life expectancy among older firms would tend to produce a population heavily weighted with young (and, therefore, small) firms, and with relatively fewer old (and, therefore, large) firms with a high expectancy of growing older and larger.

Third, to the extent that a process of economic "natural selection" determines survival of firms within any size class, the older and larger firms would tend to have increasing advantages of management, financing, and other elements that enable businesses to take advantage of opportunities for growth. In this sense, the same factors of rapidly growing markets and rapidly developing technology that breed small firms breed large firms among the survivors.

Fourth, firms of various sizes and in various industries have differential abilities to withstand "predatory" and "pathogenic" influences such as depressions, wars, inflations, etc.

Beyond these economic or market factors that may account in part for the persistent shape of the business size distribution, there are factors outside the market. Some of these have their basis in financial rather than business motivation: for example, the role of financial promoters in engineering the mergers and conglomerations of existing firms and the pressures of funds seeking investment outlets. Some have their basis in the differential effects of the tax laws. Some have their basis in "antimarket" practices by which large businesses use their economic and political power to secure or enhance their market position against each other or against small business as competitor, customer, or supplier. Some, of course, have their basis in public policy, explicitly through such protective devices as the Small Business Administration and the antitrust laws, and implicitly by such regulatory devices as "certificates of public convenience and necessity" or by tariffs, patents, and Government procurement and research. Clearly, it is impossible to account for the size distribution of the business population on the basis of market factors alone.

xix

Even if the size distribution of business changes little in the next decade, as may well be the case, the composition of small business may change a great deal. In some of its traditional sectors, small business may remain static or decline (for example, food and drug retailing) as the forces of vertical and horizontal integration proceed; but even in these sectors, growing populations and rising incomes will create markets for specialized consumer demands of new kinds in new places. In other sectors, growth may occur primarily among small businesses, particularly in business and consumer services.

Life in the interstices of the economy is not always sheltered and may be precarious, not only because the interstice may be crowded with enterprising small businessmen but also because of the superior and sometimes predatory power of big business. The rewards of survival may be great, but the odds are often long and businessmen are constantly searching for ways to shorten them. Some of these are shortcuts, like resale price maintenance, which are not likely to be permanently effective because they try to suppress market forces that resist suppression. Some are through legal protections against predatory or discriminatory practices, which, though not ubiquitous, are not without effect. Some are designed special aids, such as set-asides and credit and management assistance from the Small Business Administration.

Increasingly, small business is finding ways to improve its chances of survival by a variety of interbusiness accommodations. These generally result in shifting the balance point between integration and differentiation—sometimes toward the former, as in the case of producer- or retailer-owned cooperatives; more often toward the latter, as in the case of leased or franchised operations or a location in a shopping center. It is characteristic of these accommodations that the small businessman trades away part of his independence and perhaps part of his profit in return for reducing his risk. The variety of the arrangements is great, ranging from near-independence to near-captivity, from those situations in which the small businessman reserves most of the decision to himself to those in which he is not much more independent than a branch manager.

Small businesses now require for their success a command of many of the techniques of management and a degree of sophistication unknown even a generation ago. At the same time, the small businessman has at his disposal a wide range of specialized services to complement his own management, and to provide him sophisticated equipment and services not greatly different from those available to larger businesses: business supply and systems specialists; accounting, merchandising and marketing services; engineering and laboratory services; advertising; and packaging. In fact, furnishing such expert services is in itself one of the principal fields of small business opportunity.

Even given the soundness of the venture, adequacy of financing, skill of management, and a favorable economic and political environment, the small business encounters disadvantages in an economy in which big business plays so prominent a role in so many sectors. In many cases the small businessman is dealing with suppliers or customers with greater bargaining power. He may have to defend his market against the threat of large business competition. Increasingly he must deal with big banks, big insurance companies, big transportation companies. The demands on his enterprise, adaptability, and managerial skill are growing; the penalties of mistakes are severe.

Nevertheless, the evidence indicates that notwithstanding the hazards confronting the individual small businessman, small business as a class has a permanent, secure, and useful place in the business structure of the United States. The business population may be likened to a forest of many small trees and a few large ones, in which the survival and perpetuation of the stand of trees as a whole is assured although any individual tree may face severe competition for survival. The density of the stand and the mixture of sizes depend on the space, the ecology of soil and water, and the resistance to natural enemies. In the same way, the health of the business population—and especially of its smaller and more vulnerable members—depends on the maintenance of a favorable economic, political, and social environment.

Many aspects of this subject have been extensively documented in the past by the Small Business Administration itself or through research it has contracted for, by the Small Business Committees of both houses of Congress, by many agencies of government, and by the economics profession. Indeed, a great deal of the effort that has gone into the present study has been applied to a canvass and a sampling of the very extensive literature of statistics and research. Some topics were found to have been extremely well documented; others less so. Where the evidence was found to have been thoroughly developed in the past (notably, for example, on the subject of small business financing), the treatment in the present study has been addressed mainly to the inferences and conclusions that might reasonably be drawn from the existing evidence. Where a subject was found to be less fully treated in the literature (for example, on the effect of metropolitanization on small business), it was found necessary to develop the subject further. Consequently, the length of the various chapters and sections should not be taken as the measure of the intrinsic importance attached to the respective topics.

The Future of Small Business

CHAPTER **1** SMALL BUSINESS WITHIN
THE
DYNAMIC ECONOMY

The position and survival of small business presented no problem in the centuries preceding the industrial revolution. With but a few exceptions, all business was small business in the relatively static economies of the pre-industrial era. Big business emerged and small business encountered problems of smallness only as the increasing application of scientific research and its results generated modern technology and, with it, a highly dynamic economy.

For a hundred years it has been apparent that powerful forces in the United States economy have been working toward a greater integration of production and distribution into large units which have grown steadily larger. It has been widely recognized and amply documented that this has resulted from technological, economic, institutional, and political developments characteristic of the modern dynamic economy. Indeed, few questions of economic change and few issues of economic policy have received greater attention. It is less widely recognized, however, that the modern dynamic economy also has set in motion pervasive and persistent forces working toward differentiation in the processes of production and distribution—forces which constantly create new opportunities for small business.

As advancing technology has penetrated the economy, it has increased productivity and raised the standard of living, thus broadening the markets for the products and services of business. The more developed the technology and the broader the market, the greater the opportunities for specialization. In the past the printer achieved economies of scale by combining a newspaper with a job printing business. As the market grew and printing technology developed, the newspaper-job printer was replaced by a newspaper publisher and a commercial printer. Now, with a still broader market and more advanced printing equipment, even a large newspaper may buy Sunday supplements from a specialist; and in place of one kind of commercial printer, we have a variety of specialists in typesetting, stereotyping or engraving, in printing envelopes or business forms,

1

in duplicating, or any one of the many other separate lines that have developed in the printing industry. So in many other businesses; for example, the general metal shop has been supplemented by a variety of specialists in casting, forging, machining, stamping, finishing, and so on.

Generally, as the economy grows, products and services for which the demand previously was too small to support specialized operations attain a market size which offers new economies of scale and opportunities for specialization, particularly in the form of specialized techniques, equipment, and marketing. Existing firms find it to their advantage to externalize functions to specialists operating under more nearly optimum cost conditions. The resulting specialized firms may grow with the market, horizontally or vertically or both, as further economies of scale present themselves and provide opportunities for internal economies of production and distribution. But a growing market and changing technology generate new opportunities for economies in further specialization, and production subdivides in a new generation of small businesses.

The relationships between size, specialization, and economies of scale, internal or external, vary from time to time, from place to place, from product to product and market to market, and between one technology and another; and they are constantly changing. At a given stage of the market, technology searches for specialized means of lowering costs which, depending on the investment required, may change the scale at which costs of various functions are minimized. For some firms, this scale can be achieved internally; others achieve it by externalizing certain functions to specialists, reserving internally those functions which they can perform at or near minimum cost.

At the same time the market keeps on growing, encouraging further division of technology, function, and product, and a new set of cost-quantity relationships which again call into question the division of economies for any given firm between the internal and the external. Minimum costs are perpetually in a state of unstable equilibrium as the market and the technology change. As a result, a continuous interplay between the forces of integration and the forces of differentiation modifies time and again the structure of the economic activities supplying goods and services.

The growth of the market has comparable effects on the characteristics of demand as well. Demand increases in the aggregate, but also tends to become more specialized, particularly in an economy in which the increments to income resulting from rising productivity are widely distributed. This quality of demand—that is both massive and specialized—is the most conspicuous characteristic of the United States economy and is appearing also in other advanced economies. The market is so massive that it permits continual subdivision with little or no sacrifice of economies of scale. The combination of high wages, high incomes, and increased leisure has led to specialized demands for producers' and consumers' goods and services on a scale so vast that even a small fraction of the market in any industry may be large enough to support enterprises providing specialized knowledge, skills, processes, and equipment. This is true not only of end-products, but also of materials, parts, components, and finishes; of packaging, advertising, marketing, and distribution; of research and accounting; and of maintenance and repair.

The continuous interplay of market and technological changes creates opportunities for small business in the interstices of the mass-production, mass-distribution economy, even in the face of the well-known concentration of economic resources and economic power in giant corporations. This is not to imply that the dominant position of a few firms has no effect on small business, but to recognize that, in a dynamic economy with comparative freedom of entry in many sectors, the bigness of big business in some sectors is not incompatible with the persistence of small business in others. As Gideon Rosenbluth observed:

> Concentration, over-all, has not increased (greatly, at any rate) . . . and the number of small firms definitely has increased . . . If the share of the largest 200 firms, say, has not changed, and the number of firms has increased, this share is now held by a smaller percentage of the firms . . . As far as the problems confronting small business are concerned, this increase in inequality of size, which has continued . . . is, of course, very important. The large firms

have grown larger, and the small firms
more numerous.[1]

As a matter of fact, even in a period of such kaleidoscopic
economic and technological change as the decade after World
War II, there was no significant change in the size distribution
of the total business population of the United States or in the distribution of employment by size of firm. And, as far as can be
determined, there has been no significant change in the past
decade, in spite of market differences in the relative sizes of
the various sectors of the economy.

As long as technology of production, distribution, and
marketing continues to evolve while the market continues to
grow, the interaction of integrating and differentiating factors
can be expected continually to generate opportunities for small
business. While the integrating factors will cause more businesses of medium and large size to impinge on small business,
the differentiating factors will continue to provide interstitial
markets in which small businesses not only can compete, but
can reinforce one another by external economies of scale
arising from specialization. This is not a projection of the
status quo; it is a projection of the dynamics of change.

SMALL BUSINESS DEFINED

Because it is mainly concerned with the function of small
business within the economy, this study uses a functional,
analytical definition of small business, rather than a quantitative, descriptive one.[2] For this purpose, "small business"
refers mainly to enterprises that:

1. are businesses, in the sense that they involve all or
   most of the business functions and decisions concerning
   production, marketing, financing, and management; and

---

[1]Gideon Rosenbluth, "The Trend in Concentration and Its Implications for Small Business," Law and Contemporary Problems, XXIV
(Winter, 1959), p. 205.

[2]For a full discussion of the problems of definition, see Eleanor
J Stockwell, "What Is 'Small' Business?" in Financing Small Business
(1958).

2. do not exceed a size which, considering the nature of the business, permits personalized management in the hands of one or a few executives, as opposed to institutionalized management characteristic of larger enterprises.

This definition expresses the essential quality which differentiates small business as a component of the United States economy. It recognizes that neither amount of assets, nor volume of sales, nor number of employees alone delineates a "small business" in the context of this study. A building maintenance contractor with 500 employees engaged in routine maintenance operations may be a "small business" just as much as a manufacturer of specialized electronic components with fifty employees engaged in highly technical production, or a building materials wholesaler with a large turnover and a wide range of merchandising and financing risks and decisions. Any of these can be considered a "small business" in that the entrepreneur(s) can themselves, if they choose, operate and manage the business, make the essential decisions, and retain the rewards or bear the losses of their risk-taking and management.   By this definition the vast majority (upward of 95 per cent) of American businesses are "small."

Small business, thus defined, is self-initiated, largely self-financed, and self-managed. In this sense it is an expression of the open society and the enterprise economy. Just as the big or giant business exists by virtue of its institutionalized skills and financial and market power, the small business exists by virtue of its personalized skills and its market adaptability. It does not ordinarily wish to share with outsiders the ownership, control, or returns of the business, or the decisions with respect to the disposition of resources and earnings.

This definition does not limit the analysis by arbitrary quantitative limits. It permits focusing on the essential characteristics that distinguish small business in the various sectors and the factors which determine these characteristics. It has the analytical advantage of making it possible to use data from a variety of sources, not always strictly comparable, and to use the data most appropriate for each sector, including classification of firms by size. It facilitates identification from sector to sector of small business and the factors affecting it.

The definition used for this study applies to businesses of certain characteristics regardless of whether they are larger

or smaller than other businesses in the same or other industries. The smallest firm in an industry of large firms (e.g.,
automobile manufacturing) may still be a large business and
excluded by the present definition. Similarly, the largest firms
in an industry of small firms might qualify as "small" by
this definition.

Defining small business in this way has several disadvantages. In the first place, it does not necessarily conform to the
various statutory and administrative definitions which, per-
force, must be descriptively precise even if they are analytically
ambiguous. Conceptually, administrative definitions are addressed, at least in part, to the effect of "small business" on
the economy, in respect to competition and monopoly and the
price system, rather than to the effect of the economy on small
business, which is the focus of the present study.

A more serious limitation of the present definition is that
it is ambiguous in its application to a very large fraction of the
business population as it is recognized in law and documented
in statistics; namely, firms which in varying degrees are forms
of self-employment rather than business enterprises properly
so-called. These are clearly identifiable even though they are
not precisely defined. They are the small establishments that
are the means by which the proprietors create a market for
their personal skills. These establishments are, without doubt,
small; the question is whether they are businesses. In many
cases they involve a limited range of the common entrepreneurial and managerial functions and decisions of financing,
control, marketing, etc.—the neighborhood beauty shop, for
example. They are not unimportant; on the contrary, they are
a means by which the enterprise economy provides an opportunity for individuals to combine their enterprise and their
skill to fill a market need and thereby earn a living for themselves and give employment to others. On the other hand, they
differ in many ways from small firms which are "full-
functioning" businesses.

The limiting case and the largest component of "little"
business is the self-employed person or firm with no payroll.
This group accounts for a substantial segment of the total firms
in the services, retail trade, and construction. The borderline
between "little" business and "small" business comes as the
number of employees and the asset size of the firm increase
to the point at which the owner becomes primarily a "manager,"

or must hire a manager. This borderline is necessarily imprecise and differs with the nature of particular businesses. But because of the usefulness of "little" business as an analytical distinction, we will attempt to distinguish it in this study wherever possible.

At the other end of the scale, the distinction between large business and small business is easily drawn; but in between lies "medium-sized" business. It is not always feasible to determine where "small business" ends and "medium-sized business" begins, nor is it necessary for the present purposes. If the characteristics of small business are clearly observed, they can be related to the factors in the economy from which they chiefly derive. In any event, it is necessary to bear in mind that small business, by any definition, includes all but a small fraction of the firms that make up the business population, and probably accounts for not far from half of employment in the private nonagricultural sector of the economy.[3]

The enterprises that are the principal concern of this study are identifiable by certain characteristics relevant to the objectives of the study. They are, first, businesses, as defined by the range of their entrepreneurial and managerial functions. They are small, as defined by the personal span of their management and control. Individually, they are atoms in the economic structure; in the aggregate, their impact is very great. Their economic function is changing, but it does not follow that it is diminishing. They have in common certain characteristic opportunities and problems related to their smallness. These opportunities and problems are susceptible to policy and programmatic treatment for "small business."

It is a matter of definition in this study that the characteristics, opportunities, and problems of "small business" are not the obverse of those of "big business" and concentration of economic power. The problems generated by bigness and concentration are of the greatest political and economic importance, but they do not constitute the main source of the problems

---

[3] For example, in 1958 about 40 per cent of employees in firms covered by the business censuses were in firms with less than 100 employees. These censuses cover roughly two thirds of the private nonagricultural economy; the remaining third contains many sectors in which small firms predominate.

of small business. Small business would have problems of smallness even if big business were not so big. This is not to say that bigness, per se, is without its effects on small business. Small firms may be competitors, suppliers, or customers of big ones, and in these relationships the bigness of big firms or their dominant position in the market impinges explicitly or implicitly on the operation of the small firms.

2

THE ANATOMY
OF
SMALL BUSINESS

SMALL BUSINESS IN THE BUSINESS POPULATION

Most businesses in the United States, by far, are small. Although the available statistical measures differ in definitions and coverage, they all point to this single conclusion. If, for example, the dividing line is set at 100 employees, small units account for 90 per cent or more of the units in every industry division.[1] The average employment per unit is about thirteen, and in no industry division except manufacturing does the average exceed twenty-five.

Even though most businesses are small, it cannot be said that small business is predominant in the United States economy. A great deal of economic output is in the hands of a comparatively few very large firms. In manufacturing, for example, though over 70 per cent of firms are very small (with fewer than twenty employees), about 70 per cent of the employment is concentrated in firms with 250 or more employees, which comprise only about 3 per cent of manufacturing firms.[2] Nevertheless, there are large segments of business in which small firms play the major part—in wholesale and retail trade and service industries, for example, in which small business accounts for all but a handful of firms and in which nearly half of the employment is in firms with fewer than twenty employees. Moreover, even in industries dominated by large firms, there are segments in which small firms persist and flourish, as will be shown in detail below.

---

[1] These data are from County Business Patterns, 1962, and for this reason overstate the number of firms and understate their size in industry divisions (e.g., retail trade) where multi-unit firms are important. See Appendix A. This, however, does not materially affect the conclusions.

[2] There are unavoidable differences between statistics from different sources because of differences in coverage and definition. Conclusions take this into account.

Table 1

NUMBER OF REPORTING UNITS, 3/ AVERAGE SIZE AND PER CENT OF UNITS WITH FEWER THAN 100 EMPLOYEES, BY INDUSTRY DIVISION — 1947, 1953, AND 1962

	All Covered Industries	Contract Construction	Manufacturing	Transportation, Communications & Utilities	Wholesale Trade	Retail Trade	Services	Finance	Mining
No. of Reporting Units (000's)									
1947	2,512.3	180.6	255.2	95.2	235.5	862.9	371.1	216.3	25.6
1953	2,939.6	263.2	285.7	104.0	239.1 4/	1,015.0	382.5	243.6	28.6
1962	3,347.6	296.1	289.7	122.3	284.0	1,052.0 5/	435.5	304.4	29.2
Average No. of Employees Per Unit									
1947	13.7	9.7	58.5	26.8	11.5	7.4	7.2	7.7	35.1
1953	13.6	9.0	60.6	27.3	11.9	7.4	7.1	8.5	29.8
1962	13.0	8.2	56.6	24.6	11.4	7.6	7.3	8.9	21.3
Per Cent of Units with Fewer than 100 Employees									
1947	98.2	98.9	90.4	96.4	98.7	99.4	99.3	99.1	93.5
1953	98.3	99.0	90.1	96.2	98.6	99.5	99.3	99.0	95.1
1962	98.3	99.2	90.0	96.6	98.8	99.4	99.2	99.0	96.5

3/ For definition and interpretation of Reporting Units, see Appendix A.

4/ This figure is not comparable to the total for 1947 due to reclassification, with part of wholesale merchants reclassified to ready-mix concrete in manufacturing and part of dry-goods-apparel reclassified to textile mill products.

5/ Milk pasteurization plants reclassified to manufacturing.

Source: County Business Patterns, 1947, 1953, 1962.

Table 2

PER CENT DISTRIBUTION OF COMPANIES BY INDUSTRY DIVISION
AND SIZE — 1958

Industry Division	All Companies		Companies With		
	Number (000's)	Per Cent	Under 20 Employees	20-249 Employees	250 Employees and Over
All Industries	3,151.6	100	95	5	*
Mineral Industries	30.1	100	86	13	1
Manu- facturing	269.8	100	72	25	3
Public Ware- housing	7.5	100	86	14	*
Wholesale Trade	213.1	100	89	10	*
Retail Trade	1,688.3	100	97	3	*
Selected Services	942.8	100	98	2	*

* Less than 0.5 per cent. Percentages may not add to 100 due to
   rounding.
Source: Enterprise Statistics, 1958.

An examination of the anatomy of small business shows
that in the very smallest size classes, retail trade and services
account for nearly three fifths of the units. In the next size
classes, wholesale trade and manufacturing become prominent.
Manufacturing is the largest component among firms with 50-99
employees, and contains nearly half of firms with 100-249
employees. But even in that size class, retail trade and services account for about one fourth of all units.

Table 3

PER CENT DISTRIBUTION OF EMPLOYMENT BY INDUSTRY
DIVISION AND SIZE OF COMPANY — 1958

Industry Division	All Employees		Employees in Companies With		
	Number (000's)	Per Cent* of Employees	Under 20 Employees	20–249 Employees	250 or more Employees
All Industries	30,952.0	100	23	26	50
Mineral Industries	574.8	100	20	35	46
Manu- facturing	17,273.0	100	7	24	70
Public Ware- housing	99.9	100	33	47	20
Wholesale Trade	2,100.8	100	43	47	11
Retail Trade	8,034.1	100	47	23	30
Selected Services	2,869.4	100	46	34	20

*Percentages may not add up to 100 due to rounding.
Source: Enterprise Statistics, 1958.

These generalizations, of course, conceal the highly significant variability among divisions and subdivisions within these
broad categories. This variability in content and form of small
business and its significance for the future are analyzed in the
succeeding sections.

FACTORS AFFECTING INDUSTRY SIZE STRUCTURE AND
NUMBERS OF SMALL FIRMS

It is not within the province of this study to develop a theory
of size structure and its variations through time. This is a

Table 4

PER CENT DISTRIBUTION OF REPORTING UNITS $\underline{6/}$ BY EMPLOYMENT SIZE
CLASSES BY INDUSTRY DIVISION

	All Sizes	1-3	4-7	8-19	20-49	50-99	100-249	250-499	500 or More
All Industries*	100.0	100.0	100.0	100.0	100.0	100.0	100.0	100.0	100.0
Construction	8.8	8.9	9.4	8.9	8.3	7.5	5.5	2.9	1.5
Manufacturing	8.7	4.0	7.9	13.6	24.0	35.3	46.9	55.5	58.7
Transportation, Communications & Utilities	3.7	3.0	3.5	4.7	5.9	7.0	7.3	7.1	8.0
Wholesale Trade	8.5	6.4	10.2	13.0	13.1	10.3	7.3	4.2	2.3
Retail Trade	31.4	31.7	36.3	31.6	23.3	16.6	11.4	10.0	9.2
Services	25.8	30.6	21.9	18.2	15.7	14.5	13.7	13.1	13.2
Agriculture	.8	.9	.8	.6	.4	.2	.1	–	–
Mining	.9	.6	.8	1.4	1.7	1.9	1.8	1.9	1.6
Finance	9.1	10.8	7.2	6.5	6.6	6.5	5.9	5.2	5.4
Unclassified	2.4	3.0	2.0	1.5	.9	–	–	–	–

*Percentages may not add up to 100 due to rounding.
$\underline{6/}$ For definition and interpretation of Reporting Units, see Appendix A.

Source: County Business Patterns, 1962.

subject which has received some attention in the literature but on which there is no general agreement, either as to the relevant empirical data or their interpretation.

For our purposes it is important to have some framework for assessing the probable future of small business units in various sectors in the next five to ten years. At best we can isolate the relevant variables, and then use them for empirical analysis of particular sectors.

On the demand side are the size of the market and changes in demand through time, which may make the industry stable or fluctuating in the short run and growing or declining in the long run. On the supply side is the whole range of costs in the firm which determine economies of scale.

A market of limited size places immediate strictures on the size of the firm, and it is in such markets that small businesses have their greatest strength.

But it does not necessarily follow that a "limited" market produces a business of limited size, just as it does not follow that a vast market produces a firm of vast size. Even though a particular product, narrowly defined, has a limited market, one large firm can (and often does) produce for many such markets; or, if the limits of the market are geographic, horizontal integration can make a larger size firm possible.

The cost side of the firm must be examined to see if "limited" markets are likely to produce "limited" size firms. Economies of scale in direct operating cost may be possible if the various "products" going to different markets are closely enough related so that similar processes are used. Economies in marketing may be possible if the same marketing channels can be used for the different products.

Horizontal integration may produce economies of scale if the cost of management is reduced or if the integration confers some market power in the purchase of factors of production or in the sale of the product not available to the single-unit firm.

The small firm is more favored if the product or service is sufficiently differentiated so that it is not susceptible to easy combination with other products or services, either in production or sales. Management overhead costs may be lower in the small firm because of fewer layers of supervision.

Concomitantly, horizontal integration is most difficult where management of the single unit involves great complexity and risk, favoring the personalized management characteristic of small business.

Small firms also compete successfully in more extended product or service markets if there are economies of specialization but limited economies of scale, either internally or externally, for the larger-scale firm. This usually means that technology is relatively divisible, so that there are not significant economies of large scale in production, organization, research, and development. It usually means, too, that there are not significant cost advantages to a large-scale marketing organization, including branding and advertising.

The time dimension adds a further condition to the probable size distribution in a particular industry. Great variability of demand, either seasonally or cyclically, particularly when coupled with uncertainty regarding the product-mix and sales distribution, tends to keep the size of business units smaller. Because of the importance of the risk element, more personalized management has significant advantages. Furthermore, types of organization which reduce risk, such as subcontracting, may develop and further favor smallness of unit size.

The role of growth is more complex. Either rapid growth or a decline in demand may affect size structure. The effect depends in part on the size structure at the time of change, and in part on the age of the industry.

In a new industry (such as the various categories of electronics), a large initial growth takes place in the number of firms. As the market expands, and if economies of scale are possible, the more successful competitors increase their share of the market. Other firms remain small or may be forced out if they have not specialized in a more limited aspect of the industry, such as custom parts or components. However, in new industries where there are not substantial economies of scale, such as in most service industries, rapid growth does not result in a significant change in size structure.

In an older industry, in which scale is already larger, growth takes place to a greater extent through expansion in the size of existing firms, and new small firms generally enter and participate only peripherally. This is not only because of considerations of optimum scale, but also because problems of entry into a large-scale industry are so formidable.

Furthermore, within an industry with an uneven size distribution, financial factors often affect the growth rate of the small firm adversely. Since the small firm is largely dependent on internal financing for expansion, its rate of growth is limited, compared with a larger firm able to tap outside as well as internal resources.

In a declining industry, the relative cost position of firms in the industry determines whether a decline in production takes place largely through the elimination of small firms or a shrinking in numbers and volume of all firms. The small firms are likely to suffer most if the larger firms have benefited from lower costs as a result of more elaborate technology, or have been able to diversify into more profitable lines.

One of the serious problems in the analysis of size structure is the problem of defining the industry to be discussed. The discussion so far has assumed a highly disaggregated model with an industry for each commodity or service. But insofar as empirical data are concerned, analysis is limited to the definitions of the Standard Industrial Classification Manual. Even at the four-digit level, most categories are far from homogeneous. One category may include many products with distinctly separate markets. Thus, our analysis of changes in size structure, even at this level, may do violence to the facts since varied and distinct markets may be subsumed in the same figures.

Important gross changes in the numbers of small firms in particular categories depend on several simultaneous conditions, operating to a greater or lesser degree. For purposes of this study, it is useful to identify the categories in which important changes in numbers are likely to take place in the next decade.

Drawing on the earlier analysis, it may be concluded that a substantial growth in numbers of firms in a category is dependent on some combination of the following factors:

1. Growth of demand for the products or services in the category. This may be growth in demand for existing

products or services or additional demand for new products or services classified in the category. The latter is typical of highly heterogeneous manufacturing.

2. Lack of important economies of scale with growth in firm size; and, conversely, possible diseconomies of scale related to variability of demand, risk, or higher management overhead.

3. Ease of entry, with relatively limited capital required and management skills relatively available. Typically in the smallest firms, "little business" entrepreneurship follows from the learning of technical skills in wage employment in the same industry, as the carpenter becomes a contractor, the machinist becomes a machine shop, or the beauty shop operator starts her own shop.

A substantial decline in numbers of firms is dependent on a combination of the following factors:

1. Growth of demand for the product affecting the supply curve of existing firms in the range of increasing returns to scale. (This effect has been important in manufacturing in two groups. One is the group of relatively standard, consumer products, such as bread and milk, which historically had many small, local firms serving local markets. As the geographic market grew larger, many small firms were eliminated in competition with larger firms benefiting from mass distribution and brand promotion. The second important group in which small firms have been adversely affected by growth is the manufacture of consumer products, such as apparel, in which growth in the national market has made possible greater standardization and branding.)

2. A very slow rate of growth or a decline in demand for products or services in the category.

3. Changes within the firm or industry in technology, marketing, etc., which increase returns to greater size of firm. Such changes in the cost side of the firm or industry often work in tandem with changes in the demand side, described in (1) or (2).

4. Developments largely external to the firm and industry, such as in market distribution and transportation technology, which operate to increase returns to greater size of firm. Canning, for example, which historically had many small units widely dispersed because of a perishable source of supply, has had an attrition of small units with the development of the trucking industry and refrigerated storage facilities.

It should be noted that this group with declining numbers of firms includes both sectors with growing demand (1) and sectors with declining demand or very slow growth (2). As we have indicated, growth in demand can result in either an increase or a decrease in the numbers of firms, depending on its impact on returns to scale. A decline in demand could also theoretically increase as well as decrease the number of firms, even though profitability would be falling—for example, the pressure exerted by falling wage employment that drives workers to become self-employed.[7]

---

[7]Developing countries such as India, with millions of petty street vendors, indicate this possibility. But as long as alternative employment opportunities exist, this is not a serious possibility on a large scale for our economy.

CHAPTER **3** SMALL BUSINESS IN MANUFACTURING

INTRODUCTION

The prominent role of very large companies in manufacturing creates the popular image of the small business being eliminated by the large. But, in fact, the number of small firms continues to grow. Despite the predominant role of large companies in employment,[1] in 1958 companies with fewer than twenty employees were 72 per cent of total companies, and those with less than 250 employees were nearly 98 per cent.

Preliminary 1963 Census data are available only for establishments and not for companies, but they give some evidence of the continued growth of small firms in manufacturing. The number of establishments grew from approximately 298,000 in 1958 to approximately 310,000 in 1963. More than half of this net increase of 12,000 was in establishments with fewer than twenty employees, of which the great majority were single-unit companies.

This growth in the number of the smallest establishments from 1958 to 1963 is somewhat greater than the growth in the 1954-58 period. Nonetheless, when Census data on employment or value added by small companies (under 250 employees) are released, they will probably show a relative (although not an absolute) decline between 1958 and 1963 because, on balance, the major industry groups with large corporate strength have expanded more rapidly.

As indicated earlier, a role for small business units depends on a limited market size or advantages to the personalized management of small business. Because the large-scale business unit has been fostered in manufacturing by both mass markets and advanced technology, the extent and importance of small business units are often overlooked.

---

[1] See Appendix Table 5-C.

19

Table 5

SELECTED MANUFACTURING CATEGORIES WITH SUBSTANTIAL
NUMBERS OF SMALL BUSINESSES

I. LOCAL MARKETS

SIC Code	Category	Total Number, 1958		Per Cent of Value Added by Companies With Fewer Than 250 Employees, 1958	Per Cent of Establishments With Fewer Than 20 Employees, 1958
		Companies	Establishments		
A. LOCAL CONSUMER MARKETS					
2011	Meatpacking	2,646	2,801	38 2/	65
2013	Prepared Meats	1,430	1,494	70 2/	67
2021	Creamery Butter	990	1,058	78	78
2024	Ice Cream and Frozen Desserts	1,167	1,382	36	67
2026	Fluid Milk	5,157	5,816	49	62
2051	Bread Products	5,305	5,985	37	64
2071	Confectionery Products	1,327	1,390	35	70
2086	Bottled and Canned Soft Drinks	3,994	4,362	73	68
2097	Manufactured Ice	1,099	1,570	59	89
2711	Newspapers	7,947	8,250	32	79
	Total		34,108		70

Table 5 (Cont.)

B. LOCAL BUSINESS MARKETS

2751	Commercial - Press	12,878	13,002	61	87
2752	Commercial - Lithograph	3,696	3,746	79	73
2753	Engraving and Plate Printing	520	528	71	81
2791	Typesetting	1,181	1,188	94	79
2793	Photoengraving	897	914	93	71
2794	Electrotyping	206	226	69	51
2993	Signs and Advertising	2,691	2,725	91	83
	Total	22,329	22,329		77

C. LOCAL CONSTRUCTION MARKETS

2431	Millwork	3,112	3,163	74	77
2951	Paving and Mixture Blocks	415	563	86	84
3251	Brick	468	569	64	24
3271	Concrete Block and Brick	1,763	1,796	95	81
3272	Concrete Products	3,184	3,455	71	82
3273	Ready Mixed Concrete	3,120	3,647	87	74
	Total	13,193	13,193		76

Table 5 (Cont.)

SIC Code	Category	Total Number, 1958		Per Cent of Value Added by Companies With Fewer Than 250 Employees, 1958	Per Cent of Establishments With Fewer Than 20 Employees, 1958
		Companies	Establishments		
	D. LOCAL METAL SERVICE MARKETS				
Fabricated Metal Service					
3441	Fabricated Structural Steel	1,793	1,861	50	58
3444	Sheet Metal Work	3,075	3,159	73	78
3449	Miscellaneous Metal Work	1,532	1,591	52	75
3451	Screw Machine Products	1,785	1,792	86	77
3461	Metal Stampings	2,372	2,456	45	58
3471	Plating and Polishing	2,614	2,646	94-95	80
3479	Metal Coating and Engraving	986	1,003	83	81
3499	Fabricated Metals, n.e.c.	962	974	56	78
3544	Special Dies and Tools	5,715	5,745	81	84
3565	Industrial Patterns	1,170	1,174	99	92
3591	Machine Shops	10,098	10,151	73	89
	Total		32,552		81

Table 5 (Cont.)

D. LOCAL METAL SERVICE MARKETS (continued)

Primary Metal Service

3321	Gray Iron Castings	1,211	1,310	41 2/	35
3361	Aluminum and Aluminum Base Castings	934	955	51	70
3362	Copper and Copper Base Castings	647	665	69	69
3369	Nonferrous Castings, n.e.c.	337	345	45	61
3399	Primary Metals, n.e.c.	567	581	84-86	74
	Total		3,856		58

Table 5 (Cont.)

II. CATEGORIES IN PART LOCATED BY SOURCE OF RAW MATERIALS

SIC Code	Category	Total Number, 1958		Per Cent of Value Added by Companies With Fewer Than 250 Employees, 1958	Per Cent of Establishments With Fewer Than 20 Employees, 1958
		Companies	Establishments		
2015	Poultry	1,095	1,233	59	52
2022	Natural and Processed Cheese	1,026	1,203	63	87
2031	Canned and Cured Seafood	303	333	40	50
2033	Canned Fruits, Vegetables	1,315	1,607	44 2/	43
2036	Fresh or Frozen Packaged Fish	429	440	73	49
2037	Frozen Fruits and Vegetables	347	426	36 2/	48
2042	Prepared Animal Foods	2,016	2,379	46	70
2041	Flour and Other Grain	703	814	41 2/	69
2084	Wines, Brandy, Spirits	216	239	61	70
2094	Grease and Tallow	461	539	67	68
	Total	9,213			62

Table 5 (Cont.)

2411	Logging Camp and Contractors	12,627	12,805	83	96
2421	Sawmills and Planing Mills	15,371	15,636	67	84
2426	Hardwood Dimensions and Flooring Mills	415	436	64	40
2429	Special Product Sawmills, n.e.c.	418	478	80	78
2432	Veneer and Plywood	513	588	43	24
	Total		29,943		87
3281	Cut Stone and Stone Products	959	1,001	74	76

2/ This is the per cent of value added by companies with fewer than 500 employees.

Source: U. S. Census of Manufactures, 1958; and Small Business Administration, Size of Structure of Manufacturing Industries in the U.S., 1958.

In projecting what may happen to small business units in manufacturing in the next five to ten years, it is necessary to isolate the segments in which small business units have their greatest strength, and see whether particular segments are vulnerable, likely to remain stable, or show promise of growth.

The largest group of firms is in categories serving local markets, where the size of the market has been limited by local demand and income levels. A second group with a large small business component has been in categories in which, historically, firms were many and widely scattered because of very dispersed sources of raw materials. The third group with significant small business strength has been in categories with regional or national product markets, but with limited market size or highly differentiated products, often with a highly uncertain product-mix.

Firms in the first two groups cut across the usual major industry groups, and have been separately grouped by four-digit SIC categories for analytical purposes. Although there were only fifty-five four-digit SIC categories in these groups, they represented about 40 per cent of the total establishments in manufacturing in 1958,[3] and for this reason have been analyzed in some detail.

METHOD

No adequate time series is available for examining trends in size structure in manufacturing. The 1958 Enterprise Statistics, and the special SBA tabulations of four-digit and five-digit categories from the 1958 Census provide documentation for that single year, but there are no comparable earlier data.

The statistical material on which this analysis is based, therefore, has some limitations. Four-digit categories have been analyzed by a time series of Census establishment data

---

[3]See Table 5. Most of those categories were predominantly small, with 50 per cent or more of value added by companies with fewer than 250 employees; however, several "large-scale" categories have been included in which there were 1,000 or more small units.

for 1947, 1954, 1958, and for 1963, when available.[4] County
Business Patterns for 1959 and 1962 have been used to supplement this information where preliminary 1963 Census data
were not yet available.

This series used the total number of establishments and the
number of establishments with fewer than twenty employees.[5]
The "under-twenty" figure was used for several reasons. It is
the only size breakdown available for preliminary Census
data for 1963. It is the only size category in which the over-
whelming number of establishments are also single-unit companies. It is also the size category in which 95 per cent of new
business entries in manufacturing[6] take place so that net
growth or decline in this group, and change in its per cent of
total establishments, can give some evidence about what is
happening to opportunities for small business in the category.

In addition to this time series, the 1958 SBA tabulation by
four-digit categories was used as a further source of information on value added by companies with fewer than 250 employees. Unfortunately, no smaller size breaks under 250 were
included in this tabulation, so that a link with the time series
of establishments under twenty was not possible.

LOCAL MARKET INDUSTRIES

Every community has historically had a range of manufacturing activity called "population serving."[7] These are, for

---

[4]Changes in industrial classification in 1957 made some of these
series incorrect for the whole period, but inclusion of both old and new
SIC figures from the 1958 Census makes it possible to have two dis-
continuous series.

[5]Figures on numbers of firms and net growth that have been used
in the text have been rounded off to the nearest 100.

[6]This was the per cent in the 1951-56 period. Betty Churchill,
"Size of Business Firms," Survey of Current Business (September,
1959), p. 18.

[7]This grouping was to some extent suggested by Woody Thompson's
excellent study, An Analysis of Environmental and Management Factors
in the Success or Failure of Small Manufacturing Enterprises, Small
Business Management Research Report (Iowa City, Iowa: University
of Iowa, September, 1963).

example, the local carbonated beverages, ice cream and milk plants, bakeries, newspapers, commercial printing, brick and concrete block plants, and machine shops.

This local manufacturing activity divides into two basic groups: four-digit categories in which most firms are oriented to a local consumer market, and those in which most firms are oriented to a local business or industrial market.[8]

The number of firms has been declining, and smaller firms are vulnerable in most categories with local firms oriented to a consumer market. On the other hand, the categories that are localized to serve business and industrial customers have almost all grown in the number of firms, except for some vulnerability in recession periods.

The group of manufacturing concerns oriented to a predominantly local consumer market had about 34,000 establishments in 1958. With the increased size of the market through urbanization and improved distribution through supermarket channels, the number of firms and, more specifically, the relative number of very small firms in this group has been quite vulnerable.

These categories have predominantly standardized products, so that enlargement of the market has usually meant elimination of the very smallest units, as there are economies of plant scale at least up to the range of 50 to 100 employees. Although optimum scale of plant is not large, for example, in baking, horizontal integration may also increase the size of firm, as a large-scale marketing organization has important advantages for the promotion of a brand name. (Such brand promotion, however, may be handled by alternative systems of organization, such as franchising or cooperatives.)

In creamery butter, fluid milk, bakery products, and bottled and canned soft drinks, the number of establishments with fewer than twenty employees has been declining at a more rapid rate than in the group as a whole.

----

[8]See Table 5 for the list of four-digit SIC categories in these groups.

Except for bottled and canned soft drinks, all these categories are very slow-growing (in the case of manufactured ice and creamery butter there was actually a decline in value added by manufacture between 1958 and 1963). This slow growth, combined with the impetus to greater scale given by increasing market size, means that a downward trend in numbers can be expected to continue in all these categories, with the smallest units the most severely affected. The key to survival of the small unit in these categories is concentration on the specialized, higher-margin products in which there are greater growth potential and the possibility of developing a local following.

Bottled and canned soft drinks, which dropped 1,700 establishments between 1947 and 1963, is a somewhat different case. It has been a category with much more rapid economic growth. The character of the industry has changed, with local companies producing local brands replaced by companies franchised by national firms who furnish the flavoring, conduct national advertising, etc. Companies have become larger, although still local and mostly "small" by employment size standards. The entire drop in the number of establishments has occurred in those with fewer than twenty employees. Demand for bottled and canned soft drinks will probably increase in the next decade at a more rapid rate than other beverages and most food products because of the increasing numbers of younger people and increased discretionary income. Nevertheless, size distribution will continue to show a decline in the smallest units— both because small, local brands are at a marketing disadvantage with national and supermarket brands, and because the expansion of the market area leads to greater scale of plant.

The only categories in which the smallest units have not suffered are meatpacking (SIC 2011) and prepared meats (SIC 2013). The number of the smallest establishments grew between 1947 and 1958 by more than 700; and, although County Business Patterns data indicate a dip after that, most of the decline had been regained by 1962. At the local level, small firms in these categories benefit from the limits of advantage to scale in fresh packing.[9] Also, it is not as profitable for

---

[9] The small, independent slaughterer has been favored by two developments: the decentralization of slaughtering as a result of trucking, and the development of grocery chains. By selling direct to the chains, the small slaughtering house has a cost advantage, because it operates without the elaborate distributive organization of the big packer.

supermarkets to integrate into meatpacking as into more concentrated, higher-margin industries.[10] For these reasons, it can be expected that local firms will not suffer the attrition at the local level that has occurred in other local food product firms. In fact, the greater anticipated growth in value added expected in meat products as compared with most other foods will probably cause some further increase in the number of small firms in the next decade.

Newspapers (SIC 2711) are the only other consumer product in this local group. There is an advantage to scale because of the importance of advertising revenue and its relation to circulation, so that daily newspapers vary in size in almost direct proportion to the size of the community. This advantage to scale, and also certain advantages to horizontal integration, has meant a gradual attrition in less successful metropolitan dailies, either through merger or failure. The total number of establishments has declined less than might be expected because of the persistence of the large number of weeklies, which are much smaller in scale and serve more limited populations. Nonetheless, total establishments declined by 500 and the very smallest establishments declined by almost 800 between 1954 and 1962.

With continuous growth in the size of the market served by dailies, and to some extent the larger weeklies as well, the number of establishments can probably be expected to decrease further with a more than proportionate decline in the smallest units and, more noticeably, an increase in value added by companies over 250.

In contrast to the local consumer market group, the number of firms in the four-digit categories primarily oriented to serving local business, construction, and industry has grown, and the trend appears likely to continue. Establishments in these categories totaled more than 72,000 in 1958. Growth in market size or in demand has resulted generally in an increase rather than a decrease in the number of firms. The advantages to scale in these categories are less significant because of specialized technology, highly differentiated products, or high risk.

---

[10]Willard F. Mueller and Leon Garoian, Changes in the Market Structure of Grocery Retailing (Madison, Wisconsin: University of Wisconsin Press, 1961), pp. 87-88.

Commercial printing (SIC 2751 and 2752), serving local business, has grown both in the number of establishments and in the relative number of very small establishments—increasing by 5,500 establishments between 1947 and 1963, of which 90 per cent were establishments with fewer than twenty employees. Continued high levels of economic growth can be expected to increase the number of firms into the 1970's, although with some increase in the share of business done by larger firms. Job printing firms may begin to feel some competitive pressure in that period from wider use of electronic data processing, copying, etc. Larger, independent printers will probably also continue the trend of the last five years to merge because of the financial and technological advantages (i.e., the high cost of new developments such as the web press).

The printing service categories (SIC 2791, 2793, 2794) will be affected by the pronounced trend in the industry toward offset printing, so that future growth will take place in typesetting (SIC 2791), while the number of companies in stereotyping, electrotyping (SIC 2794), and photoengraving (SIC 2793) will continue to decline.

Another growing four-digit category similar to commercial printing in the highly differentiated custom services performed for local business is signs and advertising displays (SIC 2993). It increased by 500 establishments between 1958 and 1963, with further expansion to be expected in this category in the next decade.

Concrete brick and block, concrete products, and ready-mixed concrete, brick, millwork, and asphalt and paving block are an important segment of small business activity at the local level, accounting for more than 13,000 establishments in 1958. The number of establishments suffered some decline during the recession of 1959 but had gained 1,700 establishments in the 1963 preliminary Census figures over the 1958 total for this category. The only declining group in this category is brick, which has suffered as a result of competition with the much smaller-scale concrete-products categories. Heavier residential construction expenditure anticipated for the late 1960's can be expected to increase substantially this group of establishments.

The largest four-digit group of local categories is the metal service "satellite" firms. [11] This group accounted for about a third of the net growth in the number of manufacturing establishments between 1947 and 1958. Many satellite firms are also included in other four-digit categories so that the effect of the great expansion of the metalworking sectors is only partially shown by this group.

The eleven four-digit fabricated metal categories which serve other metalworking firms, largely on a custom or job basis, had almost 33,000 establishments in 1958. In these eleven categories are about 60 per cent of the total establishments of two major industry groups, fabricated metals (SIC 34) and machinery other than electrical (SIC 35). They accounted for 60 per cent of the growth in numbers of establishments in these industry groups between 1947 and 1958. This group illustrates the degree to which small firms have participated in the growth of the metalworking sectors as a whole.

Scale is small because most of these firms are producing highly differentiated products and services, often on a custom basis. Many perform functions that may also be internalized by larger companies, but smaller companies can compete effectively because of lower management overhead and more personalized service. Small metal service companies may also act as an overflow valve for larger companies that cannot maintain an internal department on a continuous basis on the scale necessary to handle peak periods. Consequently, the small firm may be vulnerable in a slack period as, for example, when defense orders are being scaled back, since larger companies may internalize operations to use idle facilities. [12]

The greatest growth in the metal service categories was between 1947 and 1954, resulting from the very rapid growth

---

[11]This grouping was adapted with considerable change in the categories included from a group delineated by Zenon S. Malinowski and William Kinnaird, Jr., in "The Metal Service Industry—A Case Study of a Satellite Industry," American Machinist (1960).

[12]This tendency is limited by the importance of certain satellite suppliers to the large firm. Even though a temporary saving could be accomplished by internalization, the larger firm may prefer to maintain its customary relationship to its supplier.

of demand from both durable goods and construction. Growth was slower between 1954 and 1958, and the number dipped somewhat in the recession at the end of the decade. By 1962, the number of firms in this group was again equal to the number in 1958.

Because this group of firms is sensitive to up-and-down movements in construction and in the durables, particularly automobiles, its future growth will depend on these industries. The very rapid growth of the 1947-54 period will probably not be duplicated, but relatively favorable prospects for electrical machinery and automotive equipment and for construction toward the end of the decade make it likely that this group will expand considerably in the next decade.

The last group oriented to local industry is a related primary metal service group producing castings, with almost 4,000 establishments in 1958. Except for grey iron castings which is larger scale, this group is relatively small in both the number of establishments with fewer than twenty employees and in the high fraction of value added by companies with fewer than 250 employees. As contrasted with the rest of the metal service group, this has been a relatively stable group in terms of numbers with some decline in grey iron castings compensated by an increase in the nonferrous categories.

Grey iron castings has much more horizontal integration, but like the other categories, still has some small units serving a local, custom market. However, there has been a gradual decline in establishments in this category probably related to the expansion of the size of the market being served, and the economies of scale made possible. Further change may be expected along these lines in grey iron castings while the smaller-scale nonferrous categories will remain more stable, probably with some gradual growth.

INDUSTRIES LOCALIZED TO RAW MATERIALS

Another group of industries in which historically there have been many small firms are those which developed in response to relatively dispersed sources of raw material, particularly lumber and certain agricultural products, even though their products moved in wider markets.

This group of processing industries had many small units, dispersed by the need to limit costs of transportation, storage, and distribution. As this cost structure has altered, the number of firms, and especially of the smallest firms, has been reduced. This effect has been augmented in certain food categories and lumber by relatively stagnant demand.

In food processing, reduction in the number of small firms has resulted from economies of scale arising from improved storage and transportation (as in canning), greater concentration of agricultural production (as in boilers), and changed patterns of food distribution with greater volume being purchased by supermarkets rather than through intermediate channels. The very smallest firms have declined more than proportionately in some cases, particularly in poultry processing, since 1954.

Because many food products are standardized or, as in canning, because similar processes can be used for different products, economies of scale result from the larger units made possible by improved transportation and storage. The traditional use of brokers in the trade made it possible for small firms to produce one or very few canned items. The increasing importance of the retail chains, which buy direct, has encouraged the larger canner furnishing a complete line and selling in volume. On the other hand, increasing chain strength has a somewhat adverse effect on the largest horizontally integrated firm which promotes its label by advertising. By buying directly from canners, usually without an elaborate distributive organization, the chains sell under their own label, and can undersell the brand names.

This phenomenon explains why frozen foods is one category in which the number of small firms will probably continue to expand. As contrasted with the older food sectors, which started out with many small units, frozen food processing with its more elaborate technology was pioneered by large brand-name companies. But in the last decade, new, smaller firms have gained a larger share of the market at the expense of the older brand-name companies because a ready-made distribution channel has been available through the direct purchase by the chains. A further factor in sustaining this growth in numbers into the 1970's will be the much more rapid growth of demand for frozen foods and the proliferation of more specialized products benefiting from higher incomes and luxury tastes.

Lumber manufacturing, on the other hand, has many of the characteristics of a declining industry. Softwood lumber, the largest part of the industry, has suffered competitively both at the expense of newer wood products, such as plywood, and other nonlumber building materials. This means that firms which depend totally upon softwood lumber find themselves in a deteriorating position.

Sawmilling has suffered a very severe decline, down more than 7,200 establishments between 1954 and 1963. [13] It is the small sawmiller who is particularly vulnerable and likely to become more so. [14] Demand for logs by plywood and paper mills is increasing so that the nonintegrated mill is caught between high log costs and low finished lumber prices. As a result of this price squeeze, a continuing premium will be put on both diversification and vertical integration in sawmilling. Mills which own their own timberlands have a market advantage, especially if they bought them before World War II at only a fraction of present price levels. In cutting its timber, the integrated firm takes the profit on appreciated value as a capital gain at a reduced tax rate rather than as income. Timber owners also are eligible for depletion allowance. [15]

Diversification makes it possible for the sawmiller to make the maximum utilization of logs, and utilize the residues from one operation as raw material for another. The advantage of diversification is quite separate from the advantages of vertical integration although the two generally go together. Diversification may be into plywood or pulp production or into the newer expanding fields of chip or particle boards.

———————

[13]This figure has been adjusted roughly to allow for classification changes in 1958.

[14]This section draws heavily on a research report prepared for the State of Washington by the Battelle Memorial Institute in 1964, W. Halder Fisher, Analysis of the Relationship of Softwood Log Exports to the Economy of the State of Washington.

[15]SBA policy on set-asides of public timber has little effect on the bidding up of log prices since the definition of "small" is large enough to encompass the moderate-sized integrated mill and exclude only the giants.

It is in these new wood products, such as plywood and particle board, that the greatest growth in the industry is taking place. In this category large, integrated, and diversified companies have grown up which are aggressively carrying on technological and marketing research[16] to expand still further the uses of their products at the expense of traditional softwood lumber. Thus, growth in this category (SIC 2432) will probably continue to be mainly through growth in the scale of existing large firms rather than in new small firms.

Logging (SIC 2411) is the other category in lumber with many widely dispersed establishments, almost 13,000 in both 1954 and 1958. The 1963 Census figures for logging are not yet available, but County Business Patterns indicates that some decline took place in this period, but not on the scale of the attrition in sawmilling. The group of small units in logging is less vulnerable, both because the paper industry has buoyed up demand for logs and because the contracting system in logging encourages many small units. The exemption from the Fair Labor Standards Act of contractors with twelve or fewer employees has had an important influence in causing large paper companies to use contractors, to whom they may give assistance, rather than log directly. Barring a change in minimum wage legislation, the number of logging units is not likely to decline severely in the period ahead even though there may be some moderate decrease due to improved technology and more efficient logging.

NATIONAL MARKETS—"SMALL INDUSTRY" GROUPS

The major industry groups producing for national markets in which firms are predominantly small are apparel, leather (except for shoes), furniture, and most miscellaneous manufacturing. These groups numbered about 50,000 establishments in 1958, about one eighth of the total in manufacturing. Not

---

[16]This is in contrast with the performance of the industry as a whole which has been among the lowest of any major industry group in the proportion of its resources devoted to research and development. National Science Foundation, "Research and Development in American Industry, 1963," Review of Data on Science Resources, Vol. 1, No. 1 (December, 1964), p. 6.

only was the average size of almost all categories in these groups under 250 employees, but value added by establishments under 250 was above 50 per cent in the vast majority. All have highly diversified products being sold for the most part in consumer markets. Apparel gives evidence of significant trends in size structure toward larger scale and the reduction of the number of the smallest units, as does leather, while the size structure in furniture and most miscellaneous manufacturing appears to be relatively stable.

Apparel is the only manufacturing sector in which there was a decline in the number of reporting units while employment was increasing in the postwar period. This decline took place largely as a result of the 1958 recession; and even though employment had recovered to its 1953 level by 1962, the number of units had declined by about 4,000. This entire decrease was accounted for by a decline in the units under twenty.

The decline between 1953 and 1962 was relatively greater— 1,400 units, or 26 per cent—in men's apparel, in which a more substantial part of production already was in larger multi-unit companies. The decline in the number of units was as great in the much smaller-scale women's wear—1,600 units —but less significant as a percentage of the total—14 per cent.

The expanding market for women's clothing at all price levels has made it possible for more highly specialized management skills combined with greater financial resources to develop brand names and rationalize production and marketing. Such companies have also diversified; one company will produce dresses but also items with less risk because of more stable styles, such as underwear or rainwear. The expansion of clothing sales by discount and supermarket stores purchasing directly from the manufacturer has also encouraged the development of larger multi-line companies.

Data on mergers between 1959 and 1962 indicate that a number of the largest companies in women's and children's wear are absorbing other companies. Establishments acquired were of larger size, averaging about 200 employees. The acquisitions doubled the number of plants of the acquiring companies, and increased the average number of units per

company from four to eight.[17] These acquisitions were not
only in women's and children's wear, but also in men's and
boys' wear and in knitting mills.

This tendency to somewhat larger scale in women's
clothing is significant as a relatively new departure—but it
should not be overestimated. The total number of establishments acquired was only 1 per cent of total establishments
in women's clothing.

Since there are relatively bright prospects for that part
of the apparel industry that is responsive to increased income,
there will undoubtedly be a growth in the number of firms in
particular areas of higher quality clothing and sports and
casual clothing, even though the total number of units in the
industry continues to decline.

The categories in leather products with substantial small
business strength are similar to apparel, with highly differentiated products—gloves, luggage, purses, etc. As contrasted with apparel, leather goods has been a lagging industry
with both employment and the number of firms declining. The
decline in the number of very small units has been more than
proportionate, and was most severe in handbags. With continued relatively slow growth in the industry, the attrition in
the smallest firms in most categories will undoubtedly continue
into the 1970's.

Unlike apparel and leather, the furniture group has shown
a net increase in the number of establishments in the postwar
period. There was, however, some decline in the 1958 recession, which had not been entirely recovered by 1962; but the
proportion of very small establishments remained relatively
stable at about two thirds of the total establishments.

The merger rate was relatively low in the household furniture group (SIC 251) by firms within the sector; but firms
outside the group, widely distributed in terms of industry,
acquired more firms with more employees. This reflects the
trend of larger companies to invest assets in profitable small

[17]U.S. Department of Commerce, Bureau of the Census, Acquisitions and Disposals of Manufacturing Facilities: 1959-1962, Part 1,
Annual Survey of Manufacturers (Washington, D.C.: U.S. Department
of Commerce, 1965), p. 5.

companies sometimes not even closely related to their primary line of endeavor.

The favorable economic prospects for household furniture (with the rapid increase in family formation expected to begin in 1967) make it likely that there will be a small net gain in the number of firms, with smaller firms holding their share in numbers, if not in value added.

There is little evidence yet of a change in the pattern of marketing household furniture. An increased role for super-market and discount distributive channels, as is happening in clothing, would begin to affect the smallest units adversely and encourage greater development of multi-line companies.

Miscellaneous manufacturing is largely small scale, but so heterogeneous that a projection on size trends requires analysis of its individual components. Most four-digit cate-gories are producing for national markets; but in general the market is limited by size or great product diversification, thereby keeping the size of firms relatively small.

The greatest change in size structure has been in toys and dolls (SIC 3941, 3942), where substantial changes in marketing have occurred. Brand promotion through television and the growth of toy supermarkets have promoted the growth of larger companies and the reduction in the number of very small units. In the 1958-63 period, the total number of estab-lishments declined by more than 140 units despite a very substantial increase in value added.

Most of the rest of the small-scale sectors in miscellaneous manufacturing are in categories with very little economic growth, usually leading to some decline in the total number of firms. An exception to this is sporting and athletic goods, where increased income and leisure pursuits appear to have increased the number of differentiated products and the number of small firms, despite only a very moderate increase in value added in the sector. The only other sector with any growth in the number of establishments is in jewelry from precious metals (SIC 3911), which had a faster growth in value added than any of the other small miscellaneous manufacturing sectors except toys and dolls.

A projection into the 1970's would foresee a continuation of the trend to larger scale in toys and dolls with the further expansion of supermarket facilities in this field, but relative stability in the size structure of other miscellaneous manufacturing sectors. The relatively slow economic growth of most sectors will continue to result in some decline in the total number of firms.   Only in sectors such as sporting and athletic goods where there are opportunities for the development of new, specialized products to serve the leisure market will there be the possibility for the growth of new small firms.

NATIONAL MARKETS—OTHER MANUFACTURING CATEGORIES WITH SMALL BUSINESS STRENGTH

The categories discussed so far comprise about two thirds of all establishments in manufacturing. There were, however, about 100 other SIC categories in 1958 with an average size of less than 250 employees. In almost half of these categories, companies with less than 250 employees accounted for 50 per cent or more of value added. There were also about 50 categories with a higher average size, within which there were 200 or more companies with fewer than 250 employees.

The prospects for substantial increase or decline of small firms in these categories will be determined largely by the rate of economic growth and by changes in technology, marketing, or organization.

The biggest group of categories with some growth potential in small business numbers is in the metalworking sectors (SIC 34-38). Categories in the metal service group not discussed earlier had about 34,000 establishments in 1958, almost all in producer goods manufactures and about equally divided between categories averaging less than 250 employees, and categories with a higher average size but with 200 or more small companies. Many of these larger sectors are heterogeneous, with the smaller firms operating in relatively separate markets.

Thus, although not all these sectors are as small scale as most of the metal service group, the small companies in many of them closely resemble metal service companies in their satellite relationship to larger firms, to which they furnish parts, tools, etc. Some small firms may compete with larger firms, but the small firm's advantage is in specialized management, skill, and service.

This group has been similar in its growth pattern to the metal service group, with a great expansion in numbers in the postwar period related to the growth of the consumer durable and construction industries which the group serves, but with some setback during recession periods.

Some industries in this metalworking group are relatively stable in numbers, and others (such as machine tools) have a cyclical pattern. But the group as a whole can be expected to grow in numbers in the next decade to meet the proliferation of specialized needs created by anticipated growth in transportation equipment, electrical machinery, and scientific instruments. Categories such as metal doors, sash, and trim (SIC 3442) which are related to the construction industry will receive a further growth impetus as residential construction picks up substantially by the end of the decade.

The only growth categories in which smaller units may be vulnerable are in consumer goods—those in which greater standardization of product and greater scale may result in the development of larger firms and the attrition of smaller ones. One such sector is small boat building (SIC 3732) which, although slowing substantially between 1958 and 1963, has experienced a tremendous growth since World War II. As the market has expanded both geographically and in size, the pattern of the industry has changed. The use of fiber glass and aluminum has drastically altered technology so that larger-scale production has become feasible. The emergence of larger companies and the attrition of small units have been encouraged, although the fast growth of the industry initially greatly expanded the total number of companies. As growth in the industry picks up in the decade ahead with increased expenditures for leisure, this tendency will probably be further accentuated. Similarly, the trailer coach industry (SIC 3791) has been, and in all probability will continue to be, rapidly growing, with larger companies playing an increasing role as increased market size has made possible economies of scale of technology and marketing.

Other industries in which substantial growth has taken place are characterized by highly diversified products, generally for limited markets, both consumer and producer. The greatest growth in numbers in such a category took place in a new and fast-growing industry, plastics, n.e.c. (SIC 3079), which grew by 3,000 establishments, mostly small, between 1947 and 1963. Smaller companies are concentrated in the manufacture of highly differentiated fabricated and molded products, while larger companies dominate the supply of plastic materials. Continued growth in output is predicted through the decade, although at not quite such a rapid rate, so that there will undoubtedly be a further increase in the numbers of firms.

Three other categories had substantial growth between 1947 and 1963. There were substantial increases in numbers of establishments in wooden products, n.e.c. (SIC 2499), 700; millwork (SIC 2431), 1,200; [18] and miscellaneous publishing (SIC 2741). Growth in small firms in these categories is not because of rapid growth in value added, but mainly because of the continued proliferation of specialized products by small firms, and it will probably continue for the same reason.

There has also been a limited participation and growth in numbers of small firms in two major industry groups with rapid growth rates, paper (SIC 26) and chemicals (SIC 28). The growth in both these industries has been largely through a growth in the size of existing large firms rather than through growth in numbers of firms. Only in certain specialized products have new small firms been able to overcome the advantages of scale which often cover the range of technology, marketing, and research and development. This pattern appears likely to continue as these groups continue a relatively rapid expansion into the next decade.

CONCLUSIONS

The preceding analysis has been intended to be suggestive, rather than definitive, both because statistical evidence is

---

[18] This figure has been adjusted roughly to allow for classification changes in 1958.

limited and because study in depth of all categories has not been possible. However, certain broad conclusions can be drawn from this analysis.

The future for small business in manufacturing in the next decade appears more promising than the commonly held stereotypes would suggest. First, the total number of small companies—both under twenty and under 250—will probably continue to increase.[19]

A probable net increase in the total number of small companies with one or more employees by 1970 rests on the assumption that the opportunities for new services and products of a highly differentiated kind that present opportunities for small business will outweigh the attrition of small firms caused by greater standardization of product, increased scale made possible by enlargement of the market, or acquisition by larger companies. It also rests on the assumption that output of the manufacturing sector of the economy will grow at an annual rate of approximately 4 per cent.

The proliferation of small, specialized firms in the metal working industry groups, both in the more locally oriented service group and in proprietary firms producing specialized parts and machinery, has provided the largest aggregate growth in numbers in the economy. Another major area of growth in firms has been in categories serving business and construction at a local level, in printing, and in concrete products. There has also been a substantial growth in numbers of small firms in certain categories producing highly differentiated products,

---

[19]This discussion is limited to companies and establishments with one or more employees, because neither the Census of Manufactures nor County Business Patterns includes the self-employed group. The Office of Business Economics series which includes this group shows a slightly declining total for manufacturing businesses since 1957. Apparently this is the result of the dwindling self-employed group in manufacturing, since both the Census of Manufactures and County Business Patterns show an increase in total establishments over the same period. The 1958 Census estimated a total of 52,000 manufacturing plants with no employees. The largest concentration of 13,000 was in lumber and wood products. A sharp decline in this group, due to the vulnerability of sawmills, probably accounted for a substantial part of the recent decline shown by the OBE figures.

mostly notable in the new and fast-growing miscellaneous plastics product category.

The greatest attrition of small firms has been in certain consumer categories. The enlargement of the market area and changing patterns of distribution, often combined with a slow growth rate, have eliminated many small units in certain food categories. In apparel and toys, new patterns of market distribution have helped the growth of somewhat larger firms at the expense of smaller units.

These trends in both directions will continue. [20] But it seems likely that the attrition rate of small firms in vulnerable categories will be less than in the 1958-63 period, which was accentuated by a serious recession. Concomitantly, the growth in numbers in expanding categories will probably be higher in the next decade, barring a serious recession.

To predict that the number of small companies will continue to grow in manufacturing does not mean that the relative share of small business in employment or value added will increase. The opposite is likely, particularly if economic growth continues at the present rate. Not only is the predicted growth rate higher for most major industry groups in which large corporate strength is greatest, but the pattern of acquisition of small units by larger multi-unit companies is likely to increase their percentage of total employment and value added.

Of the more than 3,300 facilities[21] acquired between 1959 and 1962, three fourths had fewer than 250 employees; but these facilities had only 24 per cent of the employment. The impact of the mergers was greatest in the facilities with 100-249 employees. This group accounted for 65 per cent of the total employment of the facilities acquired in the under-250

---

[20] See Table 6.

[21] A facility is not completely identical with the company definition of the Enterprise Statistics, 1958, with which it is compared in this paragraph. It may include more than one establishment, but only part of a company if the whole company was not acquired. For this reason, the impact on independent companies is somewhat overestimated by this comparison, since some of the facilities acquired in the under-250 employee group may have been part of larger companies.

Table 6

CATEGORIES OF PROSPECTIVE SUBSTANTIAL CHANGE
IN NUMBERS OF MANUFACTURING ESTABLISHMENTS
IN THE NEXT DECADE

1. Substantial Growth in Numbers of Establishments in:

> Local Metal Service Markets [22]
>
> Local Business Markets [22]
>
> Local Construction Markets [22]
>
> Producer Goods Categories in Metalworking Sectors
> (SIC 34-38) [23]
>
> Miscellaneous Categories with Highly Diversified
> Products [24]

2. Substantial Decline in Numbers of Establishments in:

> Local Consumer Markets [22]
>
> Categories Localized by Source of Raw
> Materials [22]
>
> Apparel (SIC 23) [25]
>
> Leather (SIC 31) [26]

---

[22] See Table 5, pp. 20-25 and discussion in the text, pp. 27-36.

[23] See pp. 40-41.

[24] Includes plastics, n. e. c. (SIC 3079); millwork, n. e. c. (SIC 2499); miscellaneous publishing (SIC 2431). See pp. 41-42.

[25] See pp. 36-38.

[26] See p. 38.

employee group. Furthermore, facilities acquired represented more than 7 per cent of the number of manufacturing companies in this size category in 1958, as contrasted with less than 0.7 per cent of the number of companies in the under-100 employee size category. [27]

Companies in the 100-250 size category are apparently more vulnerable [28] as a group to acquisition by larger companies because they can be more easily absorbed without overextending the management spread of the parent company. For this reason, it appears probable that acquisitions will continue to increase the share of employment and value added by larger companies, although affecting less significantly the number of smaller companies.

---

[27] This figure is underestimated by the sampling procedure of the Annual Survey of Manufactures which included only a sample of the concerns under 100. Figures were not inflated to estimate the acquisitions of nonsample companies. However, it is estimated that the acquisitions reported accounted for 98 per cent of the total of manufacturing employment and that the error in the number of units would probably have been more significant.

[28] This is not to say that small firms are acquired unwillingly. Acquisition of small firms seems to be taking place in our present economic climate just because the firms are successful. For the acquiring company, it is primarily a way of investing earnings and getting a more diversified operation. For the small company, it often provides a way for the owner or owners to realize capital gains or retire.

CHAPTER **4** SMALL BUSINESS IN RETAIL TRADE
AND
SERVICE INDUSTRIES

RETAIL TRADE

Retail trade continues to be a citadel of small business. Firms with fewer than twenty employees make up 97 per cent of retail firms, and only a fraction of a per cent have more than 100 employees. [1] This is characteristic of all the principal categories of retail trade except department stores.

Retailing [2] is among the easiest of entry of the principal types of business: capital requirements are relatively low, turnover of stock is relatively rapid, trade credit is widely available, technical requirements are relatively undemanding, and assistance is available in many forms and from many sources. Rising personal incomes and personal consumption expenditures offer an expanding market. It is not surprising that more than half of the business population is found in retailing.

Though retail firms are predominantly small, a few large firms play an important and increasingly influential part. This is true not only of department stores but of a few large mail order establishments and chains which are the principal competitors of tens of thousands of small retailers in the grocery, variety, drug, and, more recently, in the shoe trade. Of the 1,688,000 retail companies in the 1958 Census, only 2.8 per cent were ''multi-unit'' companies; but this relatively small group of firms did 35 per cent of retail business and employed 40 per cent of retail employees. [3] Moreover, about 20,000 of

---

[1] Bureau of the Census, Enterprise Statistics, 1958, p. 30.

[2] In the Standard Industrial Classification, ''Retail Trade'' includes gasoline stations and eating and drinking places.

[3] Bureau of the Census, Enterprise Statistics, 1958, Part 1, Table 8.

the multi-unit firms were also "multi-industry" firms, indicating some degree of integration of function.[4] These 20,000 multi-unit, multi-industry firms, with 110,000 establishments, alone accounted for about 25 per cent of all retail business. Sixty-six of these companies, each with 5,000 employees or more, employed nearly 20 per cent of all retail workers. Nevertheless, most of the chains are small: 95 per cent of multi-unit retailers and more than 90 per cent even of multi-industry retailers have fewer than 100 employees. It is primarily among department stores and mail-order houses, variety stores, grocery stores, and, to a lesser extent, among shoe stores, drug stores, and restaurants that large chains are prominent and pervasive.

Among department stores and variety stores, very large firms are dominant. Yet in other sectors deeply penetrated by large firms, small business still occupies an important place. Almost as many workers are employed in grocery firms with less than twenty employees as in firms with 10,000 or more. Among drug stores and restaurants, about three fifths of employment is in firms employing less than twenty; among shoe stores, two fifths.

At the other extreme are typical small business sectors in which very small firms predominate: gasoline stations, specialty food stores, building materials and hardware dealers, furniture stores, and miscellaneous retailing where ease of entry and specialization favor large numbers of small businesses.

If employment of 100 is taken as the upper limit of small firms in retailing, two thirds of all retail employees are in small companies and only one sixth in very large ones (Table 7). Of fifteen retail categories of the Census, nine are dominated by small business to the extent of three fourths or more of employment, and twelve to the extent of half or more. The exclusion of small business from department stores and variety stores and the pressure on small grocery and shoe stores are evident.

---

[4]The Census defines a multi-industry firm as one where establishments (exclusive of central administrative offices) are classified in more than one of the 855 industries used in the 1958 Census.

Table 7

EMPLOYMENT IN RETAIL TRADE
PER CENT DISTRIBUTION BY SIZE OF FIRM - 1958

	All Sizes (per cent)*	Small Less than 100 employees (per cent)	Medium 100-1000 employees (per cent)	Large 1000-10,000 employees (per cent)	Very Large 10,000 employees and over (per cent)
All Retail Trade	100	66	9	9	16
Building Materials, etc.	100	91	8	1*	-
Department Stores	100	2	13	24	61
General Merchandise, n.e.c.	100	76	20*	4*	-
Limited Price Variety Stores	100	16	5*	11*	68
Nonstore Retailers	100	52	14	34	-
Grocery Stores	100	44	10	12	35
Other Food Stores	100	95	5	-	-
Auto Dealers	100	91	8	1	-
Gas Stations	100	96	4	-	-
Apparel Stores	100	65	22	11*	2*
Shoe Stores	100	50	11*	18*	19*
Furniture Stores	100	87	11*	2*	-
Eating and Drinking Places	100	85	8	7	-
Drug Stores	100	79	8	9*	4*
Other Retailers	100	89	8*	3*	-

* Partly estimated from Census codes.   Percentages may not add to 100 due
  to rounding.

Source: Bureau of the Census, Enterprise Statistics, 1958.

Inspection of the 1958 employment distribution by size of
firm for numerous size classes suggested the 100-employee
size class as a convenient and useful general dividing line
between small and large firms. With this distinction in mind,
Table 8 was constructed, listing trades in ascending order of
the percentage of employment held by the over-99 employee
size class. The trades are divided into four groups according
to this distinction.

Automotive dealers and gas stations are shown separately
because their employment profile is largely determined by

Table 8

RETAIL TRADE: NUMBER OF FIRMS, EMPLOYMENT DISTRIBUTION BY EMPLOYEE SIZE CLASS AND BY TYPE OF TRADE, 1958

Group[5]	No. of Firms (000)	Employment Total (000)	Employment Single Unit Firms (Per cent)	Employment Multi-Unit Firms (Per cent)	Share of Employment by Employee Size Class, Per cent Estimated* 0-3[6]	4-19[6]	20-99	Over 99
I Automotive dealers	89	710	86.5	13.5	6	39	46	9
Gas stations	203	442	85.7	14.3	37	51	7	5
II Building material, hardware, farm equipment	99	435	77.9	22.1	30	36	25	9
Food, except groceries	93	191	82.2	17.8	8	71	16	5
Other retail	225	569	75.4	24.6	24	47	18	11
Furniture, home furnishings and equipment	95	380	72.1	27.9	16	48	23	13
Eating and drinking places	342	1,596	81.0	19.0	16	43	26	15
Drug and proprietary	52	352	68.2	31.8	9	54	16	21
General merchandise, n.e.c.	57	143	67.0	33.0	53		23	24

Table 8 (Cont.)

							(Employment (000's))	
III Apparel and accessories, except shoes	79	531	55.6	44.4	11	32	32	22	35
Nonstore retailers	77	157	52.2	47.8			30	20	48
Shoes	16	103	33.0	67.0	9		21	11	50
Groceries	247	1,095	29.1	60.9	11			12	56
IV Variety stores (limited priced)	12	342	10.8	89.4		11	-	5	84
Department stores	0.8	990	10.8	89.2	-			2	98
TOTAL	1,688	8,034	59.8	40.2	3,745			1,513	2,777

* Percentages may not add up to 100 due to rounding.

[5] For explanation of groups, see text.

[6] Based on estimated employment distribution in reporting units shown in County Business Patterns, Part 1, First Quarter 1962, Bureau of the Census, Tables 1A and 1C. For reporting units of under-20 employees, firm and reporting unit were considered to be equivalent in most cases. For those four-digit trades where data were limited to number of reporting units by employee size class, employment was estimated by multiplying the number of reporting units by the midpoint in the employee size class. The estimated distribution between 0-3 and 4-19 employee size classes derived from County Business Patterns data was then applied to the under-20 employee size class shown in Enterprise Statistics.

Sources: Enterprise Statistics, 1958, and County Business Patterns, 1962.

franchise agreements. Firms with over ninety-nine employees account for only 9 per cent and 5 per cent of the total employment in these trades. Firms of over ninety-nine employees account for 5 per cent to 24 per cent of total employment in the seven trades included in group II. Employment in groups I and II amounts to 4.9 million, or 60 per cent of total employment in the retail trades.

Firms of over ninety-nine employees account for 35 per cent to 56 per cent of total employment in the four trades included in group III: grocery stores, shoe stores, apparel and accessory stores (except shoes), and nonstore retailers (house-to-house selling, vending machine, and mail-order companies). Combined, the trades in group III account for almost 2 million employees, or one quarter of those employed in all retail trades.

Firms of over ninety-nine employees comprise 84 per cent and 98 per cent of total employment in the variety and department store trades, respectively, included in group IV. They account for 1.3 million employees, or 15 per cent of all retail trade employment. As noted earlier, the average employment per firm in these trades far exceeds that in all other retail trades.

Trades in groups III and IV are heavily chained, with 44 per cent to 89 per cent of their employment in multi-unit firms, while trades in groups I and II have only from 10 per cent to 33 per cent of their employment in multi-unit firms. [7]

In all trades except those with typically very large firms (department and variety stores), and except for automotive dealers, the four-to-nineteen employee size accounts for the largest share of employment among the size classes shown.

----

[7] These observations are based on 1958 data presented by the Census Bureau in Summary Table 5 of the House Select Committee on Small Business, Staff Report, The Status of Small Business in Retail Trade (1948-1958), December 16, 1960. Exceptions in this I and II category, where employment in multi-unit firms is significantly more important, are tires, batteries, and accessories in the automotive group, and candy and confectioners in the food stores (except groceries).

Most employment in the gas service stations firms is in the less-than-twenty employee firm size, with many employed in firms of less than four. Employees of automotive dealers (cars, accessories, tires, batteries) most typically work in firms of from four to 100 employees. Both of these groups are mostly franchised operations, i.e., producer outlets. They are served mainly by single suppliers, and sell a single or limited number of products. Except for the tires, batteries, and accessories trade, employment in multi-unit firms in the automotive trades is only a relatively small part of total employment.

In group II we find specialty trades such as food stores (other than groceries), furniture stores, hardware stores, eating and drinking places, and "other retail" that are mostly single commodity stores such as liquor, jewelry, fuel, flowers, etc. In a way, general merchandise stores n.e.c. may also be considered a specialty trade in that they are convenience stores normally serving a limited area. Most employees in these trades are in firms ranging in size up to twenty employees.

Most of the trades in group II are associated with products which are not as standardized as those found in group III and involve personal services in sales to a greater extent; they are less subject to economies of scale in store size or in number of units. They respond to population concentration and higher per capita expenditure levels by increasing numbers of firms rather than firm size.

The trades represented in group III have experienced economies of scale in multi-unit operation associated with more intense population density, with mass distribution of standardized commodities, and with a reduction in the personal service element in sales (including customers product selection, storage, and transport).

The number of retail firms has been increasing. Between 1953 and 1963, the estimated increase was 186,000, or 10 per cent, as the result of the creation of 1,613,000 new firms and demise of 1,428,000 firms. [8] The Census reported an increase

---

[8] See Appendix Tables 1-A, 1-B, and 1-C. Differences between these figures and those given in Appendix Table 6-B arise from the fact that 0-employee firms are not included in data from County Business Patterns.

of 145,000 firms between 1954 and 1958, with an increase in employment of 817,000, about three fifths of it in the employ of single-unit firms and multi-unit firms with fewer than 100 employees.[9] Over-all, the size distribution (measured by employment) was shifted slightly in favor of the larger firms but not greatly changed.

With the employment profile of the industry described above in mind, we may examine the changes which have occurred since 1948 in the position of small business. The basic data for such an analysis have been provided by the Census Bureau in a special tabulation prepared in 1960 for the House Select Committee on Small Business, covering the Census years 1948, 1954, and 1958.

The Census data are presented in terms of number of units (stores) rather than employee size class. From the Census tables for 1958 we have estimated average employment per firm as shown below.

Estimated Average Employment Per Firm

Number of units per firm	single	2-3	4-5	6-10	11-25	26-50	51-100	over 100
Employees per firm (approx.)	3.1	20	60	115	225	1,000	1,250	over 2,000

Firms of eleven or more units have been selected as the dividing point for large and small firms, as being consistent with the dividing line used for the employment profile of 100 employees. [10]

---

[9] Enterprise Statistics, 1958, Part I, pp. 32-33.

[10] It is noted, however, that for the shoe and lumber, building materials, etc., trades, employment per firm with more than ten units is substantially below the 100-employee level and below the average for all trades. If the large-small division had been made in terms of smaller numbers of units or smaller employee size classes, these two trades would have shown an appreciably higher rate of employment in "large firms" relative to other trades than with the 100-employee, eleven-unit division.

Employees per firm vary widely with type of trade as illustrated in the following trades for the 6-10 unit size firm:

Employees per Firm of 6 to 10 Retail Units

Type of Trade	No. of Employees
Department Stores	4,000
Drugs	116
Shoes	50
Groceries	140
Eating & Drinking Places	175
Furniture	150
Lumber & Building Materials	60

Table 9 shows that trades in group III were those which experienced an upward movement between 1948 and 1958 in share of sales held by larger firms (over ten units); namely, apparel, shoes, and groceries. [11] The only relevant statistics available since 1958 are estimated monthly sales data for all firms and for firms with over eleven units. These data, while not as detailed as the Census Bureau 1948-58 series, either by type of trade or number of units, in general, do follow the 1948-58 Census series and show that the trends have continued. In addition, they indicate that drug stores have shown a strong tendency toward larger firm size since 1958.

For most trades, the changes in shares of employment accounted for by multi-unit firms of less than eleven units tended to resemble the changes in the shares of larger chains rather than those of single-unit stores. The share of the smaller chains in total employment was about 10 per cent for most

[11] It is noted that the Census coverage in 1958 includes delicatessens with groceries, and excludes them from foods (except groceries); this may explain part of the movement shown in the respective trades toward, and away from, larger units.

Table 9

RETAIL TRADE: SHARES OF SALES OF FIRMS WITH 11
OR MORE UNITS, BY TYPE OF TRADE,
FOR SELECTED YEARS, 1948-58
(Per Cent)

Group 12/	1948	1954	1958
I Automotive dealers	–	2	3
Gas stations	6	6	8
II Building material, hardware, farm equipment	10	8	6
Food, except groceries 13/	14	8	7 13/
Other retail	8	12	10
Furniture, home furnishings and equipment	9	8	7
Eating and drinking places	5	6	6
Drugs	18	16	18
General merchandise, n.e.c.	7	5	(n.a.)
III Apparel and accessories, excl. shoes	16	18	20
Nonstore retailers 14/	(n.a.)	39	36
Shoes	40	40	42
Groceries 13/	36	39	44 13/
IV Variety	80	77	78
Department stores 15/	(n.a.)	(n.a.)	62
ALL GROUPS	19	20	22
Addendum:			
Single-unit firms	70	70	66
Multi-unit firms, all sizes	30	30	34

[12] For explanation of groups, see pp. 52ff.

[13] Delicatessens are included in groceries and excluded from food (excl. groceries), 1958.

[14] In 1948 included in specified trades.

[15] Coverage shifted in 1956. See Business Statistics, 1963. Source: Status of Small Business in Retail Trade, (1948-1958), House Select Committee on Small Business, Committee Print, 1960, Summary Tables I and V and text table 11.

trades and close to 20 per cent for the furniture, apparel and accessories, and general merchandise groups. [16]

In a Census study of geographic shifts in retail sales between 1948 and 1954, it was observed that retail sales in Standard Metropolitan Statistical Areas increased by 32 per cent while sales in Central Business Districts rose by only 1.6 per cent. In 1954, sales in the metropolitan areas accounted for 45 per cent of total retail sales, compared to 7.5 per cent for Central Business Districts. There was an absolute decline in the Central Business District sales in general merchandise, apparel and accessories, and drug stores.[17]

Between 1948 and 1958, the share of sales held by single-unit firms in retail sales in the aggregate dropped from 70 to 66 per cent. The greatest declines in the market share of single-unit stores were in those broad fields in which single-store retailers already had the smallest market share in 1948. The greatest decline was in food stores (11 per cent).[18]

In metropolitan areas, the chains did a far higher proportion of all retail business than in the U.S. as a whole,[19] and increased their sales between 1954 and 1958 by a much greater percentage than single-unit stores or than chains did in the United States as a whole. [20]

Detailed examination of data based on employment reported for Social Security taxes reveals remarkable stability in size

[16]Status of Small Business in Retail Trade (1948-1958), op. cit., Summary tables 1 and 5.

[17]Murray Dessel, Central Business Districts and Their Metropolitan Areas; Geographic Shifts in Retail Sales, 1948-1954. Area Development Administration, Area Trend Series 1 (November, 1957).

[18]Status of Small Business in Retail Trade (1948-1958), op. cit., p. 12.

[19]Ibid., p. 31.

[20]Ibid., p. 24.

distribution of retail business.[21] A comparison of 1953 and 1962 for all lines of retailing by eight size classes, from under four employees to more than 500, reveals little change over nearly a decade (Appendix Table 6-C). There is a marked tendency toward larger units among department stores, and a marked decline in the importance of the small food retailer. There is a general shift from four-to-seven employee class toward the eight-to-nineteen, suggesting that the small units have become bigger. (This may reflect the large number of young postwar firms in 1953 and the higher age of the survivors in 1962.)

A comparison of reporting units with less than twenty employees reveals the remarkable constancy of the composition of small business in retailing (Table 10). Over-all, there was an increase of about 3 1/2 per cent in the number of retailers with less than twenty employees, and this was reflected in most lines of trade. The decline among small food stores is evident, as is the decline among automobile dealers. On the other hand, there were increases among gasoline stations and liquor stores, reflecting increasing opportunities.

This tendency for some lines to decline and others to increase is characteristic of the adaptability of small business to changes in the character of the demand. It is shown in detail by the 1953-62 comparisons of reporting units and employment and distribution of units by employment size class for principal lines of retailing (Appendix Table 6-C).

---

[21]These data are drawn from County Business Patterns, 1962 and 1953, compiled by the Census from OASDI reports. The "reporting unit" in these tabulations differs from Census "establishment" and "company." It consists of all establishments in a county that are under common ownership; for example, all the units of a national chain in a given county. This overstates the number of large units and understates their size. For time-to-time comparisons, however, this bias may be considered constant, and for the smallest units, in which multi-county operations are unlikely, it may be negligible.

Table 10

RETAIL REPORTING UNITS WITH LESS THAN 20 EMPLOYEES
(thousands of reporting units)

All Retail Trade	1962	1953
	983[22/]	949[22/]
Building Materials, etc.	70	68
General Merchandise	49	43
Food (ex. Dairy Prod.)	137[22/]	175[22/]
Grocery Stores	99	121
Automotive	198	164
Auto Dealers	24	33
Gas Stations	142	106
Apparel Stores	81	73
Men's	15	15
Women's	22	21
Shoe Stores	18	14
Furniture, House furnishings	60	54
Furniture Stores	36	34
Appliance Stores	12	(20
Radio and TV, Music	12	(
Eating and Drinking Places	216	215
Drug Stores	44	44
Liquor Stores	23	16

[22/] Excluding dairy products retailers to avoid effects of classification change. Source: County Business Patterns, 1953 and 1962.

SERVICES

The service industries (SIC 70-79) comprise one of the largest and most rapidly growing economic sectors.[23] They are highly variegated and, although some are declining, others are fast-growing and the group as a whole will probably have the largest net increase in the number of firms of any major sector in the next decade. Generally they are characterized

[23] Professional and educational services (SIC 80-82), which also are growing very rapidly, and the balance of the service sector (SIC 83-89) are generally not commercial ventures and, therefore, are not treated in this section.

by small firms serving a local consumer market, except for the important and fast-growing business services.

The total number of companies in 1958 was 943,000, exceeded only by the number in retail trade. Of these companies, 98 per cent of the total had fewer than twenty employees, representing 46 per cent of all employment. Companies with fewer than 250 employees had 79 per cent of total employment in the sector. [24]

Except for the motion picture sector, all sectors have more than half of their employment in firms employing less than 250 employees. Less than 5 per cent of the total establishments in 1958 were part of multi-unit firms. More than 80 per cent of the establishments were single proprietorships, with the rest about evenly divided between partnerships and corporations.

Generally, because of the smallness of scale, growth in these service sectors is accomplished by a large net increase in the number of firms.

The major part of the growth in "firms" is a growth in the self-employed and the very small establishments, which are largely "little business," as defined in Chapter 1. In the period between 1954 and 1958, 43 per cent of the growth in the establishments that operated during the whole year occurred in the self-employed group, and an additional 42 per cent in the establishments employing between one and three employees.

Figures are not available on the recent growth in the self-employed in these categories, but the reporting units with one to three employees did not contribute so much to the growth of the total sector in 1959-62 as in 1954-58. If the firms with no payroll were included, establishments with three or fewer employees would probably still have accounted for 75 or 80 per cent of the increase in the sector.

Changes in size structure are relatively minor in the service categories, but changes in the relative strength of different service categories give a different balance to the

---

[24] These figures and subsequent 1958 figures for companies in industry groups are taken from Enterprise Statistics, 1958. See Appendix Table 5.

sector as a whole. By examining the relatively few categories which have experienced the most rapid growth, it is possible to get a picture of the changing structure of the services and of the areas of greatest potential growth for new small firms in the decade ahead. [25]

HOTELS, MOTELS, AND OTHER LODGING PLACES (SIC 70)

The development of the motel industry has provided the biggest increase in new businesses in this category—more than 10,000 new establishments between 1954 and 1962 with one or more employees, and an estimated additional 4,000 with no payroll.

It is noteworthy that the growth of the smaller-scale motel industry has been to some extent at the expense of the larger-scale hotel industry—contrary to the usual stereotypes.

As the pace of growth in the numbers of firms slowed down between 1958 and 1962, the relative importance of the very small establishments (one to three employees) declined, and the relative importance of the establishments with over twenty employees increased, although there was still substantial growth in numbers in all classes, with the one-to-three class still two thirds of the total.

---

[25] In order to approximate a time series for various groups and categories in the services, figures for 1954 and 1958 from the Census of Business for establishments with one employee and up have been linked with County Business Patterns for 1959 and 1962. The group of establishments with one or more employees in the Census of Business is generally comparable to the reporting unit of County Business Patterns, so that linking these figures gives a good approximation of changes in this group between 1958 and 1962. Estimates for the growth in establishments without employees, between 1958 and 1962, have been based on the relationship between the rate of growth in the latter period of the no-employee group and the group with one or more employees. Particular attention was paid to the changes in the one-to-three employee group because approximately 90 per cent of new entries are in this group. [This figure is based on the 1951-56 period in which 89.4 per cent of new entries were in the zero-to-three employee group. Betty C. Churchill, "Size of Business Firms," Survey of Current Business, (September, 1959).]

As motels have become a "big business," franchising has become a potent force, with 87 per cent of motel units operated by franchised operators in 1964.[26] In some cases financial help comes from the national franchiser, but more important is the know-how to help the local businessman meet the tough competition that has developed with the rapid expansion of the industry. This service includes feasibility surveys to decide on locations and specialized help in design, purchasing, guest referral, etc.

Further growth can be anticipated in all size classes in the next decade because of the increasing importance of motor travel, but there will be a continued decrease in relative importance of the very smallest establishments in favor of those somewhat larger. In the large metropolitan areas these units will move beyond the small business category as the borderline between hotels and motels becomes less distinct as a result of the building of large motel complexes in the downtown areas.

The other category with a substantial increase in the number of establishments is trailer parks, with the largest group in this category the self-employed, 79 per cent in 1954 and 74 per cent in 1958. The approximate increase in the number of establishments with one or more employees was 1,700 between 1954 and 1962, but the increase in the number of units with no payroll is estimated at more than 4,000. Because they are providing services rather than lodging, and are catering primarily to longer-term residents rather than transient trade, this very small size structure will undoubtedly continue, although the percentage of self-employed with no payroll will continue to decline as a percentage of the total. The category as a whole will grow substantially in the next decade because of the rapid growth of the mobile home industry, supported by an expanding older population and use of mobile homes for low-income housing.

PERSONAL SERVICES (SIC 72)

The largest group of firms in the service category is in personal services—more than 42 per cent of the total. It also

---

[26]Practical Builder (August, 1964).

includes the largest group of self-employed in the sector. The market area for personal services is often quite limited geographically for reasons of convenience; the labor component is high, and entry is relatively inexpensive—all encouraging very small scale.

Because of the high labor component, the personal services have been subject to the competition of the "do-it-yourself" trend. In some cases the industry has fought back, as did the beauty shop industry by creating hair styles that defy do-it-yourself skill. A new industry has developed in the self-service laundry by the commercialization of home equipment.

The largest number of establishments in the services is in the beauty and barber shops category. Beauty shops have shown substantial growth between 1954 and 1962 with an approximate increase of almost 24,000 establishments with one or more employees, and an estimated increase of 34,000 establishments with no payroll (about 62 per cent of all beauty shops). The number of barber shop establishments grew substantially through 1959, but in the one-or-more-employee group declined slightly between 1959 and 1962. However, the self-employed group, about 66 per cent of all barber establishments in 1958, probably continued to grow substantially. This group grew more rapidly in the 1954 to 1958 period; and the fact that every barber category, except one-to-three employees, grew between 1959 and 1962 indicates that the increasingly extensive use of the "leased chair" arrangement in small shops probably has caused a substantial number of barbers previously employed to be reported in the self-employed category.

Both beauty and barber shops will continue to grow in number because of the correlation between expenditures on personal care and increased income. Beauty shops benefit more from incremental income than barber shops and will continue to grow at a more rapid rate. Furthermore, state apprenticeship requirements may have some effect in holding down the number of firms in barbering.

The only other personal service category in which there has been rapid growth is self-service laundries, which added approximately 5,700 establishments between 1954 and 1962 (excluding self-employed operators). Part of this growth was at the expense of other laundry services (some of them much larger-scale units), which declined in number during this

period. The self-service laundries will undoubtedly continue
to grow substantially in number in the next decade. Self-service
cleaning, which is being added to this service, probably will
affect adversely the growth of other cleaning services, as
home laundry equipment and self-service laundries affected
other laundry service firms.

This trend has increased greatly the total number of firms
performing laundry services. On the other hand, traditional
personal services such as shoe and garment repair and altera-
tion have declined as independent businesses, often being
absorbed as auxiliary functions in larger establishments.

The net growth, therefore, of personal services in the next
five to ten years will be somewhat slower. The growth in
beauty and barber shops and self-service laundries (and to
a lesser extent in funeral parlors, which have a steady but
moderate growth in numbers as population increases) will be
offset by a continued decline in other laundry services and in
firms performing clothing and shoe maintenance.

MISCELLANEOUS BUSINESS SERVICES (SIC 73)

Business services are the fastest growing group of firms
in the service category. They recorded the highest relative
growth of all sectors and the highest absolute growth in the
one-and-more-employee group between 1959 and 1962. This
development is significant not only for the opportunities it
presents for small business, but because many of these firms
represent new and expanded services available to small
businessmen.

Business services are second in scale to motion pictures.
These services are still predominantly small. Among advertising firms, 56 per cent of employment was in firms with
fewer than 250 employees in 1958, and in other business
services, 68 per cent. Companies with fewer than twenty employees were 94 per cent of the total number in advertising,
and 96 per cent in other business services.

The group of establishments with no employees in business
services was also high—52 per cent of the total, with the
highest in business and management consulting services (61

per cent) and the lowest in advertising (24 per cent). The number of establishments with one or more employees went up 85 per cent between 1954 and 1962—approximately 29,000 units—and we estimate those with no employees increased by about an equal amount.

The fastest growing group within business services is business services, n.e.c. (SIC 739), which grew almost 7,000 reporting units in the one-and-more employee category in the 1959 to 1962 period, and we estimate that the number of establishments without payroll grew by more than this amount, because of the high percentage of self-employed in its two main components: business consultants (SIC 7392) and business services, n.e.c. (SIC 7399).

The other very rapidly expanding category is miscellaneous building services, which grew approximately 3,900 establishments in the group with payroll between 1954 and 1962, and an estimated 6,500 units in the group without. Both these fast growing categories represent in large part the increased contracting out of services formerly performed within companies. For smaller companies these are often services that cannot be economically performed by the firm for itself.

Other business service groups that have grown substantially are advertising, credit reporting and collection, duplicating, mailing and stenographic services, and private employment agencies. Again these services have grown with the increasing specialization of business activity and the greater tendency to contract out such specialized activity.

This whole group of business services promises to continue this pattern of growth into the next decade, with business services, n.e.c., continuing the most rapid pace of growth, in part, because it will include new types of business services as variety and technology proliferate. The computer and related electronic processes will contribute substantially to this growth.

Size structure will probably show no radical change within particular sectors, but the composition of the business service sector will be somewhat smaller scale as the smaller-scale business services gain at the expense of the somewhat larger advertising services.

AUTOMOBILE REPAIR AND SERVICES AND GARAGES (SIC 75)

This is an auxiliary service which has grown with the great postwar expansion of the automobile industry, but only since about 1953.[27] It is one of the smallest-scale industry groups, with 99 per cent of the companies with fewer than twenty employees in 1958, representing 77 per cent of the total employment. More than 95 per cent of total employment was by companies with fewer than 250 employees.

The very smallest group, with one to three employees, remained about 70 per cent of those with one employee or more as the total grew by approximately 24,000 establishments between 1954 and 1962. We estimate that firms without payroll increased by almost the same amount. Although this growth has been concentrated in the general auto repair shops, all the specialized auto repair categories have shown some growth.

Auto services other than repair have also grown, and are on a somewhat larger scale. Between 1954 and 1962 automobile and truck rentals doubled in the number of establishments with one or more employees. Like motels, this is a field where national franchising has become very important. Although the service is offered at a local level, referrals between cities permit national companies with brand names to develop.

Growth is to be expected in almost all three- and four-digit categories in this industry group in the next decade with continued expansion of the automobile industry. A possible exception is among parking lots and parking structures with one employee or more, because increasing land values encourage alternative land uses or multiple-purpose use, which include parking, or public provision of parking.

Because of the smallness of scale and the stability of the size structure in the auto repair services, most of the increase in total numbers of establishments in the industry group will be in the auto repair category.

---

[27]As auto dealers increased their repair services after the war, the numbers in this group declined until 1953, when the category began to increase in numbers.

MISCELLANEOUS REPAIR SERVICES (SIC 76)

Like automobile repairs, miscellaneous repairs are among the smallest scale industry groups, and because of this scale, growth, to a great extent, is reflected in an increase in the number of firms. More than 99 per cent of the companies in 1958 employed fewer than twenty employees, and 78 per cent of total employment was in this group. Ninety-seven per cent of total employment was in firms employing less than 250.

The fastest growing category has been electrical repair shops (SIC 762), with most of this growth concentrated in radio and television repair. The number of establishments with one or more employees almost doubled between 1954 and 1962, adding an approximate 5,800 establishments. The self-employed group remained stable, accounting for more than three quarters of the total group of establishments between 1954 and 1958. We estimate that this group increased by roughly 18,000 establishments between 1954 and 1962.

Reupholstery and furniture repair (SIC 764) has grown at a much slower rate, with an approximate increase of about 1,300 establishments between 1954 and 1962, and an estimated increase of 2,500 units in the self-employed group, which comprise two thirds of the total establishments in the category.

Miscellaneous repair shops and related services (SIC 769) also increased substantially over this period, with the bulk of this increase in the self-employed category.[28] Only the number of establishments in watch, clock, and jewelry repair (SIC 763) was virtually stationary over the period from 1954 to 1962.

The industry group as a whole will undoubtedly continue to expand into the 1970's since it services in large part consumer durables (except automobiles), which are themselves expanding categories. However, unless new durables are developed on the scale of the television industry, this expansion will be at the somewhat slower rate of the 1959-62 period, rather than that of the 1954-58 period.

---

[28] Problems of classification of these categories in the Census of Business prevent giving detailed figures.

Because of the high proportion of self-employed in this industry group (almost 77 per cent of total establishments in 1958), and the high proportion of very small establishments, most of the net growth in total establishments will continue to take place in these small size groups, creating in turn a large net increase in the total number of firms in the industry group.

MOTION PICTURES (SIC 78)

Motion pictures is the only major industry group in the services which is not predominantly small scale. Motion picture production is not, properly speaking, a "service" and typically has large production units—69 per cent of total employment was by companies of 250 employees or more in 1958. Motion picture theaters are more characteristically a local service, although multi-unit theater chains play an important role.

The whole industry group has been hurt by the growth of the television industry so that there has been substantial decline in the total number of firms. Motion picture theaters (SIC 783), the smallest scale group, declined in the total number of establishments with one employee or more by more than 5,000 units between 1954 and 1962.

This is the only major industry within the service group with a declining number of establishments; and in terms of receipts, establishments, and employment, its importance in the service group will probably be further reduced in the next decade.

AMUSEMENT AND RECREATION SERVICES (EXCEPT MOTION PICTURES) (SIC 79)

This major industry group is composed of widely different categories, but almost all characteristically small scale. Almost 97 per cent of the total companies had fewer than twenty employees in 1958, representing 53 per cent of total employment, with 90 per cent of employment by companies employing less than 250. A few of the categories in this group are not commercial ventures, but are public facilities or private membership groups, such as public golf courses and country clubs.

Between 1954 and 1958 more than half of the total growth in establishments was in the self-employed group (similar to the pattern of the personal services), with a total of almost 11,000 establishments. This growth was concentrated in race tracks and stables (SIC 7948), with an increase of about 2,700 establishments, and in theaters, bands, orchestras, and entertainers (SIC 792), with an increase of 4,800 establishments.

The greatest growth in establishments with more than one employee was in bowling alleys and billiards (SIC 793), which between 1954 and 1962 grew by almost 4,900 establishments with one or more employees. In the 1954-58 period all of the increase was in the growth of bowling alleys, with some decline in billiards and pool establishments, and it is probable this pattern has continued, although no breakdown is available. Between 1954 and 1962 there was also an increase of at least 3,000 establishments with one or more employees in miscellaneous categories of commercial amusements (SIC 7949), primarily in amusement parks and in classified commercial amusements.

Amusements and recreation services can be expected to have a substantial increase in numbers of firms in the next decade, benefiting from increased leisure time and higher incomes.

OTHER MISCELLANEOUS SERVICE SECTORS (SIC 80-89)

Certain miscellaneous services deserve brief mention because they represent to a considerable extent new business opportunities rather than the expansion of professional or nonprofit services. Medical and dental laboratories (SIC 8071 and 8072) and certain health services (SIC 809) (which includes nursing homes) represent the business opportunities created by the expansion of medical and dental services. This group grew by more than 1,600 reporting units between 1959 and 1962, and will continue rapid expansion into the next decade as part of the total expansion of medical and dental care.

Accounting, auditing, and bookkeeping services (SIC 893) are closely related to the business services described earlier, and are also a rapidly growing category with a growth of 1,900 reporting units between 1959 and 1962. This rapid growth will probably continue as new specialized services develop and benefit from increased contracting out of services previously performed within the firm, especially the small one.

5

SMALL BUSINESS
IN
CONSTRUCTION

The construction sector has been a traditional stronghold of small business because of the localized nature of the market, the ease of entry, and the need of the industry for flexibility to adapt to variations in demand, both seasonal and cyclical. Predictions on size trends and growth in the number of firms in construction in the next decade require internal analysis of the industry and of the relation of size structure to the level of construction activity. Elaborate statistics are available on the performance of the industry, housing starts, public and private construction expenditures, etc., but data on size structure are woefully inadequate. There has been no Census of Construction since 1939; information must be pieced together from public and private sources with serious limitations.

Even trends in the total number of firms present problems in measurement because of the importance of the one-man firm in this sector. The only statistics available in some detail are the figures from County Business Patterns,[1] which exclude firms with no employees. These figures show an increase from 181,000 reporting units in 1947 to 296,000 in 1962.

In contrast, the Office of Business Economics, whose annual estimates include firms with no payroll but a stable place of business, showed an increase over the same period from 268,000 to 473,000—an increase of almost twice as many firms, suggesting the importance of the self-employed in the construction sector.

----

[1]County Business Patterns has data on reporting units and employment for industry groups under the Old Age and Survivors Insurance Program (OASI). A reporting unit is a single establishment or group of establishments of the same employer within one county. Reporting units and contracting firms are probably quite close for those with one employee or more, except for the largest contractors who have operations in widely separate locations with offices of the firm in each. Data on units and employment appearing in this section are from the United States Summary, County Business Patterns, 1947, 1953, 1959, 1962. United States Department of Commerce.

Breakdown by employment size is available from the County Business Patterns figures; but, because of the subcontracting system, it understates the size of firms in the contractor group. This subcontracting pattern also means that the great postwar growth of employment in the building industry was concentrated in special trades contractors (SIC 17) with an increase of 52 per cent from 1947-62, as contrasted with 13 per cent for building contractors (SIC 15) over the same period.

Because of smallness of scale, a large part of the postwar expansion in the construction industry took place through an increase in the number of firms; but rapid growth subsided as the residential building boom leveled out. There was virtually no net growth in the total number of firms with one or more employees between 1956 and 1962, and a slight decline in employment.

Only the smaller group of highway and heavy construction contractors (SIC 16) continued to grow, reflecting the relatively faster rate of growth in public construction activity, particularly highways.

Just as important for present purposes as the growth in the number of small firms is the extent to which growth has taken place in the scale of firms.

SPECIAL TRADES CONTRACTORS (SIC 17)

Employment data can be used more accurately as an indication of size of firm for the special trades contractors than for the general contractors. The average number of employees per reporting unit, 6.6, stayed exactly the same from 1947-62, and the distribution of reporting units by employment size stayed relatively similar, strongly suggesting stability of size of firm in this section of the industry. A detailed study of special trades contractors in one metropolitan area showed that 71 per cent of trade contractors had a volume of less than $50,000 annually, as contrasted with 38 per cent for builders.[2]

---

[2]Sherman Maisel, Housebuilding in Transition (Berkeley, California: University of California Press, 1953), p. 144. By far the largest group of self-employed included in the OBE total on construction is probably in the special trades.

This is the largest section of the industry, representing about one half of the employment and more than 60 per cent of the reporting units. The bulk of the firms in the special trades derive their income from residential building, both new building and repair and maintenance.

Expansion in residential building is accomplished to a large extent through expansion in the special trades; and because of the smallness of scale, expansion results in the entry of many new firms—for example, almost 71,000 reporting units between 1947 and 1959. Just as expansion results in the entry of new firms, a decline has an important effect on reducing the number of firms, as it did by 6,000 units in the period between 1959 and 1962. This decline was exclusively in the units employing less than fifty employees, with the larger units actually gaining in number.

This illustrates one of the major reasons for the continued strength of subcontracting in the building industry. Despite the substantial increase in the scale of homebuilding since the War, subcontracting has not diminished in strength. Large builders who experimented with vertical integration in the early 1950's generally went back to the use of subcontractors except to a limited extent for painting and concrete work.[3]

The integration of a function requires not only supervisory time, but also a system of cost estimation. By the use of subcontractors, the builder can estimate his costs exactly and limit his function to the coordination of the subcontractors. Moreover, the builder gains much greater flexibility in meeting seasonal and other fluctuations with a smaller staff of direct employees. The risks of fluctuation, which are absorbed in large part by the special trades contractors, are a further reason for the relative smallness of scale of the subcontractors.

It is to be expected, therefore, that as residential building picks up in the latter part of the decade, the greater part of the expansion in both firms and employment will probably take place in the subcontracting trades with a large net increase in the number of small units in the trades.

---

[3]John Herzog, The Dynamics of Large Scale Building (Berkeley, California: University of California Press, 1965), p. 69.

The main counterpressure to this tendency will be the increasing trend to off-site fabrication of components. Prefabrication of the total housing unit has not been successful on a large scale in competing in cost, except for the low-price mobile home. Greater strides have been made in the use of prefabricated parts of the house. There is widespread use of prehung doors, windows, roof trusses, staircases, and, increasingly, of wall sections.

In a search for markets, building materials producers have been entering increasingly into the manufacture of prefabricated shells and components, and are in a much better position to pioneer than the prefabricated homes industry, which has been plagued by serious financial problems.

For example, substantial development work is now being done on "core" units (kitchen-bathroom-utilities) which would move much electrical and plumbing work off-site.[4] However, judging from the evolutionary pattern of the industry, radical change in the use of mechanical "core" units or other components is fairly remote. Builders need time to evaluate the cost advantages of a new development. Since the direct cost is usually higher, the indirect advantages have to be demonstrated. For this reason, three to five years lead time must be counted on for a new development to get more general use, and several more years before it is widespread. (And in older areas, where code problems are more severe, change takes place even more slowly.)

Consequently, the impact of change on the special trades is gradual, and it is unlikely that by 1970 the pace of off-site fabrication will be fast enough to offset the impact of increased residential building, although more offset can be anticipated over the following decade.

BUILDING CONTRACTORS (SIC 15)

The scale of building contractors cannot be measured by OASI data because of the subcontracting system. Better measures of size are either housing units produced or annual

---

[4]Richard W. O'Neil, "Technology's Promise and Performance," House and Home (November, 1963), pp. 83-116.

receipts, but unfortunately no systematic data on either are available by industry group.

Information on annual receipts for the construction sector as a whole is available from income tax sources. This shows a more significant role for larger units than data on employment.

Figures for 1961-62[5] indicate that although 88 per cent of the total businesses have annual receipts of less than $100,000 a year (largely sole proprietorships), they account for only one fifth of total receipts of the industry. But the 1 per cent of the businesses (overwhelmingly corporate in form) receiving more than $1 million in annual receipts account for nearly half (43 per cent). Only firms with over $5 million receipts at that time might appropriately have been classified "medium" instead of "small,"[6] and in the aggregate they received less than half of the receipts of the group of firms with receipts over $1 million.

Because no adequate data are available on the building contractor group as such, special attention will be focused on residential building to which the bulk of building contractors are attached. Also included in residential building are the operative builders (SIC 656) who have become a dominant force in the industry.[7]

---

[5]"Statistics of Income 1961-1962," Business Tax Returns (Washington, D. C.: Internal Revenue Service. Also see Appendix Tables 8A, B.

[6]The amount of receipts used by the Small Business Administration at that time as the limit for loan purposes was $5 million. It has been raised subsequently to $7 million.

[7]OASI figures for 1962 showed 6,000 reporting units for operative builders as contrasted with 87,000 for building contractors (which includes other types of building besides residential, its largest component). The last official estimate was that approximately 70 per cent of single family homes were built by operative builders in the last quarter of 1955 and 67 per cent in the first quarter of 1956, as contrasted with 50 per cent in 1949. Kathryn R. Murphy, "Builders of New One Family Houses, 1955-1956," Construction Review (August-September, 1958).

THE SCALE OF RESIDENTIAL BUILDING

Measures of housing output probably provide the best measure of size of residential building firms, the most important single part of the construction industry. The Census of Construction of 1939 found that builders of over 100 houses accounted for 5 per cent of the output. A subsequent survey in 1949 by the Bureau of Labor Statistics found that the figure had increased to 24 per cent.[8] The Bureau of Building and Marketing Research found in its 1963 builder survey that builders of seventy-five or more housing units accounted for 48 per cent of the total units reported.[9]

The 1964 survey of its membership by the National Association of Homebuilders indicates a comparable figure of 51 per cent of total volume by builders of over 100 housing units.[10] This represents a substantial drop from its survey of 1959 in which builders of 100 or more units accounted for 62 per cent of total volume. The biggest decline was in the builders of over 500 units, a decline from 24 per cent to 15 per cent. This decline may be somewhat exaggerated as the NAHB memberships seems to underrepresent builders of multi-units.[11]

However, it is probably safe to conclude that the nationwide percentage of building done by builders of over 75 or 100 units has probably not increased substantially in the last five years.

---

[8]Maisel, op. cit., p. 26. The percentage was 35 per cent in 1949 in the faster growing San Francisco Bay area.

[9]Practical Builder (November, 1964), p. 87. No information is given as to the size sample on which the more than 60,000 total is based.

[10]The 1964 NAHB Builder Membership Survey (Washington, D.C.: National Association of Homebuilders, 1964).

[11]Ibid., pp. 4-6. It is estimated on the basis of the sample that NAHB membership accounted for 76 per cent of single-family home production and 44 per cent of the total multi-family construction. Also, multi-unit production in the sample had only 13 per cent in high-rises as contrasted with approximately 22 per cent for the country as a whole in the spring of 1964.

Scale is dependent on favorable demand conditions, and the past five years have not seen a buoyant housing market as unfavorable demographic factors have dampened the effect of a growing GNP. This is reflected in the changing concerns of builders found in the Homebuilders' survey. The 1959 NAHB survey found that builders considered land costs and mortgage money their two most pressing problems while in 1964 their greatest concern was for lack of markets, and merchandising and selling.

Herzog's study of northern California homebuilding corroborates the scope of the change in scale of building and indicates its greater magnitude in a large metropolitan area with rapid population growth.[12] This study found the builder of more than 100 homes responsible for 34 per cent of the housing output in 1950 and 74 per cent in 1960.[13] Metropolitan areas with less substantial population growth have lagged considerably behind these figures. A 1950 comparison of the Boston and San Francisco area demonstrates the striking difference at that time: housing starts by builders of more than 100 homes accounted for only 11 per cent in Boston while San Francisco builders of more than 100 homes built 35 per cent of the total. This was closely related to the market situation created by a population increase of 52 per cent from 1940-50 for San Francisco and only 8 per cent for Boston.[14]

Not only has the builder of more than 100 houses become increasingly important in the industry, but hand in hand the "merchant" or operative builder has accounted for an increasing share of the market.

The shift to somewhat larger-scale residential building was made possible by rapid postwar growth in the industry, and has only slowed down as demand sagged. It is a response

---

[12]Herzog, op. cit.

[13]Ibid. , p. 20.

[14]F. E. Balderston, A Study of Cost and Organization in Thirteen Construction Firms (Cambridge, Massachusetts: Massachusetts Institute of Technology, May, 1953), pp. 6-21.

to the economies of scale for a larger builder, so well documented in Sherman Maisel's landmark study.[15] He found that the optimum production scale was at the 200- to 500-unit range. Beyond this range, the same procedures were duplicated, both for direct labor and subcontracts.

Indirect savings, largely through improved management, may encourage somewhat greater size—Herzog suggests 500 to 800 units as the optimal size[16]—but there are more serious limitations to growth than in many industries. Some of the impediments to the growth of "housing giants" are the loss of flexibility, increased marketing problems, production problems, and greater capital problems.

The local nature of the market is the greatest limitation to the growth of larger firms. Only if firms go into markets on a regional or national scale can they expand beyond a size determined by the local market. Housing output varies both seasonally and cyclically, putting a premium on an organization that can react quickly to changing conditions. Operating in many, dispersed locations may create severe diseconomies of management, since the risk of decision-making is so great that the principals find it too costly to delegate authority.[17]

HOW LARGE IS THE LARGE HOMEBUILDER?

Although this postwar shift in the scale of residential building is spectacular in terms of the industry, it is still largely a shift in the relationships of the "small" to each other and to the new "medium-sized" firms. Most "large" builders (over 100 units) are still small enough to face the typical problems of managerial limitations and inadequate capital for growth.

---

[15]Maisel, op. cit., especially pp. 189-222.

[16]Herzog, op. cit., p. 27.

[17]Even the large housing corporations that have gone public still have highly personalized leadership (e.g., Levitt) and operate in only a few markets at any one time.

The amount of annual receipts set by the Small Business Administration for the construction industry as the limit for "small," $7.5 million in annual receipts, is also roughly the amount at which a firm can afford to "go public" and get outside capital by a national stock issue. The number of home-building firms that have become publicly held corporations is still very small but has increased in the last five years since Levitt made the first such move in 1958. Now some twenty-two firms have stock that is widely enough traded to be listed on the House and Home monthly list. [18] If land development firms are included, the total is forty-nine.

The $7.5 million receipt figure corresponds very roughly to a volume of 500 housing units a year. The Homebuilders' member survey of 1959 found that this group accounted for 24 per cent of the volume, but by 1964 it had declined to 15 per cent. [19] As mentioned earlier, this survey was biased toward smaller builders of multi-units so that this decline may not be representative of nationwide figures. Because many large homebuilders are also involved in other types of building, undoubtedly there are quite a number of builders of less than 500 houses who have total receipts of over $7.5 million.

The over-500 or over-$7.5 million homebuilder firm can be most accurately described as a "medium" business. If it is operating profitably, it is in a position to acquire equity capital from a wide variety of sources, including a public issue. Its managerial staff is large enough to use the specialities of modern business management. As contrasted with the large single-tract builder of the early 1950's building for an assured market, the large building firm of the 1960's is increasingly diversified to minimize the greater risk its scale entails. This may include diversification within a single market into different kinds of building, expanding into related areas such as land development, mortgage lending, and real estate, and operating in more than one metropolitan area.

---

[18] House and Home (April, 1965), p. 35.

[19] The 1964 NAHB Builder Membership Survey, op. cit., p. 5.

THE IMPACT OF LARGER FIRMS IN
RESIDENTIAL BUILDING

There is little evidence yet that concentration is a danger in the homebuilding industry. Herzog's study found that in 1960 in Northern California, an area of rapid growth, the four largest firms accounted for 11 per cent of total housebuilding, and the eight largest for 22 per cent. [20] Concentration would have been greater if the figures had been narrowed to a county basis, but this local concentration is offset by increasing geographical mobility throughout the wider area over time.

Large firms producing more than 100 units do a greater per cent of the business in metropolitan areas. And as among metropolitan areas, those with most rapid population and economic growth furnish the best opportunity for the rapid growth of such firms. Not only does the firm size of local builders grow as a response to market demand, but such areas attract outside capital of large building firms.

It is in these fast growth areas of Florida, California, Hawaii, Texas, and Washington, D.C., which account for more than a third of all new housing starts, that many of the "new town" developments are being planned. [21] Large planned communities will be an increasingly important factor in these areas in the next five years. House and Home estimated that by 1969 9 per cent of all housing starts will be in such large, planned communities. Their impact in particular areas will be especially important. For example, two such developments in the Sacramento area must each capture 10 per cent of the market

---

[20]Herzog, op. cit., p. 27.

[21]Robert W. Murray, "New Towns in America," House and Home (February, 1964), p. 123 ff. Properly defined, many of the so-called "new towns" are large, planned communities or subdivisions. The new town, properly speaking, includes a substantial employing sector, either industrial or institutional, and a population with a wide range of income. Because large planned subdivisions will receive Federal help from the Housing Act of 1965, while new towns will not, and because of the zoning obstacles new towns have encountered in many places, it would appear that most of the growth in the next five years will be in the large, planned subdivisions rather than in "new towns."

by 1970 to be successful. However, this would still be far from an oligopoly position.

What is the impact, if any, of the larger firms in the local market upon the smaller firms? Entry cannot be restricted and will continue to be easy for the small contractor, due to the minimal amount of capital needed.

A period of decline in housing demand or of credit restriction affects the smaller builder much more seriously. Because of his capital limitations, he is in a position neither to hold inventory nor to switch quickly to different types of building. This adverse effect is not due to any action of the larger builders as such, but simply to their superior capital resources.[22] However, the handling of unsold inventory by large builders, and also FHA handling of its repossessed homes, can augment the problems of the smaller operative builder who cannot compete in price cutting or easy credit terms.

PROSPECTS FOR THE HOMEBUILDING INDUSTRY IN THE DECADE AHEAD

The unfavorable demographic influences that have slowed residential building will alter radically by the end of the decade. Beginning in 1967, the number of new households will increase sharply.

These demographic changes and continuous growth in the Gross National Product led the National Planning Association to predict housing starts in the range of 1,900,000 for 1970—a net increase of almost 400,000 from present levels.

A resumption of upward growth of housing demand will encourage growth in size of firms, and at the same time provide an umbrella for the continued entry and more rapid growth

[22]The Herzog study, op. cit., pp. 41-46, documents the greater stability of the larger builders through a tight money period. The larger builder has a longer lead time, so that he can shorten his span of backlog of commitments and, to the extent that he must pay higher discounts, he is in a better cost position to absorb them. Land profits help the big builder, so that he can afford a loss on construction if he can make a profit on land.

in the number of small firms. But an upward trend in housing starts does not preclude shifts in local demand. In fact, the existence of large firms from outside that can enter "boom" markets, as well as local firms capable of quick expansion, means that overbuilding, in certain categories of building, at least, can take place quickly, as happened recently in Sacramento and Phoenix. An increasing premium is put on the large firm that can diversify in the local market and expand beyond one geographical area.

The shift to the building of multi-family units is part of this diversification as well as the shift to commercial building and related fields of endeavor such as mortgage lending, real estate, and land development.

Builders of over 100 units account for a much larger share of multi-family units than of single-family homes, so that the population shifts which favor the net growth of the young and the old and stimulate demand for multi-family units will further increase the number of larger firms.

Land development companies with their lucrative investment potential are now becoming the giants of the industry as a result of the inflow of outside capital from oil companies, insurance companies, and building material producers. These development firms are not necessarily builders. Their impact on the building industry will depend, therefore, not only on the fraction of the market they capture, but on the extent to which they build directly, use contractors, or sell or lease land to outside building firms. But it seems likely that except for certain custom-built or higher-priced units within large planned communities, the great proportion of units will be built by builders large enough to reach the economies of scale, at least 100 units or more.

Government policy also will have a significant role in the pace of change in the size and type of firm. Special provisions that have given more favorable credit terms to multi-units and urban renewal have encouraged the shift to greater production of multi-units. Tax advantages to investors have encouraged new apartment construction. The proposal that FHA give land loans for new planned subdivisions and new towns, if enacted, would give further encouragement to the growth of larger firms.[23]

---

[23]See explanatory footnote 21.

However, the Herzog study gives evidence that most of the increase in share of the output by larger firms will probably be accounted for by an increase in the number of large firms rather than in large firms becoming larger,[24] unless large planned communities or "new towns" by single building companies become a dominant force. The smallest homebuilding firms will grow in number, as increasing income expands the market for the higher-priced, custom-built house in which the small builder has the greatest aptitude, but their total share of the market will probably decline.

NONRESIDENTIAL CONSTRUCTION

Inadequate as data on homebuilding firms are, there has been much greater interest in them because of the size and greater homogeneity of the homebuilding industry. Nonresidential building contractors are probably only a very minor fraction in the total number of firms because the scale of projects is much greater, encouraging large scale. Moreover, there is often an overlap, so that larger firms that are building apartments may be building office buildings too.

They have many characteristics in common with the firms in the highway and heavy construction field. Much of the contracting is with public bodies or large institutional customers on the sizable contracts, requiring substantial capitalization to meet performance bonds.

But the size of the firm is still limited by the localization of construction, even though demand may be more related to regional and national trends. Serious limitations on expansionism result from the problems of management span in many scattered physical locations, and maintaining an even flow of contracts.

---

[24] Herzog, op. cit., pp. 25-32. Most of the great expansion in production by larger builders in the San Francisco Bay area between 1950 and 1960 was accomplished by the entry of new firms rather than by the expansion of existing firms. Herzog believes that more concentration did not take place because of (1) lack of economies of large scale and (2) a relatively high degree of mobility among large-scale builders.

Nonetheless, subject to these limitations, a somewhat larger scale in nonresidential construction can probably be anticipated in the next decade as a result of the continued expansion of local markets through increasing metropolitanization, industrial growth, and increased demand for public facilities.

Firms operating in the highway and heavy construction field resemble the nonresidential building contractors just described, with greater scale resulting from the greater value of contracts, and from the heavier capitalization needed for much more expensive equipment.

Their markets are also less narrowly local because of the importance of state and Federal contracts. Particularly firms that contract with the Federal Government or with large national corporations can more easily operate on a regional or national basis, although the problems of developing managerial organization to operate at many widely scattered sites are still crucial.

Employment data from OASI indicate that the scale of firms is the largest for this section of the industry. Average employment per reporting unit increased from 21.7 per reporting unit in 1947 to 26.0 in 1953, but declined to 19.4 by 1962 because of the increase in the number of small firms. However, the number of units employing more than 500 was greater than in building and special trades contractors combined.[25]

Information on size structure is so inadequate that predictions for the decade ahead become very speculative. But it would appear that sustained demand in the public sector will continue to encourage the growth in numbers of firms as well as some growth in scale of the largest firms. But this scale is still limited by the management problems and risk entailed by the spatial and intermittent characteristics of construction.

---

[25]The fact that most of the larger firms are operating at widely scattered sites over a state or region and so appear as several reporting units, means that the size of firm is actually much larger than employment data would indicate.

6

SMALL BUSINESS ORGANIZATION
AND
MANAGEMENT

FORMS OF ORGANIZATION AND OPERATION

The traditional forms of business organization are the proprietorship, the partnership, and the corporation. Which of these a business elects is largely determined by the size and kind of business, its mode of financing, and the circumstances of the individual firm. Most small businesses are proprietorships—the simplest and most flexible form, legally and operationally, as well as in matters of taxation. They are usually businesses which are predominantly an outgrowth of the personal energies and competence of the proprietors. This form of organization is also in specific ways financially more restrictive and riskier. In 1963, the U.S. business population included over 9 million sole proprietorships, about a million partnerships, and over a million corporations.

Businesses above the smallest size are likely to elect the corporate form, which in addition to limiting the liability of the owners, opens wider possibilities of financing. It facilitates separation of investment and ownership from management, where this is advantageous. It subjects the business to corporation income taxes, unless the business is organized as a "small business corporation" to permit shareholders to treat earnings and losses as ordinary personal income. Shares in the business can be sold and the proceeds invested in the business or accrued to existing shareholders as capital gains.

When the advantages and disadvantages of the traditional forms are analyzed, it does not appear that the choice of one or another in itself has much effect on the chance of survival of a small business. Some small businessmen have turned to other devices—of operational rather than legal significance—to reduce the risks, or to insure a market, or to enable them to improve their technical or managerial efficiency, or to realize economies of scale in transactions with, or in competition with, larger businesses.

One of the oldest of such devices is the cooperative. Though more widely used in agriculture, cooperatives have been used by small businesses as a means of joint buying, joint marketing, and joint research, on a scale which would be beyond the reach of individual small firms. Cooperatives are generally formed to permit members (who are also stockholders) to pool their business strength by acting in concert to buy, sell, or invest on more advantageous terms than would be obtainable by them acting as individuals. Small grocers or druggists can join together to buy goods through cooperative buying, or through a cooperatively-owned wholesale business, on a large scale; to establish brand names; or to cooperate in advertising programs and merchandising. Small producers can pool their products for sale through a cooperative marketing agency to obtain better terms from large buyers.

The cooperative, though useful, has limited application to small business. It can help bring economies of scale in buying and selling to small business engaged in more or less standardized operations, capable of pooling for the purpose of simulating the operations of larger, more integrated companies. But by the same token, its use is limited because it does not lend itself to the differentiation and specialization characteristic of so much of small business.

A form of operation more suited to many kinds of small business is franchising, which is becoming increasingly widespread.

In its early historical application, a franchise was "a system under which a manufacturer granted to certain dealers the right to sell his product or service, in a generally defined area, in exchange for a promise to promote and merchandise the product in a specific manner."[1] As franchise selling has evolved to encompass a wider segment of the economy, the definition has broadened to include "any contract under which the independent retailers or wholesalers are organized to distribute given products or services."[2]

---

[1]William P. Hall, "Franchising-New Scope for an Old Technique," Harvard Business Review (Jan.-Feb., 1962), p. 62.

[2]Ibid.

For the franchisee, the agreement represents his licensed right to conduct a specified business, usually under a specific trade name and usually in a designated territory. The agreement is usually a continuous arrangement, requiring the franchisee to maintain specified standards of performance. For the market supplier or franchisor, the agreement will bind him to provide the franchise dealer with assistance in organizing the business and training its employees, and in operations and merchandising. In many instances, the franchisor will also provide management aid to the franchisee. In return for the right to conduct the business and for assistance provided, the franchisee will pay a fee or royalties or agree to buy part or all of his supplies from the franchisor. Such an arrangement represents essentially a system of distribution.

Four types of franchising have evolved in recent years, and in each type, retail sales represent a major share of the volume.[3]

(1) Manufacturer - Retailer—In this category, manufacturers may franchise the entire retail outlet, such as automobiles and gasoline stations; or a single department in a store which undertakes to sell no other line of merchandise in a particular department, such as women's wear; or, a line within a department, such as TV's and radios.

(2) Manufacturer - Wholesaler—The prime example is the franchising of a brand or line of soft drinks to a wholesale bottler-distributor.

(3) Service - Sponsor Retailer—In this case the program is built around a service sponsored by the franchisor. This category includes, for example, food drive-ins, motels, and auto rentals. The sale of a product, such as food, may be involved and sometimes the franchisor performs a manufacturing or wholesaling function for all or part of the products. In this category of franchising, fees often form an important part of the franchisor's income.

---

[3] Ibid., pp. 62-63.

(4) Wholesaler - Retailer—These are relationships be-
    tween a distributor seeking to realize economies of
    scale in merchandising a private brand line, and a
    retailer seeking an affiliation to realize economies of
    scale in buying private brands. The franchise is granted
    exclusively to one retailer in the franchise area and
    becomes his private brand with which he can compete
    with brands of the chains. The franchisor earns his
    profit on the sale of merchandise and ordinarily does
    not rely on franchise fees for a significant part of
    his revenue.

There are various ways in which franchisees are financed.
Some franchisors give the franchisees the option of paying a
lump sum at the beginning, or of making payments, including
an interest charge, over some specified period of time. Other
franchisors require a down payment and will either finance the
balance themselves or will guarantee a bank loan with the
dealer's inventory as security.

Nationwide car dealerships and gasoline stations are evidence that franchising has been long practiced, but there has
been a rapid growth in franchising in recent years. The
International Franchise Association estimates that in the
thirteen largest franchise groups, 338,292 franchised outlets
account for approximately $60 billion annual volume per year.
Approximately two thirds of the total number of outlets in
this group are gasoline stations, and another 10 per cent are
automobile and truck dealers. It is the remaining 20 per cent
or so that have experienced a phenomenal growth, from almost
nothing at the end of World War II to an estimated 100,000
outlets in 1963.

This growth has taken place primarily in the retail and
service industries. An analysis of 556 firms listed in the 1964
edition of Franchise Annual shows that 74 per cent of the firms
were in the retail service trades. [4]

---

[4]U.S. Congress, Senate, Distribution Problems Affecting Small
Business, Part 1, "Franchising Agreements," Hearing before Subcommittee on Antitrust and Monopoly of the Committee of the Judiciary,
89th Cong., 1st Sess. (Washington, D.C.: Government Printing Office,
March 23, 1965), p. 97.

One of the major reasons for the rapid growth is that franchise techniques offer the franchisor quick expansion at a relatively low cost because a substantial part of the investment is contributed by the franchise holder. By doing this, the franchisor can make rapid gains without commensurate investment and risk. It is also a means for a company to increase sales and profits from regional or national operations without itself having to undertake to staff distant and scattered outlets for its products. Franchising thus presents an alternative to centrally-owned chains which require large amounts of capital investment. At the same time it allows a company to match, at least to some extent, the distribution and purchasing advantages of large chains and discount houses.

The franchise system also offers many benefits to the franchisee. Foremost is the reduction of risk it offers to many businesses.

It offers a small businessman a better chance of survival and success than if he sets up his business from scratch. He receives technical, managerial, operational, marketing, and often financial assistance from an experienced franchisor who has evolved an established and successful pattern of operation. Many decisions that might be crucial for the independent businessman are made for the franchisee.

Another advantage to the franchisee is that the amount of capital required is often less than for an independent business. An analysis of 179 firms by the Department of Commerce's Task Force for Equal Opportunities showed that about 36 per cent required an investment of $5,000 or less and about 70 per cent required $7,500 or less.

For his part, the franchisor has the strongest incentives to assure the success of the franchisee. His growth and profitability depend on the number and the abilities of his franchisees as businessmen and managers. The spectacle of numerous failures would deter the more capable and better financed prospects.

Because the franchisor cannot afford to let his franchisees fail, he frequently will go to great lengths to keep them afloat.

The result is a low failure rate, said to be less than 10 per cent[5] for the industry as a whole. Most of the big franchisors are so managed that their reported failure rate is less than 1 per cent of these franchises. Usually available to the franchisee of the better managed organizations are scientific site selection, market analysis, packaging facilities, tested architectural interior and exterior design, leasing and financing aid, merchandising, promotion and advertising aid, accounting procedures and inventory control, staff training, and help with all the usual problems of management.

In return for reduced risk, the franchisee yields part of his independence and his freedom of choice and decision. The constant supervision that some parent companies maintain over their franchisees may be unpalatable to a businessman who prizes his independence. The franchise is a "half-way house" between entrepreneurship and employment.

Generally, one of two policies is followed by franchisors in the pricing of goods and services. Typically the franchisor may either issue a suggested price or set prices in terms of his own competitive situation. When price competition enters the situation, the latter policy may be the only one feasible. Less common is the practice of specifying the price at which the franchised product or services must be sold. Control such as this generally indicates that the franchisees are expected to follow very closely the operating methods developed by the franchisor. Other franchisors take a middle position and issue a list of maximum prices which the franchisee may not exceed.

Franchising permits a wide range of operating relationships between franchisor and franchisee. In some cases the latter is hardly more than an agent or branch manager, with little choice in the customary entrepreneurial and management decisions. In others he may perform most of the functions of entrepreneur and manager, using the name and certain basic products or services of the franchisor. The franchise form is very flexible and adaptable, as indeed it must be to accommodate businesses as various and specialized as automobile

---

[5] "It's Wise to Franchise," Dun's Review and Modern Industry (March, 1962), pp. 38-40.

dealerships, soft drink bottling, motels, mattress manufactures, doughnut stands, filling stations, and swimming pool construction.

Franchising also presents opportunities for minority groups to overcome their lack of past experience and to advance their economic and social independence.

Another established form of operation which is becoming increasingly common in distribution is the leased operation. This is most commonly an arrangement between a general merchandise retailer (e.g., department store or "discount house") and a specialist in a line of merchandise (e.g., beauty shop, watch repair, photographic studio). The specialist contracts for space in the general merchandise store, paying a percentage of sales, usually with a guaranteed minimum. The specialist gains the benefits of the store's name, location, traffic, conveniences (such as charge accounts), and good will. The store management gains the benefit of being able to offer a wider range of goods and services and of making intensive use of its space. It gains the advantage of top management in the speciality without itself having to assume the risks and burdens of merchandising a specialized operation with which it is unfamiliar and which may have many pitfalls.

Both parties to the contract realize the economies of scale and the economies of specialization which, given the nature of the specialty, would otherwise not be available to them. Such an arrangement is advantageous usually when the volume of business in a given store is too small to support the specialized management (e.g., watch repair) or when the merchandising operation requires a large number of outlets to achieve economies of scale in styling, manufacture, or purchasing (e.g., millinery or auto accessories).

PROFESSIONALIZATION OF MANAGEMENT

When the "causes of failure" of small business are analyzed, "poor management" is cited more often than any other. In one sense this is a tautology: the scope of small business "management" is so broad that any business failure is by definition a failure of "management" to gauge the market, to obtain the necessary financing, to operate the business efficiently, to control costs and set prices, to merchandise and market, etc.

Perhaps this is too broad a definition, and many sins are laid at the door of management which are not always within management control—undercapitalization, for example. But it is undoubtedly true that small business requires a broader and more sophisticated approach to management today than ever before, and that the requirements will become more rigorous as time goes on. If the range and complexity of management decisions and operations of a small business are less than those of a large one, the requirements of versatility, adaptability, and discernment may be greater. Small business, as we have seen, thrives on specialization in a large business environment. To know that specialized market and how to exploit it is the peculiar requirement of small business management, along with the range of functions common to all business management. The importance of this aspect of small business is recognized in a great deal of the research and activity of the Small Business Administration.

In the past, unevenness in the quality of management, as among the technical, the financial, the sales promotion, and the internal accounting aspects of business operation, has been a conspicuous characteristic of small concerns. Under the increased competition of today, the small entrepreneur is faced with a need for highly developed skills of many kinds. The fact that many small businesses, whether in manufacturing or in trade, ordinarily find their opportunities in specialized markets does not relieve them of the requirements of sound management in financing, operating, merchandising, promotion, and control. On the contrary, in order to exploit the advantages of specialization, the small business often may need tighter and more resourceful management than its large business counterpart.

Small business, by definition, is personalized rather than institutionalized in its management, and it is incumbent on the small businessman to employ sound, and sometimes sophisticated, management practices to sharpen the advantages of his personal knowledge and skills. His special advantage may lie in specialized technical knowledge or distinctiveness of design or high quality, or aggressive merchandising or fast service, but his ability to compete effectively requires close attention to all aspects of management.

Underfinancing, or high costs, or poor quality or service, or ignorance of his market can offset his advantage.

Consequently, managerial competence demands a wider range of skills and abilities of the small business operator, generally, than it does of managers in larger organizations. The small business manager usually cannot afford staff specialists. He must develop the skills himself or employ them. He must understand the techniques of development, production, financial analysis, planning and control, training and motivating personnel, advertising, sales promotion and sales management, and others. He must learn to evaluate economic conditions and plan accordingly. He must know what Government rules and regulations are applicable to him and what he must do to comply, and what responsibilities—to customers, employees, the public—are his and how to discharge them.

Technological improvement, better communication systems, faster transportation facilities, and the growth of management consultants, among other things, have provided a variety of tools available to management. For example, the computer, one of the most important technological advances available to management, can be used in planning, budget analysis, record keeping, marketing analysis, inventory and sales analysis, and many other functions. The availability and application of these tools may apply as well to the small business as to the large, although the application is on a small scale. In addition, there are Government agencies, universities, and thousands of publications to assist in the management of any kind of business.

Examples can be drawn from many fields:

(1) Computers—A small company, while unable to afford the purchase of costly computers, has available to it computer service companies (many of them small firms) which will work for a small company on an hourly basis. This includes anything from checkwriting to inventory control and sales analysis. The development of shared time is under way and may be expected to spread as costs decline.

(2) Consultative Services—Small business can draw, as needed, on outside management assistance and technological services to supplement their own capabilities. A small company can obtain help from a number

of outside non-Government sources that are especially
geared to filling this kind of a need. These sources
include:

(a) Consulting firms.
(b) Banks and other financial institutions.
(c) Business   service   centers   of   colleges   and
universities.
(d) Research laboratories.
(e) Nonprofit foundations.
(f) Trade associations.

In addition to these non-Government sources of assistance,
there are many Government sources, including such Federal
agencies as the Small Business Administration, and Government laboratories offering a wide variety of services and
publications useful to the small firm. Whether the problem
involves setting up retail inventory controls, organizing a
company, financing a new venture, or marketing a new product,
help is available, if the small business manager recognizes
his needs.

(3) Assistance from Suppliers or Customers—To an increasing extent large companies are realizing that it
is good business to help their small distributors, suppliers, or customers in the solution of operating, merchandising, record keeping, training, and similar management problems. Many large suppliers now provide
a wide range of management services, and access
to technical information is free or at a nominal
cost.

There are literally hundreds of thousands of small companies filling a multitude of needs in the interstices of our
national economy and filling them profitably. These are the
businesses that have met the requirements of good management. There is no substantial evidence that the increasing
complexity of individual business operations has to change the
success level of small business. What has changed is that the
small businessman can no longer successfully run his business
entirely by the "seat of his pants."

It appears that the trend toward professionalization of management raises three serious questions about the future of small business:

(1) If the trend continues, and perhaps accelerates, will small business thereby lose any part of its persistent share in the economy? There have been great advances in management techniques since World War II, and the trend continues unabated. During this period small business in the aggregate has lost no ground in the total economy. Many small businessmen have succeeded in adopting and using these new and better tools, if only as a condition of competitive survival. Many small business service firms now bring to other small businesses the equipment and techniques formerly available only to large companies. Further improvements in education are equipping the smaller businessman to understand and apply the new management concepts.

(2) Will any areas of the economy be foreclosed to small business because of the trend toward more scientific management practices? The tremendous capital requirements needed to compete in mass production and merchandising and in certain technically oriented industries, and not the advent of professionalized management, have probably foreclosed some sectors to the smaller firm. There are, however, significant counter trends even in these sectors. For example, through the use of scientific methods for depth analysis of the entire business operation, large corporations are now able to determine functions which, because of requirements of specialization and scale, cannot be economically performed "in house." This is creating new markets for small business in specialized manufacturing and business services.

Advances in management of large firms may spill over to small ones. A gasoline retailer still has to keep books, but the holder of his franchise tells him how and provides the forms. An automotive or electronics repairman has to adapt to new and more complicated equipment, but in many cases not without help from the manufacturer in training and technical aids. Obversely, small business has already found a place among those who are offering scientific management services, such as computerized bookkeeping or inventory control, on a commercial basis to a wide range of customers. In its total effect, professionalization of management may have opened to small business at least as many doors as it has closed.

(3) If, as often alleged, poor management has been the major reason for small business failure, can the advent of professionalized management reduce the mortality rate of small businesses? This question is difficult to answer. Probably there is a size level (different in different lines of business) below which a business can make only limited use of sophisticated techniques. This is the same size group where the greatest birth and death rates occur. Probably the application of professionalized management is most relevant to those firms which survive and grow to a point of some size and stability. These are also the firms of greatest value to the economy.

CHAPTER **7** THE DEMOGRAPHY
OF
SMALL BUSINESS

The most conspicuous characteristic of the business population in the United States is its vitality and continuous growth. In many ways, in its cycles of "births" and "deaths" and its propensities to multiply, it exhibits many of the characteristics of a living population—perhaps more analogous to a forest than to an animal population. Like a forest with its crop of seedlings and its mixture of species and sizes, the business population has been shown to be a population with high "birth" rates, high rates of "infant mortality," a small but persistent excess of births over deaths, and a median age currently of about eleven years.[1]

The business population (98 or 99 per cent of it small) is more than a reflection of economic and market conditions. It has an organic quality, rooted in the socio-economic system of the United States: the ecology of the open society; the enterprise economy; the qualities, attitudes, and experience of the people; the manner and level of living and working; the value system; etc.

The number of businesses grows with the aggregate economy and with the passage of time.[2] Different size and industry segments grow differentially, according to circumstances of the market and the changing opportunities it offers; and the whole is affected by outside influences, such as the limitation of opportunities during World War II and the removal of those limitations afterward. But the dominant trait for the past thirty years has been regular and (except for the War) almost uninterrupted growth. Moreover, immediately after

---

[1]The median age in 1954 (6.75 years) was lower than at present because of the extremely large numbers of births in the immediate postwar years. In 1947 half of businesses were under three years old. Betty Churchill, "Age and Life Expectancy of Business Firms," Survey of Current Business, (December, 1955).

[2]Betty C. Churchill, "Rise in the Business Population," Survey of Current Business (May, 1959), p. 16.

the War, the business population rebounded sharply, almost exactly to the level that could have been anticipated for 1947 had the War not intervened. (One is tempted to say, "Like the marriage rate.")

This regularity of growth is the more impressive in the light of the high rates of turnover within the business population. Annual rates of births between 1951 and 1956 averaged 86 per 1,000 in the business population as a whole, and ranged among industries for the most part between 50 and 100 per 1,000.[3] Similarly, annual discontinuance rates (which do not include businesses transferred from one ownership to another) averaged 71 per 1,000 and ranged from industry to industry about as widely as births. Yet in spite of these highly variable movements of the individual sectors at different rates and in opposite directions, the business population has shown a smooth trend of growth since the War. It seems to suggest that the smooth trend is itself a primary phenomenon, expressing a complex of socio-economic forces in American life, and that the differing rates of change of sectors within the business population express the manner in which the business population at any time responds to changes in the structure of demand and economic opportunity.

The suggestion here is that there exists an "autonomous demand" for the status of "businessman" in certain segments of the labor force; that this is inherent in the nature of the United States society; that it persists (unless externally restrained) through a variety of transitory changes in the economy. When one examines the various correlation studies undertaken to "explain" or project the size and composition of the business population, one is struck with the embarrassment of variables which correlate very highly with the total number of business firms: gross product, employment, population, and the passage of time.[4] One is tempted to conclude that the business population is correlated with the United States.

---

[3]Ibid., p. 19.

[4]National Planning Association, Projections of the Number of Firms by Industry and State, Regional Economic Projection Series (April, 1964).

As the population grows, so does the number of would-be entrepreneurs.[5] Population, likewise, is probably an element in the "supply" of business opportunities. Of greatest importance in determining the "supply" is the growth of the gross national product, which itself reflects the growth of the private and public market for goods and services, the volume of savings for private capital, and other elements vital in generating business enterprises.[6]

The business population continues to grow despite conspicuous risks facing new enterprises, and especially small enterprises. It is estimated that even in the relatively favorable decade of 1944-53 only two thirds of new or transferred business survived one year and only about half survived two years.[7] A "life table" from early postwar experience shows this very high "infant mortality": in most industry divisions, only one fourth to one third of firms could expect to complete their fifth year. Beyond that, survival rates rise sharply.

Thus at any given time, the business population with a median age of about ten years consists of two sectors: the sector of relatively stable older firms, most of which are five years old or more; and the sector of young firms with high rates of entry and discontinuance. In the early 1960's, an entry rate of about 9 per cent was required to maintain a net increase in the business population of about 1 per cent.

Much of the high turnover is among "little businesses," as defined earlier, and reflects shifts of individuals between employment and business activity which is an alternative or

---

[5]It is possible that the labor force, as the economically active segment of the population or, perhaps, males aged thirty to fifty as the supply of potential entrepreneurs, would be more significant than the total population in the demand for business opportunities.

[6]As a measure of the character of the market and the rate of personal saving, gross product or income per capita might be even more revealing.

[7]Churchill, "Age and Life Expectancy of Business Firms," op. cit., pp. 17-18.

substitute for employment. This is suggested, for example, by the much-higher-than-average rates of entry and discontinuance in contract construction, transportation (trucking and hacking), eating and drinking places, and filling stations. High rates of turnover in the business population apply also to the "small business" component: to small mines and quarries, sawmills, automobile dealers, and small factories in the apparel and machinery industries.

The most recent data indicate that in the early 1960's there was a brisk entry rate, even in the industry divisions, notably manufacturing and construction, in which there was no net increase. In those years new businesses were formed at an annual rate equivalent to something over 9 per cent of the business population, and businesses were discontinued at a rate of about 8 per cent. The total population has increased at a smooth and very slowly diminishing rate of about 1.3 per cent per year over the period 1949-63, tapering to about 1.1 per cent in the past five years. This very closely matches the hypothesis that the "demand" for business opportunities is related to the size of the economically active population.

The supply of business opportunities appears to reflect the size and composition of the economy and its characteristic forms of production, distribution, and consumption. This is clearly evident in the changing composition of the business population (Chart I), which shows how the number of firms in the several industry divisions accommodates to the changes in the composition of aggregate demand: the declining relative importance of manufacturing, the rapid postwar buildup of construction, the relative stability of trade, and the currently growing importance of the services.

It is because would-be entrepreneurs are highly sensitive to business opportunities that the number of enterprises— mainly small business—responds so markedly to shifts in demand; for example, while entry rates (1951-56) were very low among retail food, drug, and hardware-farm implement establishments, they were very high among automobile dealers, filling stations, and restaurants.[8] In this way the over-all economy exerts a powerful short-run influence on business births. Currently, birth rates are still high in construction

---

[8]Churchill, "Rise in the Business Population," op. cit., p. 19.

(though lower than a decade ago) and in the service industries (sharply higher than a decade ago), but relatively low in manufacturing and trade.

In nearly all industries, as expected, the entry rate (new firms per 1,000 existing) varies inversely with the size of the firm, with high entry rates among small firms and low entry rates among large firms.[9] Even within small business size classes very finely divided (0-3 employees, 4-7, 5-19, 20-49, 50 or more) and within rather detailed industry classes, in most cases the entry rates were highest in the small classes and declined with size, the entry rate being almost invariably lowest among firms with fifty or more employees. In the total enterprise population the entry rate in the smallest size class was about eight times as high as in the largest, in service industries it was four times as high, and in retail trade six times as high; but in some industries it was thirty times as high or more. Such differences by size occur in all industries.

The entry rates indicate a fair degree of ease of entry—6 per cent per annum or more—in most sectors and a high degree—above 10 per cent—in many. Where entry rates are conspicuously low, they may reflect the limited opportunities that result from increasing preemption by large business (as in food manufacturing and general merchandise, food and drug stores) or a kind of business that is diminishing in importance (as in hardware and farm implements). Where rates are conspicuously high, they reflect the leading edge of economic growth as, for example, in 1956 was reflected in eating and drinking establishments, electrical manufacturing, and everything to do with automobiles.

A great deal of the high turnover occurs among firms with less than four employees, many of them "little business" as defined earlier; but high entry rates are evident in succeeding size classes of small business in many industry classes. In some industries entry rates of 5 per cent occur in business size classes up to twenty employees, but in most industries there is a sharp falling-off among firms above seven employees. Above twenty employees, only a handful of industries show rates of 5 per cent or more. It appears that even among small business, entry is easy only among the very small; and

---

[9] Betty C. Churchill, "Size of Business Firms," Survey of Current Business (September, 1959), p. 18.

above fifty employees entry rates over 1 per cent per annum
are rare.

Comparable data on rates of discontinuance by size of firm
are not available; but the stability of size distribution of the
business population even in a period of rapid economic change,
1945-56, suggests that the variations among size classes in
exit rates are similar to the variations in entry rates. [10]
Trends in average employment per firm indicate some variation from year to year and from industry to industry: manufacturing firms notably have become fewer and larger.[11] Notwithstanding industry differences, the average size of firms
has not changed much in ten years.

So persistent are these functions of "births" and "deaths,"
that it has been possible to construct "mortality tables" for
the business population. [12] The very high "infant mortality"
is conspicuous in all years and all industries: in each year
from 1944 to 1953, about one third of firms newly established
or in new ownership did not survive the first year; more than
half did not survive the first two years. In this period the
survivorship rates varied significantly by industry (notably
low in retail trade, and high in wholesale trade). In most industries the median age of firms at "death" was between 1.75 and
3.25 years; wholesale and financial firms lived a little longer;
retail firms were shorter lived. The median age of firms in
operation varied similarly from industry to industry and rose
from year to year as the effects of the very high immediate
postwar birth rates were assimilated in the business population. By 1954 the median age ranged in most industries between

---

[10] Appendix Table 4.

[11] The Office of Business Economics figures include the self-
employed with a fixed place of business, so that this series differs
from County Business Patterns and the Census of Manufactures, which
only include establishments with one employee or more. In manufacturing, the dwindling number of self-employed has resulted in a
slight decline in total number of firms in the OBE series, while the
number of establishments in both County Business Patterns and the
Census of Manufactures continued to increase.

[12] Churchill, "Age and Life Expectancy of Business Firms," op. cit.,
pp. 15 ff.

CHART I

TRENDS IN THE UNITED STATES BUSINESS POPULATION, 1947-63, AND PROJECTIONS TO 1976

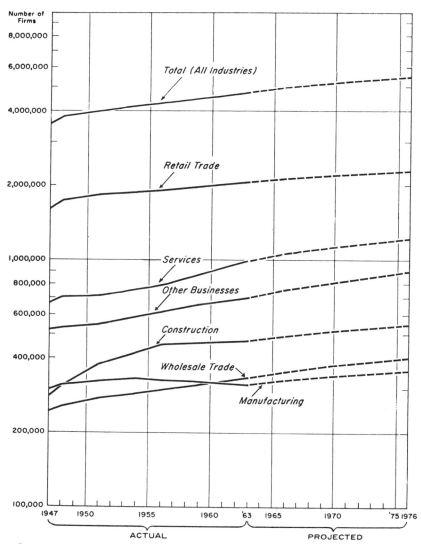

Source: Office of Business Economics, Projections from National Planning Association, with adjustments for service industries.

six and eight years. Recent evidence suggests that it has since risen to about eleven years (Chart II).

Clearly the high "infant mortality" rates represent a severe pruning among newly started firms as they are subjected to the tests of the market and other hazards of business operation. On the other hand, after about four years the mortality rates decline sharply and the prospects for survival from year to year are very high.[13] The "infant mortality" rate seemed to intensify in the late 1940's and early 1950's, probably reflecting the rise in business formation immediately after the war; but there has been a marked rise in the median age, apparently of the order of 50 per cent, in the past decade.

It is relevant to ask: Why is the infant mortality rate so high? And the corollary question: What is the relationship between birth rates and infant mortality rates?

As to the first question, there is an accumulation of evidence which suggests that high rates of mortality are inherent in the nature of American small business enterprise. In the first place, it is estimated that only about half of business liquidations were for the purpose of avoiding or minimizing losses.[14] The remainder of discontinuances are for personal or other circumstantial reasons related to the narrow base of small business ownership, management, and markets: for example, the liquidation of proprietorships on the death or retirement of the proprietor; the discontinuance of a business that was formed for a limited or temporary purpose; the shifts between proprietorship and employment and back again, characteristic of certain occupations; the sale of a business to new owners; etc.

Some evidence of this point can be adduced from the records of business receipts and profitability as reported by the Internal Revenue Service for 1961-62.[15] In every industry division, among proprietorships and partnerships (almost invariably "little" or "small") there are thousands of "firms"

---

[13] Ibid., p. 18, especially Table 3.

[14] Ibid., p. 16.

[15] Internal Revenue Service, Statistics of Income, 1961-62.

CHART II

ESTIMATED CUMULATIVE AGE DISTRIBUTION OF THE
BUSINESS POPULATION TO THE MEDIAN AGE, 1954 and 1964

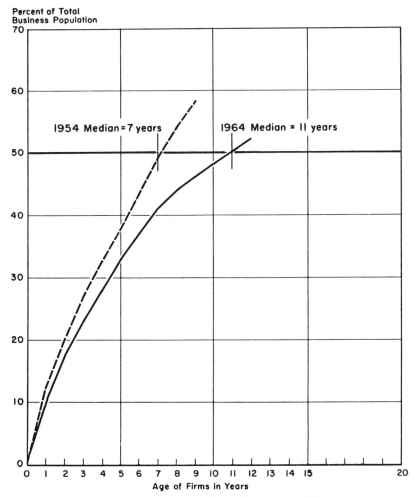

Source: <u>Survey of Current Business</u>, December, 1955, p. 19,
as adjusted by recent data.

with annual business receipts below $5,000, ranging from about half of all proprietorships in construction and service industries to one third or one fourth in manufacturing and trade. It must be inferred that these are "little businesses" which consist mainly if not entirely of the sale of the proprietor's services, in many cases probably not full time.[16] This is further suggested by the rather high ratio of net profits to receipts (except, of course, in small retail proprietorships). To the extent that these are businesses, they should probably be regarded as fringe or marginal. Using net receipts under $5,000 as the criterion, the number of businesses that would fall in this class of marginal business might be estimated at somewhere approaching 2 million:

Construction	over	300,000
Manufacturing	under	100,000
Wholesale	over	100,000
Retail	about	400,000
Services	about	1,000,000

Within this component on the fringe of the business population it is reasonable to expect that there would be a very high turnover. These are firms whose attachment to the business economy may be tenuous and transitory, whose participation may be casual or circumstantial, whose resources of capital and management may be too limited to permit them to gain a firm, permanent foothold even where this may be their objective. This is not to deny their economic function. On the contrary, it recognizes that they come into being to take advantage of opportunities that the economy creates and encourages. But high rates of entry and exit are inherent in the nature of the opportunities.

Among the business births each year are many which will survive for many years. The recent evidence[17] is that about

---

[16] Some of these, of course, were businesses not in operation for a full year which nevertheless were required to file tax returns.

[17] Some of the recent evidence is from reliable sources which are confidential and cannot be cited by name. The data from these sources have been made available in their entirety to the Small Business Administration.

one third will live to age five and about one fifth to age ten, after which the survivorship rates from year to year are very high. From this point on, deaths are from "natural causes": the sale of the business as a going concern; liquidation because of retirement, death, or other personal reasons; the termination of a lease or forced removal; etc.

That small businesses, aside from the marginal and transitory component, can be profitable is evident from their record in producing income for their owners. Among businesses with receipts under $25,000, the net incomes of proprietorships (as reported for tax purposes) range for most industry divisions between 20 and 40 per cent of receipts (lower in retail trade because cost of merchandise is relatively greater). At annual receipts of $100,000, net profits for most industry divisions average between 6 and 8 per cent; at annual receipts of $1 million, they average about 3 per cent of net receipts.

Comparable results are shown for corporations (with income expressed in relation to total assets). When returns to owners are defined to include officers' compensation and interest paid, along with net profit, small corporations are seen to yield good returns on the average (even when the average includes firms whose tax returns showed net losses); and the rate of return so defined, as a per cent of assets, is higher among the smaller than among the larger corporations.[18] This reflects in part the fact that owner-officers of small corporations find it advantageous to draw a relatively large part of their income in salaries rather than in taxable profits, and this compensation is larger in relation to profits in small corporations than in large ones in which officers' compensation is very small relative to profits. (See Appendix Tables 11-A to 11-M.)

The point is not to demonstrate that small businesses are more "profitable" than large ones, in the sense of making more money, but to obtain additional insight into the nature of small business and the reasons that lead to their formation and survival. It would seem that even the criteria of "profitability" may not be the same for small businesses as for large ones. In one way or another, many small businesses

---

[18] For a discussion of the method of measuring returns to owners of small corporations, see Appendix B.

owe their origins and continuance to their ability to provide
a satisfactory income to the owner(s)-manager(s) rather than
"profitability" to investors in the conventional sense. It appears
that many who believe they have the ability and who can assem-
ble the necessary capital from private savings (their own or
others) see in a small business not only independence but the
opportunity for greater income than they could otherwise
command. The small contractor or manufacturer with receipts
of $50,000 will earn on the average the same as a factory
worker who is employed full time the year round.[19] He is his
"own boss," and he need not fear being laid off. For this he
may have to work harder and face the risks of failure, which
may be even greater than being laid off. If his business reaches
$500,000 a year, his income will be on the average $20,000 or
$25,000. Similarly, the small corporation with $100,000 of
assets can yield its owner-operator $15,000 in compensation
and profits. The risks are great, but the rewards are alluring.

From confidential sources we have a statistical description
of 2.5 million firms comprising the more settled part of the
small business population which is currently within the commercial credit system. These sources by definition under-
weigh the youngest businesses, the industries with highest
turnover, and the service industries not generally active users
of commercial credit; nevertheless, about four fifths of the
firms included have net assets of less than $50,000 and 98
per cent have net assets under $500,000. Even in manufacturing,
92 per cent have assets under $500,000.

Notwithstanding their small size, more than half of them
have good credit by reasonably rigorous pragmatic tests.
"Larger" firms (over $50,000 of assets) have better credit
than smaller ones of the same age, and older firms have
better credit than younger ones of the same size. But the
differences are not very great, and age seems to be as important as size in determining creditworthiness. The same
sources indicate that the median age has lengthened significantly in the past decade.

The accumulation of evidence suggests that the "infant
mortality" among business firms is high because of the highly

---

[19]These comparisons are based on average return (including
entrepreneurial compensation) in relation to business receipts and
assets, as reported in Statistics of Income, 1961-62, op. cit.

individual circumstances that bring new businesses into being: motivation, resources of money and management, personal judgments about the prospect of success, and a personal and often a narrow base of capability and skill. These and similar factors, more noneconomic than economic, make new businesses fragile and vulnerable to mistakes or changes in personal circumstances as well as to economic forces. It would seem that the very influences that generate high rates of new business would result in high rates of discontinuance. Given the ease of entry, the overresponse may be inherent in the nature of the stimulus.

This impression is strengthened by the record of growth of the business population. The high correlation with the growth of the economy and the growth of the population suggests that as the country grows larger and richer, it generates business opportunities which find eager takers, more, in fact, than the market supports. In this sense, the high infant mortality is an inevitable function of the high birth rates, which in turn are a function of a continuous "supply" of entrepreneurs (or more properly, a "demand" for business opportunity and businessman status), competing for a limited supply of opportunities. The concomitance of high birth rates and high "infant mortality" rates suggests that the "infant mortality" rates would be lower approximately to the extent that the birth rates were lower—given the level of opportunities afforded by the aggregate output, the wealth, the rate of growth, and the forms of organization of the economy.

As in other populations subject to the Malthusian constraint, the survivors of the thinning out process may find themselves in a tolerable balance of demand and supply, subject at times to predatory or pathogenic enemies or an inhospitable environment for specific reasons. It is a principal purpose of this book to examine and appraise the more important of these. While doing so, however, it is necessary to keep in mind the record of viability and profitability of small businesses which have passed the stage of infant vulnerability.

8

PRINCIPAL FACTORS
AFFECTING
SMALL BUSINESS

THE AGGREGATE ECONOMY

Nothing about the business population (and hence, about the small business population) is clearer than the close relationship to the growth and fluctuation of the economy as a whole. This is apparent throughout the thirty years or more for which reliable data on both are readily available. The occasional deviations only prove the rule.

A decade ago the Department of Commerce demonstrated the close correlation of the business population from year to year with Gross National Product (deflated for price change) and with "time." The latter is a bundle of secular trends expressing changes in the United States population, economy, and society, measured by the number of years since 1929.[1] The content of this bundle of trends is significant. It has since been identified by the National Planning Association as including, probably, the structure and product-mix of industry, the state of technology, and various social institutions and attitudes.[2] This is a more precise formulation of the findings of the Commerce Department and of the statement earlier in this book that the business population is "correlated with the United States."

These studies show very high correlations between the number of firms and the Gross National Product, gross product originating in various industries, and nonagricultural employment, not only for the business population as a whole but for

---

[1]Betty C. Churchill, "Rise in the Business Population," Survey of Current Business (May, 1959), 16.

[2]National Planning Association, Projections of the Number of Firms by Industry and by State, Regional Economic Projection Series, Report No. 64, (April, 1964), pp. 47-57.

broad industry segments and for states, at a given time and over a span of years.[3]

The long-term relationship is evident in the record back to 1929, showing the effect of GNP and "time" on the business population.[4] "Time" must be taken to include not only human population growth but changes in the modes of production, consumption, and living. In the very short run these latter changes are not significant. Accordingly, we find the changes in the business population ("index of net business formation") to be one of the sensitive indicators of cyclical changes in the economy, as identified by the National Bureau of Economic Research. This analysis shows that net change in business population, measured quarterly, fluctuates in close correspondence with the business cycle, reaching a cyclical low during each of the recognized postwar recessions and cyclical highs in the intervening recoveries.[5]

The NPA analysis implicitly takes into account the long-run effects on the business population not only of changes in total output but also of changes in "product-mix" of output and in "technology." These variables are closely related to changes in per capita output, per capita income, and levels and modes of living. A point in evidence is the contrast between the experience during the depression and the experience during the War: in the early 1930's the size of the business population followed the economy downward as the forces inherent in the relationship were free to operate; but in the early 1940's the business population did not follow the economy upward because the "supply" of business opportunities was depressed by wartime constraints and the "demand" for business opportunities was depressed by the absence of 10 million adult males from the civilian labor force. Immediately after the wartime constraints were removed, the business population rebounded to its historic or normal relationship to the economy.

---

[3]Ibid., pp. 31-46.

[4]The correlation coefficient is .984. Churchill, op. cit., Chart on p. 16.

[5]U.S. Department of Commerce, Bureau of the Census, Business Cycle Developments (May, 1965), p. 12, also note 1, p. iii.

It is clear that the behavior of the aggregate economy, in all its manifestations discussed here, will be a principal—if not the principal—determinant of the future of the small business population.

It may be inferred, further, that this relationship expresses itself in specific ways. In the first place, the breadth, depth, and richness of the economy determines the extent of the market and consequently the division of labor which generates small business opportunities in a highly structured, diversified, complex economy. This is a reflection not only of the aggregate size of the economy but the level of output, income, and consumption per capita which gives the economy its character. The effect of these is clearly reflected in the specialized character of the small business population.

Moreover, a high level of after-tax incomes generates a large volume of personal savings, which in one form or another provide a substantial part of the capital for investment in small business. Annual aggregate personal saving is currently above ten times what it was thirty years ago and twice what it was ten years ago. Moreover, as incomes rise, savings are more widely dispersed through the population and the economy. Granted that a large part of this is in illiquid or semi-liquid forms, nevertheless widespread liquid savings plus borrowings against equities in owned homes and insurance are common sources of financing small businesses.

The greater "demand" for small business opportunities arising from the labor force and from the personal sources of capital, the greater "supply" of opportunities arising from the greatly enlarged economy and the division of labor; all are affected by the level and distribution of personal income. As the aggregate of income determines the extent of the market, the distribution of income at any given stage of technology determines the degree of specialization of demand for goods and services and the generation of opportunities for satisfying it.

We have seen in the United States how widespread purchasing power and leisure have created demands that go beyond standardized goods to highly diversified products and services, both in final and intermediate demand. At the same time, technological development makes possible new economies of scale in production of goods and services to meet highly differentiated demands. This tends both to broaden the demand through lower prices and to generate opportunities for new businesses specializing in order to realize economies of scale. As the demand grows still further, the specialized production concentrates in larger units which are the survivors in the competition among the smaller ones. At the same time, new technologies and new differentiated demands generate still further opportunities for specialization. If technology stood still and innovation ceased while demand grew, eventually all production would tend to integrate into units at least large enough to realize economies of scale of the prevailing technology; and among these, the more effective competitors would tend to grow at the expense of the less effective. On the other hand, if demand stood still while technology and innovation continued to develop, the differentiation of the product would tend to limit the economies of scale by subdividing the market.

In the United States economy, both expansion of demand and technological change are developing rather rapidly, and both integrating and differentiating forces are at work. The growth of demand increases the scale of production to the point where "specialized" products become "standardized"; while continuous, rapid innovation generates new specialities and introduces specialized inputs into "standardized" production in the form of materials, processes, components, management controls, packaging, marketing, etc. These may have either or both of two consequences: first, the production of the specialized inputs generates opportunities for small businesses to realize economies of scale by virtue of specialization; and second, the availability of the specialized inputs to small businesses enables them to realize external economies of scale in competition with businesses large enough to internalize such economies. Thus, the simultaneous growth of technology and demand continuously creates interstices in the economy which are fertile ground for new and small business.

SMALL BUSINESS AND TECHNOLOGICAL CHANGE

It has already been pointed out (Chapter 1) that there is a complex and continuous interrelationship between technological change and market growth in creating opportunities for small business. In the context of that relationship, technological change generates two kinds of opportunities: those growing

out of the role of small business as innovator, and those growing out of the impact of innovation, whatever its origin, on
small business. By its terms of reference, this study emphasizes the second.

For the present purpose, technological change or innovation
(the terms are used here interchangeably) refers to the introduction into the economy of new processes, materials, or
products resulting from the application of technology. (In this
it is distinguished from market innovations of design or style.)
The innovation may be in the form of improved productivity in
the processes of production or distribution, or in the form of
new or improved products introduced in the market. It may
be the result of a basic invention, or of incremental technological improvements of market significance.

SMALL BUSINESS AS THE SOURCE OF TECHNOLOGICAL CHANGE

Fundamental advances in scientific and technical knowledge
(basic research), their experimental application (applied research), their specific application to economic uses (innovation,
or applied technology), and successful market development
(including production, financing, and marketing) are necessary
stages in the process of technical change. But the stages are
not institutionally or organizationally indivisible.[6] Basic research can be—and often is—physically and institutionally
separate from experimental or specific innovative applications;
and innovation, in turn, may be separate from market development. The role of small business and the degree of its participation may be different in different stages.

Though there tends to be a concentration of research
activities (as of assets and sales) in large firms, smaller
businesses are by no means precluded from research, even
basic research. While much corporate research conforms to
the commonly held image of the large laboratory, with scores
of scientists and technicians, there is a considerable volume
of research that is as well, or even better, carried on in small
units, personally by highly qualified scientific and technical
personnel.

---

[6]For an enlightening discussion of this classification in relation to
business size, see testimony of David Novick in Hearings Before the
Subcommittee on Antitrust and Monopoly of the Senate Judiciary
Committee, 89th Cong., 1st Sess., Part 3, May and June, 1965.

A similar distinction can be made between "inventive" activity, covering roughly basic research and experimental application (the "R" in "R and D"), and "innovative" activity, covering the product development and introduction (the "D"), by which technological change reaches the economy. Novick has pointed out that invention is "unpredictable" with respect to size of firm; that is, that "the likelihood of successful invention does not increase significantly, or that it increases much less than proportionately, as greater quantities of resources are allocated."[7]

This unpredictability or randomness is supported by many examples of important discoveries and inventions made by a very small number of exceptional individuals, working with limited resources, along with those made by organized, institutionalized research effort. It appears that in the creative process of invention, the individual is more significant than the institution or its size. For advantages that can be hypothesized a priori for the large organization (greater resources of personnel, more elaborate equipment, organized research), there are contrary advantages for the small one (greater flexibility, greater selectivity of personnel, stronger motivation, the fact that they may be younger firms with less vested resistance to radically new ideas).

Thus, it is not surprising to find that the independent inventor or small business is the source of many significant inventions. A much-noticed study[8] of sixty modern inventions—mostly basic—documents the place of the individual or the small firm, even in the era of expansive institutional research.

It is not unreasonable to conclude that small (though not very small) business can be a significant source of "inventive" activity. While this activity is of great long-run significance, it appears to absorb only a small fraction of "R and D" expenditures, and it does not in itself constitute technological change or induce economic change. Such changes result from the innovation process, which accounts for the largest part of "R and D" and its economic consequences.

---

[7]Ibid., p. 1249.

[8]J. Jewkes, D. Sawers, and R. Stillerman, The Sources of Invention (London: Macmillan, 1958).

Successfully applied technology or innovation can be conveniently (and roughly) divided into two major categories. On the one hand are innovations of great and pervasive significance to the entire economy, such as electric light, the automobile, radio and television, quick freezing, synthetic fibers, and the computer. On the other hand are incremental improvements, which individually may be of minor importance but which over time have a great cumulative effect on the economy and its productivity through lower costs and improved performance. The difference between today's machine tools, today's mining equipment, today's refrigerators, and those of forty years ago is evidence of the cumulative importance of such innovation. It is through such incremental innovations that basic innovations are brought to more advanced and sophisticated stages of production and marketing. They are especially important in an enterprise economy because they are the stuff of competition.

There is substantial evidence that a relatively small business may be as efficient as a large one, often more efficient, in product research and especially in product development. The high quality of small technical staffs, their identification with the company and its future, and their ability to work closely and flexibly with production personnel give them advantages over the more highly institutionalized approach of the large firm. The more specialized the field, the more likely the advantage will lie with the small firm and its small research staff.[9] On the other hand, in more comprehensive development, the larger firms may have the advantages of a wide range of specialists and specialized equipment.

If the small businessman is successful in making an important discovery, or if someone else's invention is available to him, his ability to exploit its market potential successfully may be competitively limited. The resources required to introduce an innovation commercially are much greater than those required to demonstrate its feasibility.[10] Thus, the history of invention records many examples of the struggles of inventors to obtain assistance in financing or production, and of the difficulties encountered by producers in trying to market new

---

[9]Arnold C. Cooper, "R&D Is More Efficient in Small Companies," Harvard Business Review (May-June, 1964), pp. 78-82.

[10]See testimony of Robert Schlaifer in Hearings, op. cit., p. 1235.

products.[11] No matter who the inventor, the advantage in commercial development, production, and marketing is more frequently with those with large financial, technical, and organizational resources, mainly large companies.

Large established firms are not always willing to undertake the introduction of radical innovations, and it sometimes falls to small or new firms to do this. The safety razor, the xerographic photocopy process, and the transistor are examples. The commercial exploitation of the first represented a fusion of an individual inventor, a few individual financial supporters, and an administrator-businessman. The second involved an individual inventor, a nonprofit laboratory developer, and (originally) a small established firm in the business equipment field which successfully financed, produced, and marketed a series of products based on the process. The third, though invented by a research group in a huge private firm, was successfully exploited commercially by many other firms of varying sizes, several of which were, more or less, created to produce and market the transistor (including one firm established by one of the inventors).

If major inventions and their market exploitation represent a limited area of direct participation by small business, opportunities for incremental innovation are plentiful. Although not often as dramatic as the major technological breakthroughs and glamorous discoveries, the quantity, and occasionally the significance, of the thousands of technological improvements and refinements in basic products or processes is impressive. In some manufacturing industries such as machinery, metal and plastic fabrication, and printing, small business' contribution has been especially great. The trade literature is replete with examples. There is still prospect of success for the builder of the better mousetrap.

Special note should also be made of the occasional crossing of the conventional lines between big and small business, between institutional and individual effort, and between academic and commercial development in relation both to invention and market exploitation of new products or processes. The last two thirds of the Thompson-Ramo-Woolridge Corporation was originally created as a small business by two academic scientists who saw opportunities for exploiting commercially some

---

[11] Jewkes, Sawers, and Stillerman, op. cit.

of their theoretical and technical knowledge. One of the key associates of the group at Bell Laboratories which developed the transistor left to set up a small company to produce it, though the company eventually became part of a larger enterprise. In the Boston area a number of "brain companies," especially in applied electronics, owe their existence to inventor-professors who decided to become part-time or full-time entrepreneurs or advisors to business.

SMALL BUSINESS AND PATENTS

The opportunities and constraints that describe the role of small business as inventor and innovator apply also to the effects of the patent system. To the extent that small business continues to be a source of invention, it can benefit by the opportunities which patents confer, to certain exclusive rights to the economic exploitation of inventions. Where small business has the resources to develop the innovation for production and to exploit it in the market, the patent system protects its opportunity to do so. Where small business lacks resources for development, ownership of the patent provides a means of sharing the rewards with investors capable of market exploitation. Recent experience provides examples of both.

The economic effects of the patent system are obscure and in some degree opposing. On the one hand, the patent system has encouraged invention and innovation as sources of growth of the economy generally, and of specialized opportunities for small business specifically. Benefits to small business can accrue either from general technological advance or from ownership or licensing of patented products or processes. On the other hand, a patent, by definition, confers a limited monopoly on its owner; and where it is used perversely as an anti-market restraint, this monopoly power can restrain both technology and competition. This is especially a danger where concentration of patents becomes an instrument of concentration of financial and market power. It is not clear that the patent system per se operates differentially to favor or penalize small business. As long as it is procedurally and legally efficient, the system as a system appears to be neutral in its impact on small and large business.

But the patent system does not exist in an economic and legal vacuum. As an instrument of public policy far older than the American Republic, it has reflected the times it has served.

It was particularly well suited to encourage the exploitation of the landmark inventions of the Nineteenth Century. In the Twentieth, it has become entangled in the issues of "big business" and "big government."

A corollary of the bigness of business has been, as we have seen, a concentration, in some fields, of resources applied to invention and innovation, and in some a corresponding concentration of patents. This need not be attributed to superior efficiency of bigness, nor to discriminatory operation of the patent system. More directly it reflects the scale of the effort, reinforced by cross-licensing and pooling agreements. These have proved to be powerful market—and sometimes antimarket—devices which in some cases have resulted in retarding technology or suppressing competition. Such cases have been the occasion of antitrust action by the Government to end abuse of the patent system by breaking up patent pools and opening patents to general use. Notable among these actions are the 1956 and 1958 consent decrees of Western Electric and RCA to release nearly all of their existing patents free of royalties.[12] These actions helped small business, at least in principle, to compete in areas formerly closed to it. Another case in point was the antitrust action eliminating Eastman Kodak's exclusive processing of its color film, thus opening the business of processing to a great many small processors.[13]

A similar issue of patent policy has arisen from the vast program of Government-financed research and development since World War II. Notwithstanding the presumption that inventions growing out of Government research contracts are the property of the Government (as specified in early postwar statutes), recent statutes have permitted some agencies to waive the exclusive patent rights of the Government "if the

---

[12]U.S. v. Radio Corporation of America, Civil Action No. 97-38 (S.D. N.Y.) Final Judgment, October 28, 1958.

U.S. v. Western Electric Co., Inc. and American Telephone and Telegraph Company, Civil Action No. 17-49 (B.N.J.) Final Judgment, January 24, 1956.

[13]Eastman Kodak v. U.S. No litigation. Civil Action No. 6450. Complaint filed in Western District of New York, December 21, 1954. Consent Decree, December 21, 1954.

interests of the United States will be served thereby." This has been widely practiced by the Department of Defense in the belief that the hope of patentable inventions would serve as an incentive to research contractors. Considering the concentration of Defense research contracts, this could scarcely fail to favor big businesses as against small ones.

A Presidential policy directive in 1963 established general guidelines and principles, applicable to all Federal agencies, governing the disposition of patent rights to inventions made under Government contract, and established an interagency Patent Advisory to coordinate and review application of the policy. The directive strengthened the presumption in favor of Government retention where the invention is intended for general public use or concerns the public health or welfare, or where the patent is in a field principally developed or funded by the Government. This has resulted in some tightening of the practice of granting waivers and presumably, therefore, in wider access to patents. But the issue remains in dispute, awaiting legislative resolution.

It is by no means an academic issue. Because the Agricultural Research Act, for example, permits no private patents from Government-financed research, valuable inventions like the aerosol bomb, frozen orange juice, and flame-resistant cotton are available to business, small and large. By contrast, many Defense research contractors are receiving exclusive commercial rights to inventions and innovations, including some whose applicability and full value are still unknown. And these contractors, of course, are very often big businesses. The more rapid the pace of invention arising from Defense research and development, the greater will be the advantages to the holders of these exclusive rights.

EFFECT OF TECHNOLOGICAL CHANGE ON SMALL BUSINESS

The effect of technological innovation on small business can best be viewed as part of a continuing, dynamic interplay between the forces of innovation, on the one hand, and the forces of the market, on the other. It is essentially a "ripple effect." The impact of the innovation is at the center, and the successive rings of "ripples" represent the successive effects on the economy. The first ring may be taken to represent primary impact on the industry immediately affected. The second ring represents the impact on affiliated industries involved in producing the new product or components of it. The third ring might represent auxiliary activities created to distribute, serve, and maintain the new product in use. Subsequent rings might represent industries created to meet new markets derived from uses of the product.

The ripple effect can be expressed also in more precise economic language. Consider the technological innovation of mass production applied to an industry which has been composed of many small producers, making an essentially custom-tailored product for a limited market.

The innovation of mass-production techniques permits manufacture to be performed on a much larger scale through a reorganization of the production process. Essentially what is involved is the rationalization of the many stages and skills required into distinct functions which can be separately performed by individual workers specializing in particular activities. This division of labor and standardization of the production process results in greater output of the final product per unit of labor and in lower costs.

However, the introduction of mass-production techniques is not uniform among the many producers, nor are its results equally beneficial. Some adapt more successfully than others to the new technology. Some competitors disappear or merge with rivals, leaving fewer and larger producers. New competitors emerge to exploit the new technology.

The lower cost of the product increases the market demand, which enhances the returns to scale up to the point where increased scale no longer diminishes costs. It also stimulates growth and expansion among suppliers of materials and components to the producers—the second ripple.

Standardization of manufacturing processes and the growth in the market induce increased standardization and economies of scale among the suppliers as well. In some operations these forces also lend themselves to consolidation of supply functions in fewer and larger hands. However, in other operations increased needs for specialization also arise, conducive to a proliferation of small enterprises based on the special skills involved.

The demand for machinery, for example, becomes increasingly complex. Instead of a few basic, simple types which perhaps lend themselves to production by a few large firms, the new production techniques need a variety of types, some very intricate and requiring advanced specialized technical know-how. The market for some of these specialities may be relatively small and economies of scale attainable only by concentrating output in small specialized firms. New small firms are, therefore, created to develop and produce special machinery based on new technology or technical skills. The processes of growth and of specialization go forward simultaneously within the supplier industries.

The effects of the technological change extend outward beyond the affiliated supplier industries to the auxiliary distribution and service industries involved. Growth is evidenced among wholesalers and retailers—existing firms expand and new ones enter the market. Effects are also felt among a variety of related industry groups, such as transportation, finance, communications, professional and business services, etc., which serve those directly affected by the change. Where, and as, the forces of standardization and specialization apply to them, similar processes of structural change become evident: consolidation of certain functions among fewer large firms, and proliferation of specialized functions among a large number of smaller enterprises.

Finally, as the product attains wider use, it may bring about changes in patterns of production or consumption, sometimes even in patterns of living; and these changes create new markets for products only remotely related to the original innovation, but derived from it.

The interplay of forces can be illustrated by reference to developments in particular industries, most dramatically in those industries directly and indirectly associated with the automobile. In the early years of the motor vehicle—the stage of evolution of production technology—the market and the apparently open character of the technical and scientific techniques needed to produce cars were conducive to manufacturing by many relatively small enterprises. The operation was not unlike that of a custom tailor or special order shop, with major emphasis on semi-skilled and skilled labor.

The technological breakthrough within auto manufacturing that revolutionized the industry's structure was the process of mass production. This development elevated greatly the economies of scale, reduced production costs and prices, expanded the market, and squeezed out unsuccessful small enterprises while making large ones out of the remaining few.

The interaction between technological change and the market within the automobile industry itself had its counterpart in the group of affiliated industries supplying the automobile industry. Economies of scale coupled with growth in their markets helped to create large units in supplier industries producing standardized materials—steel, glass, and rubber—and even in some supplier industries producing highly fabricated components.

However, while production of the automobile and of many of its component parts can increasingly be performed efficiently by a few large producers, growth and diversity of the market and increasing product differentiation and product improvements together invoke growing needs for specialization.

A variety of specific parts or components that find their way into the final automobile product can actually be produced more efficiently by specialized producers, often very small, outside the giant auto producer itself. [14] This tendency may be enhanced as the final product becomes increasingly diversified to satisfy varied functions, or incorporates an increasingly large number of complex components, particularly of an optional or discretionary character, reflecting diversities of individual consumer tastes.

The principle that new opportunities develop for small specialty producers complementary to their larger competitors can be documented from trends in the automobile-related industries. Consider just a few of them within manufacturing itself: small businesses supply materials, components, and machinery to new car manufacturers; new replacement and processed parts and equipment to jobbers and consumers; and specialty vehicles and accessory equipment like truck and bus bodies and auto trailers.

---

[14] One small metal fabricator, for example, designs and produces a small, but complex and essential part for one of the Big Three automobile manufacturers because his specialized experience and personnel enable him to do it better, as well as more cheaply.

In 1958, the most recent year for which data are available, businesses with fewer than twenty employees represented almost two thirds of all firms in the motor vehicle and equipment manufacturing industry, and even a larger proportion of all firms in various fabricated metal and machinery industries which produce various parts and components for the motor vehicle industry.15

Should anyone think these opportunities for small business within manufacturing itself have run their course, he need only reflect on some of the latest options offered the motoring public: seat belts, air conditioning, TV, high-fidelity systems, remote control garage-opening devices, automatic car-washing equipment, etc., many of which are produced by small enterprises.

Up to this point, the illustrations have focused on effects of the automobile in the first two rings: producing of motor vehicles and of the materials or components furnished by affiliated supplier industries. The effects extend to the important third ring, which includes those retail, service, maintenance, and financing functions directly linking the auto and parts producers to ultimate consumers. These are the auxiliary functions which are essential to the distribution and maintenance of the basic product.

Consider the large variety and great number of basic retail and service establishments, virtually all small, owing their existence to the growth of the automobile. Virtually every filling station, new- and used-car dealer, and repair and service shop is a small operator. They number in the hundreds of thousands altogether.

The ripple effects of the motor vehicle extend outward to derived rings. The automobile induces demand for roads, which expands continuously as car ownership increases. The "road," our fourth ring, is the domain of the construction industry, which is populated by a great many small firms. Side effects, or additional ripples, also extend backward to the group of industries supplying materials used in road construction, including cement, steel, and petroleum.

15U.S. Bureau of the Census, Enterprise Statistics, 1958. See Appendix C, Table 5-A.

The motor vehicle also induces demand for gasoline and lubricant products of the petroleum industry, our fifth ring. While it is largely the province of large firms, certainly the number of producers of specialized drilling and exploration equipment, as well as wildcatters and assemblers of leases, owe their existence to the automobile.

Another important ring is the "roadside," embracing the host of typically small retail and service establishments associated with the highway. Many of these types of opportunities for small businesses have existed for many years. But traditional opportunities have grown substantially and newer ones have been created to serve the consumer on wheels: motels, doughnut shops, drive-in restaurants, automatic car-wash, and rent-a-car facilities are among them.

Still another ring is commercial transportation. The giant trucking industry, created entirely as a result of motor vehicle technology, is after many years still a stronghold of small enterprise. The same situation prevails in the taxicab and, to some extent, in the bus or motor coach business. The new technology expanded greatly the market for commercial transport of both people and goods.

At certain times the ripples of several technologies intersect, as with the radio and the automobile. While television has cut into the market for radio as a mass-market communications medium, the automobile has enabled radio to grow as a specialized medium. The radio broadcasting industry is populated mainly by small enterprises.

The preceding pages have sketched the many direct and indirect effects of one major innovation, the automobile, on the economy, and especially on the small business sector. The automobile was selected for illustrative purposes because of the maturity of its development and its spectacular effects. Its ability to illuminate the stages, direction, and character of changing technology's effects in the economy, including those affecting small business in particular, is probably unique. Other innovations of materials, processes, products, and techniques almost as dramatic and widespread in their effects could be cited: for example, the vacuum tube, radio and television; freon and the small refrigerating unit; synthetic plastics; and the transistor and the computer.

The relationship of technological change to small business in the American economy may be summarized as follows:

a. The role of small business as the source of invention is significant, if limited; its role in innovation, especially incremental innovation, will continue to be significant.

b. The effects of technological change on small business are generally to expand the range and quantity of opportunities available in a series of ripple effects. Where the innovation is a new material, small businesses may become fabricators; where it is a new process, they may use it in producing goods or components; and where a new kind of product is developed, they may produce it or components for it and, especially, sell and service it.

c. Opportunities for small business in manufacturing of basic products or of materials and components used in them depend primarily on the stage of maturity of the industry or product involved, the commercial availability of necessary technical knowledge (e.g., patents), and the size of the market. For dynamic new industries or products in early stages of development, small businesses may be important primary producers or suppliers of components to them. In more mature industries, or for older products having large markets, large firms may dominate. However, increasing product variation and complexity may offer new opportunities for specialized inputs by small entrepreneurs of particular product categories or of components.

d. Limits to the economies of scale in selling and servicing consumers render trade and service industries the natural habitat of small enterprises. The effect of innovation is to create new consumer demands for their facilities.

CAPITAL MARKETS AND CREDIT

The capital requirements of business too new to have accumulated internal resources or too small to tap the organized financial markets present a perpetual problem to small business. The problem was noted by Adam Smith[16] and has occasioned more comment and controversy probably than any other subject concerning small business.[17] There is no need to repeat or even to recapitulate that discussion here. But it is clear that the money and credit system and the capital market of the United States operate in specific and characteristic ways which impinge differentially on large and small business.

The effect of business size on financing is most pronounced in respect to long-term money which large firms can obtain through debt and equity securities sold in the capital market. This method of financing involves the most remote relationship between the suppliers and users of funds and, therefore, is feasible only through elaborate institutions in an organized market, subject to complex safeguards. These range from the investment banker's extensive investigation of the enterprise to be financed, to the Government's regulation of the security business. They involve sizable expenses for each financing operation. The economies of scale are substantial: a large public financing is much less expensive in relation to the amount involved, and subsequent security flotation for an enterprise already publicly financed is apt to be less complex

---

[16] "The banks (the trades and undertakers seem to have thought), could extend their credits to whatever sum might be wanted, without incurring any other expense besides that of a few reams of paper. They complained of the contracted views and dastardly spirit of the directors of those banks, which did not, they said, extend their credits in proportion to the extension of that trade of the country; meaning, no doubt, by the extension of that trade the extension of their own projects beyond what they could carry on, either with their own capital, or with what they had credit to borrow of private people in the usual way of bond or mortgage. The banks, they seem to have thought, were in honour bound to supply the deficiency, and to provide . . . all the capital which they wanted to trade with." An Inquiry into the Nature and Causes of the Wealth of Nations, Cannan Edition (London, England: 1922) Vol. I, p. 291. Cited by Paul Donham and Clifford L. Fitzgerald, Jr., Harvard Business Review (July-August, 1959).

[17] See particularly Financing Small Business, Report to the Committees on Banking and Currency and the Select Committees on Small Business, U.S. Congress, by the Federal Reserve System, April 1958, the most comprehensive treatment of this subject.

and costly than the first. For a small first issue, on the other hand, the costs in relation to the yield are often prohibitive.

Inevitably, long-term financing through the security markets is inaccessible to most small business firms and difficult and costly for those large enough to make use of it. Evidence indicates that initial capital for small business is typically supplied by personal savings or secured borrowing (against real property or life insurance) of the entrepreneur or his family, by loans or investments from personal acquaintances, by windfall lump sums (inheritances, etc.) and similar sources. Beyond this, in his attempts to raise initial capital or capital for operation or expansion, the small businessman may find his needs and objectives inconsistent or incompatible with the terms and objectives of potential investors or lenders.

It has been said of small businesses that "they want venture capital on a loan basis," [18] meaning that they want long-term money not fully secured, without surrending or diluting their equity or their freedom to make policies and decisions in their personal interest. On such terms, organized capital markets are normally beyond reach; and long-term loans are hard to come by and require secure collateral. Private equity money, when it is available at all, is more likely to be available on terms intended to return a quick profit, preferably a capital gain, to the investor. Such investors normally demand close scrutiny and some control of the business, particularly of the personal drawings of the entrepreneur. It might be said of this kind of financing that the demand and the supply are on different curves, which hardly intersect.

The fact that small business inevitably is lacking easy access to the organized security markets is of crucial significance to its financial problem. For in the economy of the United States the larger corporation obtains long-term funds sufficient to finance not only its long-term investment requirements but also at least a sizable portion of its working capital needs. The American corporation's balance sheet typically shows an excess of current assets over current liabilities, financed by equity capital. This is by no means common in other industrial economies, let alone the less developed countries.

---

[18] George Garvey in Financing Small Business, ibid., p. 13.

In the United States, however, it greatly influences the stand-ards of creditworthiness throughout the economy and especially within the financial system.

The financial system operates as a rationing device in allocating scarce (that is, limited) financial resources among competing demands. Leaving aside certain ambiguities in the definitions of "demand," "supply," and "price" in the money markets, there seems to be little doubt that in this competition the small business is under certain disabilities that do not equally affect its larger counterpart: it is more likely to need money; its choice of sources is more limited; the terms are generally more burdensome in respect to security, interest, and maturity. The rationing operates rather differently for different kinds of small business financing. Short-term com-mercial and trade credit are ordinarily available, commen-surate with the cash flow required to repay them; but term credit usually requires security which is often limited or not available.

Term loans have been offered by financial institutions in the United States only in the last twenty years. Initially they were made available only to prime risks, i.e., the longest and financially most stable corporations. Their use has been ex-panding gradually, but even today most banks and insurance companies extend term loans only to those customers whose standing also permits ready access to the stock market, or else against ample security and under burdensome conditions. Small business can rarely obtain term credit from these sources. In recent years, public and semi-public financing institutions, such as development banks and small business investment corporations, have offered term loans to smaller firms and some banks have begun to do the same. Generally, however, small business firms still can obtain term loans only from private sources, much like equity capital.

Short-term bank credit always has been available to those small firms which could supply ample security or convince banks of their creditworthiness. Of course, they have to pay a higher rate of interest than prime risks or even other well-established borrowers to compensate for the larger risk assumed to be involved. Nevertheless, when small firms seek credit in amounts beyond those which their assured cash flow clearly warrants, most banks will make it available only against pledge of assets rather than take a slightly higher risk at a correspondingly higher rate of interest.

The availability of short-term credit from both financial and trade creditors appears to be a function of the age of a business and its size. To the extent that the business, though small, is established and time-tested, the terms of credit approach more nearly the large business norm; but the newer and smaller the business, the more rigorously the rationing devices operate to limit its access to funds it needs. As Table 11 clearly shows, younger businesses are more restricted in their access to commercial credit than older ones; and at any age, the restrictions are more severe on the smaller businesses. This is true of trade credit, which most nearly represents a "market" appraisal of risk. Trade credit standing, in fact, may understate the pure risk, since trade credit is a concomitant of sales which are themselves normally profitable and establish a close contact between the supplier of merchandise and funds and his customer. Moreover, there is normally a wider spread of risks by trade creditors, and of obligations by trade debtors, than in bank borrowings of small business. In formally assessing risks as between larger and smaller businesses, and as between older and younger ones, banks are likely to make sharper distinctions than trade creditors.

Table 11

INDEX OF RELATIVE TRADE CREDIT STANDING
OF BUSINESS BY SIZE AND AGE

(The proportion of businesses with good
credit in the surveyed populations = 100)

Age Classes	Size Classes			
	All Sizes	Small	Medium	Large
All ages	100	97	108	129
Under 5 years	88	86	97	n.a.
5-10 years	97	96	101	n.a.
Over 10 years	105	102	111	129

Source: A statistical study of data on credit standing of a large and representative sample of business firms conducted for Robert R. Nathan Associates, Inc.

From Table 11 it appears that the proportion of businesses with good credit standing increases with the age of the business: compared to the average of all businesses, the incidence of good credit was 88 per cent of the average among young businesses and 105 per cent of the average among old ones. Similarly, the incidence of good credit increases with size: from 97 per cent of the average among small businesses to 129 per cent of the average among large businesses. The incidence of good credit rose with age in every size class, and rose with size in every age class.

It is hardly surprising that credit standing is greatly influenced by age. The very high birth rates and death rates of the business population make it clear that a large proportion of young businesses have but a slim chance of survival. While financing difficulty may be one of the responsible factors, there are many others; and easier credit often would only result in greater losses for creditors and larger waste of resources for the economy as a whole. Undoubtedly, however, there are exceptions: young businesses which would have a good chance of survival and growth if only financing were more readily available. The economy as well as the entrepreneurs would benefit by nourishing these growth nodes.

As has been noted above, banks generally have been slow to develop financing modes to accommodate these promising businesses. It is significant, however, that there appear to be marked regional differences in this respect. It seems clear, for example, that the enterprising and aggressive banking practices in California have encouraged and financed small growth businesses that would not have been able to obtain financing under similar circumstances or on similar terms in other parts of the United States where banking is more conservative or more traditional. The emphasis on the quality of entrepreneurship and management and on the market prospects and the opportunities for growth, rather than on collateral security or balance sheets, has made it possible for some small business in California to qualify, to the mutual advantage of borrowers and lenders.

Aggressive banking has also offered a variety of leasing arrangements to help equip business, thus reducing capital requirements. These and similar practices, however, are the result of differences in concepts and practices of banking, not lapses from "good banking standards." Where these special

banking practices are not so readily available, the greater
need for working capital financing and the greater difficulty in
meeting standards of creditworthiness have contributed significantly to the development of special institutions and practices outside of the banking system.

Such institutions base their extension of credit on special
forms of security or on close supervision of the use of funds.
Among them are insurance companies, which sometimes make
funds available to small business; finance companies and
factors; trade credit of special kinds—extended, for example,
by customers to suppliers; leasing and franchise financing.
These supplement the more common means whereby private
financial or nonfinancial institutions with access to the money
markets on favorable terms use their financial strength to
accommodate small business. Many gaps are filled in these
ways. Others are filled by improvisations such as the occasional
issue, to friends mostly, of medium- or long-term debentures
by small businesses themselves or, occasionally, by flotation of
security issues; but, lacking organized primary or secondary
markets for these securities, they are an expensive and uncertain means of financing.

Beyond these varied market mechanisms, Government support, notably through SBA loans, has a noticeable impact though
it has not closed the gap between the financial requirements of
small business and the private funds available. SBA makes only
loans which banks will not make; nevertheless, the SBA loan
program is essentially an extension of the commercial banking
system, with somewhat easier requirements and longer ma-
turities. The emphasis on "bankable" loans and on the marketa-
bility of its paper assures that SBA cannot depart at will from
banking standards. Similarly, SBIC's have in general been
vehicles primarily for achieving the investment objectives of
investors (whether for community development or for individual
profit) rather than vehicles primarily to meet the financial
needs of small business. Where these coincide, the results
have been beneficial. In some cases the SBIC emphasis on
equity financing (or financing convertible to equity) has limited
its acceptability to small business.

Cutting across all the institutional means of financing small
business is the role of the country's general credit condition
as it is affected by monetary and credit policy. There is some
evidence (though it is disputed) that small business is more

vulnerable than large business to the impact of the credit stringency that ensues from "tight money" policies.[19] It would be surprising if this were not true. Small business may be generally more vulnerable to the economic and business consequences of tight money because it is more dependent on credit, having more limited internal resources. It usually has fewer alternative sources and means of obtaining credit when credit is tight. It may be more affected by the tightening of lending practices because it is normally not in the position of the preferred borrower or most profitable customer of the bank. It may have more difficulty in meeting tightened loan standards with respect to creditworthiness, compensating balances, repayment schedules, longevity of banking connections, etc. It is difficult to find grounds a priori or in the evidence of experience for concluding that tight money does not operate differentially against small business, still less in its favor. This may be particularly true of the smaller among small businesses.

On the other hand, when ample loan funds are available, the numerous and varied institutions whose profits depend on lending are competing for loan customers. Under those circumstances, there clearly is a better chance to obtain financing for those small businesses which upon careful investigation are found worthy of credit though they might not qualify by rule-of-thumb application of conventional credit standards. It is, of course, the same competition among lenders which sometimes leads to the financing of ventures whose creditworthiness is questionable by any reasonable standard when loan funds become so ample as to exceed the needs involved in healthy expansion of the economy. Easing the financing difficulties of small business by indiscriminate relaxation of standards generally would entail too high a price in waste of economic resources.

The key issue of monetary and credit policy—in this respect, as in respect to its general economic effect—thus is: How much is enough without becoming too much? This is characteristic of an enterprise economy regulated by market mechanisms

---

[19] Deane Carson, The Effect of Tight Money on Small Business Financing (Brown University for the Small Business Administration, 1963); especially pp. 128-29. Also, Financing Small Business, op. cit., pp. 436-38.

that are modified by Government policy, though by no means fully controlled by it. As indicated by the cursory review above, the market mechanisms which ration the flow of investment capital and credit tend to control more stringently the rivulets supplying the many young and small businesses than the streams going to the fewer well-established and large firms, if only because the latter can more readily meet any objective credit standard. In accord with its very nature as a personalized enterprise, small business depends for its financing more heavily on close appraisal and individual recognition of its creditworthiness and earning potential, and such recognition has been more difficult to institutionalize—though many good banks are finding means of doing it.

Much of the discussion of the financing of small business consequently revolves around a single ambiguous word: "discrimination." In one sense, of course, all financial decisions and operations imply "discrimination"—discriminating among investment or loan decisions on the basis of prospective risk and profitability. Investment and credit standards are established accordingly, and the net discrimination is measured by interest rates and other conditions of financing. Implicitly, this is true not only of bank and other "conventional" financing but also of all forms of financing, such as trade credit, where the price of the financing may be implicit in a transaction which is basically nonfinancial.

To the extent that such discrimination is based on market factors and reflects market judgments, it can be looked upon as the market mechanism for allocating financial resources— call it "discriminating." As such, it is a necessary function of an enterprise economy, notwithstanding that, as a result, many small businesses will not obtain all the financing they seek at a cost that is not prohibitive, and that, as a result, some will not be able to stay in business, including perhaps some whose long-run prospects might be bright. As noted above, high rates of mortality are implicit in the high rates of entry, and the rationing of financial resources is one means by which the market works its way.

Practices become "discriminatory," however, when they impose conditions which are not based on market considerations and judgments or when they systematically favor one class of borrowers over another. Neither the banks nor the

Federal Reserve System will admit to such discrimination.[20]
Nor is such invidious discrimination necessary to explain the
financing difficulties of small business. In large measure, they
are inherent in a system that relies on market tests for the
allocation of resources. The market tests are imperfect, and
often financial institutions have elected to lean to the safer side.
It is possible to design institutions and devices to provide
means to offset the handicaps of the young and small business
inherently worthy of financial support; but whatever means
might be chosen would entail highly individualized evaluations
to distinguish the promising prospect from the inherently poor
risk, to avoid the alternative of fostering economic waste. The
evidence suggests that such institutions and devices can be
employed more widely and effectively than they have been
in the past.

EFFECTS OF THE FEDERAL TAX SYSTEM ON SMALL BUSINESS

The heavy income taxation of the past twenty-five years
has been cited as a special and differential disability of small
business. High rates of personal income taxation have limited
personal saving as a source of small business capital as well
as the accumulation of reinvested earnings in proprietorships
and partnerships. High rates of corporation income taxation
have slowed the growth of earned surplus of small business
and encouraged pretax drawings by their officers. It is undoubtedly true, as one authority observed, that

> Most of the tax handicaps to which small
> business is said to be subject could be re-
> moved quite easily if this country were in
> a position to make a substantial reduction
> in taxes . . . . If all businesses were taxed

---

[20] E.g. " . . . bankers tend to subject almost all borrowers to the
same general test of creditworthiness, but they have found from
experience that certain lines of business and types of collateral offer
possibilities of greater risk than others. By and large, terms do not
seem to vary significantly as between loans to small and larger businesses, except that interest rates are usually higher for the former."
Financing Small Business, op. cit., p. 436.

less heavily, the small firms would find
themselves in a relatively stronger position financially, because they would be able
to retain a larger percentage of their
profits.21

Some observe that high rates apply equally to large businesses or point to the slight concession in taxing the first
$25,000 of corporate earnings at a preferential rate (a maxi-
mum difference in tax liability of $7,500). The heavy dependence
of small business on personal saving and retained earnings
means that high tax rates per se would have a differential and
unfavorable effect on small business even if other tax provisions did not. The undistributed profits tax of the 1930's and
the excess profits taxes of World War II and the Korean War
eroded the internal earnings base on which small business so
largely depended. This kind of erosion is particularly true of
"the minority of nonroutine businesses which have growth
potential" 22 whose growth is limited by shortage of capital and
by the difficulty of realizing high enough aftertax earnings to
make them attractive to outside investors.

On the other hand, the Federal tax laws make certain concessions to small business as such. Proprietorships and
partnerships are exempt from corporation income taxes. Small
corporations benefit by the preferential rate on the first $25,000
of earnings, and have greater flexibility in the distribution
of income between officers' compensation and corporate
earnings.23 There are also provisions permitting losses to
investors in small corporations under certain circumstances
to be treated as ordinary income losses of the investors, thereby
shifting part of the risk to the United States Treasury.

Congress never intends to discriminate against small businesses or small taxpayers. Yet very high rates have provided
the rationale for statutory exceptions which often are distorted
to create "loopholes" which have a discriminatory effect.

21E. Gordon Keith, "The Impact of Taxation on Small Business,"
Law and Contemporary Problems, Vol. XXIV (Winter, 1959), p. 113.

22Ibid., p. 101.

23Financing Small Business, op. cit., p. 541, footnote 2.

These loopholes begin as measures to correct or offset un-intended or unwanted effects of high tax rates (personal or corporation) under certain circumstances. Often they are framed or applied in such ways that benefits accrue mainly to large taxpayers rather than to small ones. Such devices, for example, as the liberalization of depreciation allowances and the investment credit, designed to generate cash flow and stimulate investment, are more significant to large businesses than to small ones. The new business in its early and often profitless years derives only limited benefits from concessions on income taxation. The effects of these measures are not positive disadvantages to small business, but they are more likely to be positive advantages only to larger businesses. More positive disadvantages to small business are the penalty tax on unreasonable accumulation of earnings (rarely enforced but always a threat), and the less liberal treatment of deprecia-tion of used equipment. Small business, often operating in competitive markets in which it has no control over prices at which it buys or sells, is on the whole less able than big business to escape or lighten the burden of taxes by passing them on in the form of higher prices.

Several specific Federal tax provisions have had specific effects on small business. The preferential rates on capital gains influence the terms of investment in small firms with growth potential. Such firms, in order to attract capital from high-income investors, must offer the prospect of very high rates of return with a prospect of the sale of the equities to realize a capital gain in several years. The rate of growth sought by such investors—doubling the investment in three to five years—is achieved by very few firms; returns of 8 to 10 per cent of ordinary income are not very attractive. For the same reason the successful small businessman is under con-tinual temptation to sell his small business to a larger one (competitor, customer, supplier, or investor) and take his re-turn in capital gain.[24] By this device he discounts risk and reduces his tax liability to one half or less what it would be if he waited to accumulate returns from business earnings. To what extent this contributes to the high turnover of small business ownership has not been estimated.

Capital gain in combination with estate taxation also en-courages sale of a proprietorship or a closely held or family

---

[24]Keith, op. cit., p. 108.

corporation before the death of the principal. An estate locked into a small business is caught between the risk of a high valuation by the Treasury for tax purposes and the risk of a low price in a forced sale or liquidation. To avoid these risks the small businessman may prefer to take advantage of a favorable offer to realize a capital gain and a more liquid estate.

The arithmetic of the alternatives open to the small businessman is illuminating. Assume a business with net taxable income of $25,000 a year after all allowable deductions, perhaps held at or near this figure to take advantage of the graduation in the corporation tax rate. The corporation tax at 22 per cent is $5,500. The remaining $19,500, reinvested in the business and realized as a capital gain later on, would be subject to a maximum tax of 25 per cent, or $4,875, on distribution. Thus, the effective rate on the $25,000 earnings to the owner of the corporation would be just above 40 per cent, if his personal income was high enough to reach the maximum tax rate on capital gain, not allowing for the advantage of having the interest-free use of the $4,875 until the capital gain is realized. If his is a typical small corporation, officers' compensation plus profits might equal about 6 per cent of business receipts: for example, on $1 million receipts, a total of about $60,000, composed of the $25,000 in profits and $35,000 in compensation. His marginal tax rate before withdrawing profits would be of the order of 35 per cent; on the aftertax distribution of $19,500, the marginal rate would be 50 per cent or more. If he elected to be taxed as a proprietorship, the effective rate would be even higher. The higher the individual's income, the greater is the incentive to accumulate earnings in the corporation for realization as capital gain, and by the same token, the greater the incentive to sell or merge.

In the case of the small business with $100,000 net earnings, assuming receipts of $2.5 million and compensation of $50,000, the case for reinvestment and resale is even more compelling.

Insofar as the income taxes operate to encourage reinvestment of earnings, they are conducive to the growth of financial strength of successful small business. (The unsuccessful ones, of course, are unaffected.) For the dynamic, fast-growing, profitable business this presents an opportunity to create a market for the shares in the business which the owner can realize profitably with a minimum tax liability. It also helps him to attract outside capital in the form of equity capital or loans with privileges of conversion to equity. For such a business it offers a kind of flexibility in the management of compensation, earnings, and taxes not usually available to public corporations. The case is less clear where small businesses, though profitable, are slow-growing, with less need for reinvestment of earnings and a less ready market for sale of share for capital gain. Here the alternative may be reinvestment of corporate earnings outside the principal business, or withdrawal of earnings and advantageous reinvestment of the aftertax personal income.

Given the pervasive effects of high taxation of income of both individuals and corporations, it is difficult to find much solid evidence that the Federal tax system in general results in a marked net discrimination against small business as such. To be sure, heavy taxes are burdensome; but neither the accumulation of personal savings, nor the flow of investment into new business, nor the rate of births and growth of the business population since the war appear to have been much affected by the high tax rates, at least in the aggregate.[25] It has been said that the effect of the tax laws has been to make conservative investors more cautious and aggressive investors more venturesome.[26]

The effects of taxation on small business could, of course, be changed by changing the level or configuration of corporation and individual income taxes. A 10 per cent rate on the first $25,000 of corporate earnings would further reduce the tax liability by about $2,500; a graduation that extended, for example, through the first $100,000 might reduce the effective rate on $100,000 from above 40 per cent to, say, 30 per cent. These are not negligible sums for small business, but neither would they alter fundamentally the effects of the tax system on modes and incentives of small business financing, though the changes in degree would be significant.

_____

[25] Financing Small Business, op. cit., pp. 143-45.

[26] Ibid., p. 543.

GOVERNMENT POLICIES AFFECTING CONCENTRATION
AND SMALL BUSINESS

The recognition of the intrinsic value of small business to
the society is embedded deep in the political consciousness of
the United States. For the first century of the Republic, small
farms and small business dominated the economy and wielded
great political power. The rise of big business after the Civil
War provoked a vigorous political protest that found expression
in a quarter-century of reforms, from the Interstate Commerce
Act and the Sherman Act to the Federal Trade Act and the
Clayton Act, by which the Government sought to restrain the
spread of bigness and modify its impact on the structure and
operation of the economy. A quarter-century later the hard-
ships of the Depression stimulated a new wave of concern for
the trend toward concentration of economic power. The plight
of small business produced direct measures of "relief" such
as resale price maintenance, chain store taxes, and the
Robinson-Patman Act. During the 1940's and 1950's, the
concern generated more positive and more sophisticated measures of aid to small business in such forms as procurement
set-asides, financial aids of various kinds and technical
assistance, notably in the past decade through the Small
Business Administration.

It is beyond the scope of this study to recount the history
and the particulars of the public concern and public programs
for the welfare of small business.[27] For the present purpose
it is necessary only to point out that the concern is neither
uncomplicated nor unambiguous, and that the complications
and ambiguities are reflected in the programs. Side by side
with the ideal of the sturdy small businessman is the ideal of
mass efficiency and the awesome respect for "captains of
industry." The small businessman has many political friends
and no political enemies; he has two Congressional committees
as watchdogs of his interests, and a special agency of Government dedicated to his welfare. Statutes and executive orders
are enacted to protect him and to soften the impact of the
market and of legislation such as minimum wages, social

---

[27] For an excellent summary see Ramsey Wood, "Public Policies
Affecting Small Business" in Financing Small Business, op. cit.,
pp. 306-321.

insurance, etc. Even much that is urged for the benefit of bigger business is rationalized in terms of the benefits—concomitant, incidental, or alleged—to small business. Yet the country has not been willing as a matter of policy to act against bigness as such, for fear of jeopardizing the very benefits which mass production and mass distribution have conferred. The commitment to small business is matched by the commitment to the market of the "free competitive economy," and the concessions to small business have been cautiously meted to avoid too great an offense to the market. On the other hand, the defense of the market against oligopoly has been constrained by the power of bigness.

This is not to imply that the concern for small business is lacking in sincerity or in results. It is true that the various measures on behalf of small business have a certain patchiness to avoid head-on conflicts with big business, and the restraints on the exercise of the power of bigness are often evaded. Nevertheless, the United States is the only developed country with a declared and enforced policy against cartelization, and the total policy of discouraging the abuse, or even the aggregation, of concentrated economic power has had a considerable cumulative effect as a "force-in-being." More precisely, while the trend toward bigness has not been reversed, the opportunities for small business, though changing in kind, continue to increase.[28] Mergers and acquisitions continue; indeed, the sale of his business on favorable terms is a favored way for a successful small businessman to realize his success. But with the Antitrust Division of the Justice Department and the Federal Trade Commission looking over its shoulder, the large business is cautious about swallowing up smaller competitors, suppliers, or distributors where the effect may be "substantially to lessen competition." Court decisions defining "competition" in fairly narrow industrial and regional strata have heightened the caution.

It is perhaps in terms of practices rather than structure that the restraints have had their greatest impact, partly because the effects are more overt, partly because the attack on offending practices can be carried on without a frontal assault on bigness. Many examples come to mind: the Standard

---

[28] For a review of the evidence on this point, see Rosenbluth, op. cit., pp. 192-207, especially p. 205.

Stations case,[29] in which gasoline dealers were freed from the
constraint to deal exclusively in the tires, batteries, and
accessories marketed by the oil company whose gasoline they
sell; the Eastman Kodak case[30] which denied the film manufacturer the exclusive right to process its color film sold by
dealers; the strictures against tied sales; the attack on recip-
rocity requirements by which a large integrated purchaser
attempts to use his buying power to force his suppliers to buy
their supplies, in turn, from one of his affiliates; the attack on
abuses of patent rights to control entry or fix prices; the
Robinson-Patman Act and the restraints on discriminatory
pricing.[31]

Moreover, small business has a continuous forum before
the Small Business Committees where abuses can be aired and
legislators and administrators alerted. Perhaps even more
important is the fact that the public views reflected in these
legal restraints and in antitrust policy generally have deeply
affected the attitudes of American business, beyond the reach
of law enforcement. Practices accepted in other countries as
normal business procedures, while not completely absent in
the United States, are used far less frequently and are hurting
small business rather less.

The existing restraints, both legal and institutional, have by
no means eliminated the structural conditions or the practices
by which bigness confers advantages over smallness. In certain
manufacturing industries the increasing scale of financial,
technological, and market demands inherently favor bigness;
this is true also of certain distributive industries. Notwithstanding procurement policies setting aside modest amounts
for small business, defense contracts go mainly to big business.
Mergers and acquisitions extinguish small businesses and make
big business bigger. These phenomena do not lend themselves

---

[29]Standard Oil v. U.S., 337 U.S. 293, 1949.

[30]Eastman Kodak v. U.S. No litigation. Civil Action No. 6450.
Complaint filed in Western District of New York, December 21, 1954.
Consent Decree, December 21, 1954.

[31]Some would add the resale price maintenance laws to the enum-
eration of protections to small business, but others regard these laws
as anachronistic and irrelevant to the problems of small business.

so readily to interventions of public policy. Nevertheless, there is little reason to doubt that, in the absence of existing policies and statutes in its defense, small business would operate under far greater disabilities of smallness. This would be true both of small producers in competition with big producers, and of small customers and suppliers dealing with big business.

There are, in addition, practices which, far from supporting the market economy, are burdens on it. Some of these are business practices that escape the law or lie beyond its reach. The hearings of the Small Business Committees are a running chronicle of these practices. Recent examples are the complaints against dual pricing and dual distribution, patent abuses, refusal to sell to certain buyers, displacement of small business in renewal and highway programs, and the discrimination against small business in leasing space in shopping centers. In time, some practices are brought under statutory or administrative control to right the balance of advantage; but there is no reason to expect that all advantages of bigness can be neutralized or even, where they express the judgment of the market, that they should be. Some price may well be paid to preserve the benefits derived from vigorous small business in some, but not all, of the circumstances under which the free market mechanism might terminate these benefits.

The case is different where the advantage of bigness is not a function of the market but of Government intervention in the market. There are persistent and documented allegations of the effects of some Governmental regulatory actions in promoting monopoly or oligopoly and suppressing freedom of entry for small business. Notable among examples is the administration of the Motor Carrier Act by the Interstate Commerce Commission which has tended both to restrict entry and suppress price competition in the trucking industry.[32] In air transport between 1938 and 1958, while commercial air traffic in the United States increased tremendously, not one trunk line air carrier was certificated by the Civil Aeronautics Board, while the existing trunk carriers grew larger and larger and some even disappeared in mergers. The entry of two small carriers (each

---

[32]See Walter Adams, "The Regulatory Commissioners and Small Business," Law and Contemporary Problems (Winter, 1959) pp. 147-68. Also Ramsey Wood, op. cit., pp. 314-15.

employing about 500 persons—one on a trunk line route certificated by CAB, and one on an important intrastate route and
therefore beyond the reach of CAB) showed how fares could be
reduced and traffic increased by less restricted entry and more
intense competition. The same effects have resulted from the
admission of a limited number of nonscheduled carriers to
charter service, but the more extensive activities of such
carriers in the transportation of individual passengers during
the earlier postwar period were terminated to protect the
established industry. Similarly, there are instances in which
Government intervention in the form of tariffs, licenses, health
regulations, safety specifications, or even in the name of public
morals has served to solidify the position of dominant elements in the market at the expense of freedom of entry and
competition.

Thus, we see the ambivalence of public policy. On the one
hand, we observe the use of public resources to help small
business overcome the handicaps inherent in smallness, and
the invocation of public authority to protect small business
from abuses and strengthen its position in the market place
by curbing monopolistic practices and concentration of economic
power. On the other hand, we notice toleration of practices,
sometimes with Government sanction, which diminish competition and encourage concentration. It is hard to tell which
tendency prevails at any given time and even harder to foresee
the future impact of ambivalent public policy.

SMALL BUSINESS AND LABOR

INDUSTRIAL RELATIONS

Some of the oldest, strongest, and most advanced unions
are in industries or activities which are typically small
business. Where unions are successful in organizing the
majority of small businesses in an industry which is typically
composed of small units, and contracts for uniform, but
flexible, standards of wages and working conditions, the results
can benefit the industry as well as its workers. Some small
business industries, notably apparel, have provided impressive
examples of management-labor cooperation in rationalizing

relationships among firms as well as between employers and workers.[33]

However, a very sizable portion of the small business sector of the American economy, especially the portion represented by very small enterprises in competition with larger ones, is still not unionized. The established unions have been, and most still are, reluctant to carry on organization campaigns and to enforce union standards and regulations among small, widely scattered, and fiercely resistant business units. Like other organizations, unions try to concentrate their expenditures where they are likely to yield the highest return. In the trade and service industries, for example, the tendency is to organize the large chains and department stores and ignore the corner grocer. Some unions have not organized the small businesses within their industrial jurisdictions even where these businesses are characteristically suppliers to larger ones in the same area which have been organized. Notable exceptions are, of course, the large industrial unions, such as the Steelworkers and Auto Workers, which have extended their organizational efforts throughout whole areas and into businesses of all sizes and types in order to protect and equalize employment conditions for their members.

It has been said that the industrial relations department is one of the union's chief contributions to management organization.[34] Union organization stimulates management to a sharper awareness of the importance of industrial relations and of specific procedures and standards for dealing with employee grievances and with such matters as promotions, hiring and firing, and work and vacation schedules. The advantages of unionization to small business management may include greater acceptance among employees of such things as shop rules, hiring procedures, and layoff regulations, and an actual reduction of grumbling and grievances, once collective bargaining is securely established.

---

[33] A.D.H. Kaplan, Small Business: Its Place and Problems, Committee for Economic Development Research Study (New York: McGraw-Hill, 1948).

[34] W. F. Whyte in Research in Industrial Human Relations (New York: Harper and Bros., 1957), p. 171.

The great fear of small businessmen, in industries which are a mixture of small and large firms, is that the big industrial unions will impose upon them terms which are arbitrarily geared to the resources of large and diversified businesses, with little regard for their applicability to smaller units. Rigid job classification, for example, is anathema to small businesses where flexibility is essential. The nature of a small business often requires that its employees be versatile and that they be permitted to shift from one line of work to another, or to combine two or more jobs. The typical small enterprise does not have the leeway of the larger one in realigning jobs or in reallocating work in different plants. Neither does it usually have the financial resources to provide the whole range of employee fringe benefits available to larger enterprises, especially where payrolls constitute a high proportion of total business costs, as in service activities. The resentment of the small businessman toward the labor union in mixed-size industries could probably be reduced if union leadership showed greater awareness of the special conditions under which the smaller unit must operate.

Small business units which have pooled their individually small bargaining power in the form of trade associations are in the best position to bargain collectively with a union. From the union's point of view, such associations, even though local and of limited membership, offer more efficient units for negotiation and service than individual, scattered, small businesses.

UNION-WIDE COLLECTIVE BARGAINING

The policy of union-wide or "pattern" bargaining will undoubtedly continue among various major labor unions (United Automobile Workers, United Steelworkers of America, and United Packinghouse Workers, i.e., unions dealing with large-scale, national firms in important areas of their jurisdiction).

The companies, or bargaining units, affected by this type of collective bargaining practice, vary widely in terms of product line, location, financial condition, competitive circumstances, and size. They include many small businesses. The United Steelworkers, for example, has collective bargaining agreements not only with the large companies in the basic steel industry, but with many heterogeneous companies not in the steel industry, including foundries, forge shops, smelters, stamping establishments, and primary aluminum facilities, as well as manufacturers of farm machinery, construction equipment, trailers, cans, dairy supplies, plumbing fixtures, refrigeration equipment, industrial instruments, general hardware, gears, springs, toys, etc. These bargaining units account for more than 85 per cent of the Steelworkers' contracts. They range in size from twenty-five employees to more than 5,000. Under union-wide bargaining, the United Steelworkers makes a "key bargain" with the major steel companies and then attempts to apply or transmit this standard or "pattern" to all the other bargaining units with which it has contracts. A similar procedure is followed by the United Automobile Workers, which sets a "pattern" with the major auto producers and seeks to apply it to the many smaller automotive as well as nonautomotive companies within its jurisdiction.

Union-wide bargaining is sometimes viewed as a menace to the survival of small business because it threatens to impose arbitrarily upon independent small companies wages and working conditions based on agreements with large and presumably prosperous companies, regardless of the local problems and price competition of the small companies. To some extent this is the case. In general, however, unions following the policy of union-wide bargaining, while pressing always for the substantive terms of the key bargain with the large companies, have shown a willingness to compromise with smaller ones.

In the steel industry, as pointed out by Professor Seltzer in his definitive study on the subject, independent small business firms can and have negotiated terms with the Steelworkers which have fallen short, in various ways, of the key bargain.[35] The likelihood of divergence seems to depend greatly on the initiative of the individual independent employer and on his circumstances. Smallness has actually been an important variable in the process of bargaining for deviation. The smaller the collective bargaining unit, the less likely the union to press for adherence to the key bargain. In fact, the

---

[35] George Seltzer, Small Business and Union-Wide Bargaining (Minneapolis, Minnesota: University of Minnesota, April, 1962).

United Steelworkers Union has apparently considered small size in itself an indirect indicator of relatively poor financial condition.[36]

The same general conclusions are to be drawn from the postwar experience with union-wide bargaining in other industries. Studies of pattern-following in the tire and meat packing industries show that deviations occurred most frequently among the small firms, and that in tire manufacturing, significant deviations were confined exclusively to such companies. The results of the policies followed by the United Packinghouse Workers are reflected in wage differentials. Average straight-time hourly earnings, reflecting wage rates, were higher in every occupation in meat packing plants with 500 or more workers than in smaller plants.[37] The United Automobile Workers has also shown a considerable degree of flexibility in bargaining, with the size of the business unit a major variable affecting policy. During the period 1946-57, below-pattern collective bargaining agreements were concluded by the UAW with 86 per cent of both auto and nonauto companies in the Detroit metropolitan area having fewer than 100 employees, and with 50 per cent of the auto companies and 64 per cent of the nonauto companies having between 100 and 500 employees.[38]

There is every reason to believe that the trend toward adapting pattern settlements for small businesses involved in union-wide bargaining will continue.

LABOR LEGISLATION

It appears very likely that the portion of indirect labor cost represented by the taxation of payrolls and by Government regulation will increase in the near future for businesses of all

---

[36] George Seltzer, "The United Steelworkers and Union-Wide Bargaining," Monthly Labor Review (February, 1961), pp. 129-136.

[37] U.S. Department of Labor, "Industry Wage Survey Meat Products, November 1963," Bulletin No. 1415 (June, 1964).

[38] Harold M. Levinson, "Pattern Bargaining: A Case Study of the Automobile Workers," Quarterly Journal of Economics (May, 1960), pp. 296-317.

sizes. The cost of the Medicare Program is a case in point. Certain other prospective legislation, however, would, if enacted, have a differential effect on the costs of small businesses as opposed to large ones, especially on the costs of those small businesses which, for one reason or another, are exempt from the application of the current laws.

A very large number of small businesses are exempt from Federal legislation providing for the taxation of payrolls simply by virtue of their small size. There is a specific size-of-firm cutoff at four employees, for example, in the Federal Unemployment Tax Act. Other small businesses are exempt from Federal legislation by statutory exception, because the activities in which they are engaged, such as local trade and service, have been considered intrastate in character and, therefore, not subject to regulation by the Federal Government. Some states have enacted labor legislation along the lines of Federal laws for the intrastate businesses, both small and large, within their jurisdictions. However, the standards of these laws are generally below Federal standards, and most of them also provide for the exemption of small enterprises.

Under the stimulus of programs designed to reduce poverty and economic insecurity, a gradual encroachment on these exemptions, and a consequent increase in the indirect labor costs of small businesses, is to be expected. Some legislation along these lines has been introduced in the First Session of the Eighty-ninth Congress and in some state legislatures.

MINIMUM WAGES

Many thousands of small businesses are excluded from the minimum wage provisions of the U.S. Fair Labor Standards Act, either by the application of the general interstate commerce rule or by special exemption. The Act excludes businesses employing about 3.3 million retail trade workers and more than 4 million workers in the services, particularly hotels, laundries, and hospitals.[39] In addition, certain groups of workers are excluded through special provisions of the Act; for example, employees of small logging firms and small retailers.

---

[39] AFL-CIO, American Federationist (August, 1964).

Minimum wage laws to cover intrastate employers not covered by the Fair Labor Standards Act have been enacted by thirty states. However, many of these states have excluded whole industries from coverage, either by specific exemption or simply by failing to issue a wage order for them. Minimum-size-of-firm limitations have been set for other industries. Only thirteen states had established minimum wage rates for intrastate employers as high as the then current Federal minimum of $1.25 an hour.

In May, 1965, the President recommended to the Congress that the $1.25 Federal minimum hourly wage provision of the Fair Labor Standards Act be extended to cover about 4.4 million additional workers in the following industries:

Industry	Number of Workers
Retail trade	1,500,000
Laundries & cleaning establishments	175,000
Hotels & motels	275,000
Restaurants	425,000
Hospitals	890,000
Logging	87,000
Motion picture theaters	75,000
Taxicab companies	100,000
Construction	250,000
Other industries	650,000

Much of the extension would be accomplished by applying a uniform test of more than $250,000 in annual sales, thus bringing under coverage for the first time many businesses, predominantly in trade and service activities, which had previously been exempt because of their relatively small size. The total of employees in these small establishments whose hourly wage would have to be raised to $1.25 has been estimated to be at least 1.5 million.

The effect of an increase in the minimum wage on the total costs of any individual business will depend to a large degree on: how many workers are currently receiving less than the minimum, by what amounts their wages are less than the minimum, and how large an element the total payroll is in the cost of doing business. Most of the activities proposed for extended coverage are, in fact, trade and service industries which typically have a high proportion of workers in low-wage occupations and a high ratio of labor cost to total sales. Depending heavily, as they do, on providing extra services, such small businesses may be less able than larger ones engaged in the same activity to compensate for an increase in the hourly wages of a large proportion of their employees by reducing total labor costs through offsets, and may have to make adjustments or else absorb the cost.

Some light on the varying economic effects of a minimum wage increase on small and large trade and service businesses is shed by a recent study by the New York State Department of Labor of the effect of the State's Retail Trade Order of 1957 which established a $1.00 hourly minimum for all retail trade businesses, regardless of size.[40] The Order applied to 86,000 establishments of which about 80 per cent had fewer than eight employees each. Nearly three fourths of the stores in the State were unaffected by the $1.00 minimum wage order of 1957 because no employee was below the minimum. But nearly 8 per cent of the stores had increased payroll costs of 10 per cent or more, and about 3 per cent had increased payroll costs of 25 per cent or more. In nearly all branches of retail trade, the cost of raising the minimum (expressed as a per cent of payroll) was highest in stores of the smallest size—those with one to three employees—in part, because small stores tend to have a relatively high proportion of workers in low-wage occupations.

The proportion of part-time workers was also a differential factor. These workers earned less per hour on the average than regular full-time workers and required larger increases to bring them up to the minimum. Part-time help was relatively important in stores with one to three employees, such as small grocery stores, drug stores, candy stands in movie theaters, etc.

No stores were reported forced out of business by the Order, and more than 70 per cent of the 23,220 stores having to raise wages simply absorbed the costs. This group included nearly 2,000 stores with fewer than twenty employees; their increased wage costs amounted to 15 per cent or more of payroll. The rest took action to accommodate the new minimum

[40] Economic Effects of Minimum Wages: The New York Retail Trade Order of 1957-1958, New York State Department of Labor, 1964.

by reducing total labor costs in varying ways, through offsets or adjustments. Small stores were able to offset a higher proportion of the increased wage cost than the larger stores because any layoff or cut in hours was likely to save a larger relative share of the total payroll. However, some small stores with substantial increases in wage cost did not have enough flexibility to make offsets. For example, some self-service stores and two-employee stores could not reduce staff, or even cut hours, without seriously impairing their ability to carry on. Layoffs were much more prominent in stores with four to ninety-nine employees than in the very small ones.

As minimum wages rise, it is clear that industries in which payroll is a large element of the cost of doing business and in which there is a relatively large proportion of low-wage labor will be more affected than others. Many of the activities in which small businesses predominate are in this category. Included are: restaurants, movie theaters, motels, auto and other repair services, amusements, cleaning and dyeing, laundries, barber shops, beauty services, job printing, logging, and lumbering. If business conditions in general are favorable, it may be conjectured that even small enterprises would probably be able either to absorb whatever additional labor costs would result from some increase in the statutory minimum wage, or to make offsets or adjustments. Small business units in general, however, have fewer alternative ways of compensating for increased labor costs than do large ones. Inflexibility is especially characteristic of one-employee and two-employee operations such as candy and stationery stores and many service and repair shops.

There is a strong possibility that, under public pressure, the statutory Federal minimum wage will be raised and that the minimum hourly wages in some industries under some state laws will gradually be pushed up at least to the present $1.25 Federal level.[41] State legislatures will also be urged to bring under the coverage of minimum wage regulation many small businesses now exempt from Federal coverage.

---

[41]The AFL-CIO is urging a $2.00 an hour minimum in Federal Legislation.

OVERTIME PAY

The standard workweek under the Fair Labor Standards Act is forty hours. For hours worked in excess of forty, the law establishes an overtime premium of one and one-half times the regular rate of pay.

Many workers who are covered by the minimum wage provisions of the Federal law are exempt from the overtime provisions. For example, local transit employees and gas station attendants at stations with annual sales of $250,000 were covered for the first time by the 1961 Amendments to the Act, but only by the minimum wage provisions. A bill extending the coverage of the overtime provisions of the FLSA to the same groups of employers as are covered by the minimum wage provisions was introduced in the Congress in May, 1965. The bill would require double wages for all hours worked in a week in excess of forty-eight in the first year after enactment. The cutoff would be reduced to forty-five hours in three yearly steps. Time-and-a-half pay would continue to apply to hours worked between forty and the cutoff. It would also end the current exemption from overtime protection of about 103,000 transit employees and 86,000 gasoline station attendants.

UNEMPLOYMENT INSURANCE

The coverage provisions of state unemployment insurance laws are influenced by the taxing provisions of the Federal Unemployment Tax Act. Since 1954, when amendments to the Unemployment Tax Act reduced the size-of-firm limit from eight to four employees, smaller businesses have been brought into the program in all states. Currently, twenty-eight states cover workers in firms with four or more employees, and four states cover firms with three or more employees. Only eighteen states cover all firms with at least one employee,[42] and only seven states cover firms with at least one employee at any time during the year.[43]

---

[42]Puerto Rico and the District of Columbia also have this provision, making a total of twenty jurisdictions.

[43]U.S. Department of Labor, Comparison of State Unemployment Insurance Laws as of January 1, 1964, BES No. U-141, Washington, D.C., 1964.

It has been estimated that, in 1962, about 1.8 million workers were not covered by unemployment insurance because they were employed by small firms in the thirty-two states which exempt very small businesses. It is estimated also that about 1.0 million additional workers in the remaining twenty states were not covered because they did not work for a covered employer of one or more workers at any time.

According to testimony by the Under Secretary of Labor in 1959, about 45 per cent of the uncovered workers were at that time in retail trade, 26 per cent were in service activities, and 9 per cent were in finance, real estate, and insurance. The remaining 20 per cent were broadly distributed, with a large proportion working as secretaries or receptionists in professional offices.[44]

Small businesses were exempted from coverage at the beginning of the Federal Social Security Program because it was believed that, at least at first, it would be too difficult and too expensive to collect taxes from the large number of very small employers. Modern electronic data processing equipment has made the administrative cost of securing and processing taxes and wage reports from small employers less of a problem. Employers of one or more at any time are now covered by unemployment insurance taxes in twenty states; they have been covered under the Federal OASI program from the start.

There appears to be little doubt that the Federal unemployment insurance program will be expanded, perhaps in the near future. Legislation already has been introduced in the Eighty-ninth Congress. The proposed omnibus bill would extend coverage to employers who employ one or more at any time during the year. It also provides for an increase in the taxable wage base. If such legislation is enacted, there will be an increase in payroll taxes for unemployment benefits for businesses of all sizes, and several million very small businesses will be faced with the payment of such taxes for the first time.

---

[44] U.S. Congress, House, Unemployment Compensation, Hearing before Committee on Ways and Means, 86th Cong., 1st Sess., (April 7, 1959).

SMALL BUSINESS AND GOVERNMENT PROCUREMENT

The past, present, and future market for goods and services furnished by small business to public bodies is a function of two factors: (a) the total level of Government procurement; and (b) the proportion of that total accruing to small business. The latter, in turn, is dependent primarily upon the basic character of the public programs for which goods and services are needed, and to some degree upon various procurement policies adopted, which may affect the ability of small business to compete effectively.

In this section, the above elements are considered in relation both to the Federal Government (with separate treatment of military and civilian departments) and to agencies of state and local governments.   First we analyze recent trends in Government procurement and in small business' share of that total market. Then Government procurement policies in relation to small business, especially by military agencies, are considered. Finally we project the total level of Government procurement and evaluate small business' possible level of participation.

RECENT PATTERNS OF GOVERNMENT PROCUREMENT
FROM SMALL BUSINESS

Small business sales of goods and services to Government bodies have shown an over-all pattern of growth in recent years. In fiscal 1964 sales to the Federal Government alone amounted to about $6.6 billion, up from $4.6 billion in fiscal 1958 (see Table 12). [45] Modest growth may have characterized similar sales to agencies of state and local governments over the same period, perhaps exceeding in value those made at the Federal level (no suitable data are available).

It is important to note that growth in Federal procurement from small business between 1958 and 1964 was approximately

---

[45] The definition of small business used for procurement by the Federal Government varies with the industry group. For manufacturing, the size standard for the most part is 500 employees, and in certain cases 250, 750, or 1,000 employees. For this reason, certain business classified as "small" for procurement purposes may actually be "medium" business by our earlier definitions in Chapter 1.

Table 12

SMALL BUSINESS SHARE OF FEDERAL PROCUREMENT, 1958-64

Fiscal Year	Federal Procurement		Procurement From Small Business		Small Business Share (per cent)	
	($ millions)					
	Total	Civilian	Total	Civilian	Total	Civilian
1958	27,168	1,598	4,636	768	17.1	48.1
1959	29,275	1,632	4,793	840	17.3	51.5
1960	28,574	2,038	4,467	847	15.6	41.6
1961	30,922	2,280	4,782	964	15.5	42.3
1962	35,230	3,413	6,098	1,279	17.3	37.5
1963	38,281	4,801	6,074	1,279	15.9	26.6
1964	38,324	6,259	6,582	1,550	17.2	24.8

Note: Includes all prime contracts of military and civilian agencies awarded to business firms except AEC. Military includes research and development contracts.

Source: Department of Defense ("Military Prime Contract Awards"); General Services Administration ("Procurement by Civilian Executive Agencies").

the same as growth in total Federal procurement. The share of total procurement going to small business ranged only between 15.5 per cent and 17.3 per cent, with no pronounced trend in its share (see Table 12).

A somewhat different pattern emerges when military and civilian purchases of the Federal Government are considered separately. Military agency procurements have been far more important to small business than those of the civilian agencies. However, there has been a significant and consistent increase in the relative importance of civilian, as compared with military procurements. This shifting relationship reflects a far more rapid growth in procurement by civilian departments, a trend which is expected to continue.

However, a more detailed analysis of trends in procurement by civilian agencies of the Federal Government indicates that the share going to small business has been declining rapidly—falling by almost half between 1958 and 1964 (see Table 12). Thus, while small business' volume of Federal civilian agency procurement doubled in that six-year span, total procurement increased fourfold.

The explanation for this remarkable pattern is the emergence of the Federal space program (NASA), which made relatively few purchases from small business. It expanded so rapidly in three brief years that its total procurement now exceeds that of all other Federal civilian agencies combined (see Table 13).

If NASA is excluded from the figures of civilian agency procurement, small business' share of the total between 1958 and 1964 remains relatively constant, fluctuating between 42 and 52 per cent (see Table 13). Its share of NASA procurements has trended down from 12 to 7 per cent.

Procurement trends of the Defense agencies in recent years have revealed patterns contrasting sharply with those of the civilian agencies. First, growth in total procurement has been modest since 1958, showing signs of leveling off in the three years preceding recent expansion of military programs in Southeast Asia (see Table 14).

Table 13

SMALL BUSINESS SHARE OF FEDERAL CIVILIAN PROCUREMENT
(EXCLUDING NASA), 1958-64

Fiscal Year	Total Civilian Procurement (exc. NASA)	Procurement From Small Business	Small Business Share of Total (per cent)
	($ millions)		
1958	1,598	768	48.1
1959	1,632	840	51.5
1960	2,038	847	41.6
1961	2,280	964	42.3
1962	2,359	1,156	49.0
1963	2,533	1,088	43.0
1964	2,738	1,310	47.8

Note and Source: see Table 12.

Table 14

SMALL BUSINESS SHARE OF MILITARY
PROCUREMENT AND SUBCONTRACTS, 1958-64

Fiscal Year	Military Pro- curement	Small Business Share	Total Military Subcontracts	Total from Small Business	Small Busi- ness Share of Total
	($ millions)	(per cent)	($ millions)		(per cent)
1958	25,570	15.1	9,026	3,242	35.9
1959	27,643	14.3	9,144	3,336	36.5
1960	26,536	13.6	9,666	3,587	37.1
1961	28,642	13.3	9,407	3,495	37.2
1962	31,817	15.1	10,560	4,011	38.0
1963	33,480	14.3	11,411	4,341	38.0
1964	32,065	15.7	9,278	3,630	39.1

Note: Includes subcontracts made by the larger prime contractors only.

Source: See Table 12.

Second, the small business share of military procurement
has remained relatively stable since 1958, fluctuating in a
narrow range between 13.3 per cent and 15.7 per cent (see
Table 14).

This pattern of stability in small business' share of the
military prime contract dollar has been reflected also in
military subcontracts, as shown in Table 14.

Third, the share of military procurement represented by
small business has been less than one third its share of Federal civilian procurement (excluding NASA). Thus, each dollar
of civilian agency procurement (again, excluding NASA) has on
the average more than three times the value to small business
of a dollar of military procurement.

PUBLIC PROGRAM AND POLICY CHANGES IN PROCUREMENT

Fundamental changes in the character of public programs
can alter significantly the types of goods and services needed

from outside suppliers. This can, in turn, have a large impact on small business, whose facilities are better adapted to some types of procurements than others. One illustration, indicated earlier, is the significantly greater participation of small business in procurements of civilian as compared with military agencies, reflecting basic differences in requirements between the two groups.

In addition, the character of, or changes in, the procurement program of any particular military or civilian agency affect small business. As indicated in Table 15, small business' share of prime defense contracts in 1964 was relatively most important in the areas of soft goods, construction, miscellaneous purchases of less than $10,000, subsistence, building and other supplies and equipment. It is significant that in the important area of aircraft and missiles, which account for almost 44 per cent of total procurement, less than 2 per cent was awarded to small business. In those areas where small business accounts for 40 per cent or more of the awards, the actual dollar amount is about 20 per cent of the total procurement program.

Small business' participation in defense procurement is also affected by shifts in emphasis between "operational" and research and development programs. The small business share is 16 to 18 per cent of operational procurement but only about 3 1/2 per cent of the cost of R&D.

Two basic developments in defense programs in recent years have undoubtedly had an adverse impact on small business, although they appear to have been largely offset by other factors which are discussed later. The first development was the adoption, about 1953, of the "weapons system" approach to the selection and management of prime contracts. Under this system a single prime contractor was given wide discretion in deciding whether to produce itself or to subcontract needed items and in selecting subcontractors. This system permitted "swapping" of subcontracts among a handful of the largest defense producers and in many ways placed smaller subcontractors at the mercy of the prime contractors for getting work and financing sizable jobs. It also tended to give prime contractors considerable control over innovations developed by small firms, whose fortunes are largely determined by make-or-buy decisions at prime level.

Table 15

MILITARY PRIME CONTRACT PROCUREMENT, BY CLASS,
FISCAL YEAR 1964

Program	Dollar Amount All Firms	Dollar Amount Small Business (In $ Million)	Small Business Share (Per cent)
TOTAL	$26,920.4	$4,841.9	18.0
Guided Missile Systems	5,579.3	89.2	1.6
Airframes and Spares	4,404.0	73.0	1.7
Electronics & Communications Equipment	2,918.3	302.3	10.4
Services	1,800.0	412.2	22.9
Ships	1,484.5	151.5	10.2
Construction	1,360.0	767.4	56.4
Aircraft Engines and Spares	1,108.8	19.5	1.8
Petroleum	765.4	171.4	22.4
All Other Supplies and Equipment	689.1	218.8	31.7
Ammunition	660.6	100.3	15.2
Subsistence	579.4	307.1	53.0
Other Aircraft Equipment	549.2	103.0	18.7
Noncombat Vehicles	425.0	49.7	11.7
Combat Vehicles	320.4	28.0	8.7
Textiles, Clothing, and Equipment	262.2	176.0	67.1
Weapons	211.5	57.7	27.3
Construction Equipment	91.8	13.4	14.6
Medical & Dental Supplies & Equipment	74.7	20.1	26.9
Photographic Equipment and Supplies	65.6	16.5	25.1
Production Equipment	59.5	11.3	19.0
Materials Handling Equipment	53.9	16.0	29.6
Other Fuels and Lubricants	21.1	8.3	39.1
Military Building Supplies	19.1	10.7	56.3
Containers and Handling Equipment	1.6	0.3	15.9
Transportation Equipment	0.7	*	–
All Actions of Less Than $10,000	2,710.4	1,395.3	51.5

*Credit of less than $50,000 resulting from cancellation or adjustment of contracts.

Note and Source: See Table 12. Figures exclude research and development contracts.

The importance of the make-or-buy decision under the "weapons system" approach is likely to increase if there are cutbacks in defense procurement outlays. Under such conditions, prime contractors may be unable to resist the temptation to produce components or undertake development that had previously been subcontracted. Small businessmen who depend on subcontracts from large manufacturers for components of such hard goods items as missile systems, airframes, and electronics, and those small businessmen engaged in research and development work, would be particularly affected. However, since the procurement categories involved are those where small business participation is minimal, the impact, over-all, might not be great.

In the last few years, the Defense Department has adopted a number of policies designed to ameliorate the negative effects of the above-discussed developments on small business and to improve its competitive position in obtaining both prime and subcontracts.

INCREASE IN COMPETITIVE AWARDS

In its attempts to buy at the lowest acceptable bid, the Department of Defense has been increasingly shifting from sole source to a price-competitive basis. In fiscal 1961, 32.9 per cent of the awards were placed on a price-competitive basis and a goal of 40 per cent was set for fiscal 1965. [46]

COMPONENTS BREAK-OUTS

Standard procedures have been established under which special research teams select, up to one year in advance, parts and components which can be safely "broken-out" from the end item for separate competitive procurement. This procedure clearly enhances the ability of small business to compete.

---

[46] Statement of Thomas D. Morris, Assistant Secretary of Defense, Installations and Logistics, before the Subcommittee on Government Procurement of the Select Committee on Small Business, U.S. Senate, June 2, 1964.

DECREASED USE OF COST-PLUS-FIXED-FEE CONTRACTS

The decreased use of cost-plus-fixed-fee contracts, down from 38 per cent to 12.5 per cent since 1961, has brought more attention to competitive subcontracting and even closer attention to buying rather than making items which are procurable at the same or less cost from subcontract sources. This shift has, however, made competition for subcontracts more vigorous, since purchases from suppliers by prime contractors now have greater effects on the latter's costs and profits.

INCREASE IN AWARDS SET ASIDE FOR SMALL BUSINESS

The Department of Defense set-aside program has been steadily increased during the past five years. This is a program to assure that a predetermined volume of procurement will be made from small business. Department of Defense policy requires that every purchase of over $2,500 be screened by Small Business Specialists in the Military Departments and Defense Supply Agency for possible small business opportunities and set-asides. Set-aside awards have more than doubled in value from 1960 to 1964, and have increased from 19 per cent of small business awards to 30 per cent.

CONTRACTOR PERFORMANCE REVIEW

In selecting contractors and in negotiating profit and fee rates on noncompetitive contracts, the Defense Department has introduced techniques for considering past performance and success in reducing costs. Among factors considered are the contractor's effectiveness in administering subcontracts, including the degree of competitive bidding, and awards to small business or to companies in distressed labor areas.

INCREASED ADVERTISING OF PROCUREMENT BIDS

To improve small business' knowledge of contracting opportunities with military agencies, the Defense Department has almost tripled the proportion of its intended procurements which are advertised by the Department of Commerce. This substantial increase has probably been due both to substantially greater advertising efforts by defense agencies as a matter of policy and to changes in programs for which procurement is needed, lending themselves more readily to competitive bidding. The influence of the latter factor would seem principally to account for the opposite recent trend in the advertising of planned procurements by Federal civilian agencies, as shown in Table 16. Planned procurements which are not publicized consist of modifying actions or purchase orders under existing contracts, classified contracts, and procurements of unusual or compelling urgency.

FORMAL GOALS FOR PRIME CONTRACT AWARDS
TO SMALL BUSINESS

Since fiscal 1962, each military agency has been required to establish a specific target, in terms of per cent of awards to small business, for each of its procurement programs. Performance against these targets is reviewed monthly by the Material Secretaries and the Director of the Defense Supply Agency. In this way procurement personnel are required to analyze the small business potential one year in advance, to set goals, and to strive to reach them.

Table 16

ADVERTISING OF DESIRED FEDERAL PROCUREMENTS
1958-64

Awards Publicized to Prospective Bidders

Fiscal Year	Civilian		Military	
	Value in $ Millions	Per Cent of Total Procurement	Value in $ Millions	Per Cent of Total Procurement
1958	1,185	74.2	--	--
1959	1,235	75.7	--	--
1960	1,632	80.1	$ 4,366	20.5
1961	1,780	78.1	6,427	27.9
1962	1,488	63.1	10,390	39.8
1963	1,578	62.3	13,237	48.4
1964	1,624	59.3	15,012	57.3

Note: Excludes NASA and AEC.

Source: see Table 12.

PROCUREMENT INFORMATION CONFERENCES FOR SMALL
BUSINESS AND LABOR SURPLUS AREA FIRMS

During the period 1963 to 1965, the Department of Defense has conducted over 150 procurement information events in cities throughout the United States to assist small business and firms in labor surplus areas to compete more effectively for defense contracts. These conferences are conducted by procurement officers and small business specialists of the military departments and the Defense Supply Agency. Frequently the procurement conferences are conducted jointly with the Small Business Administration, the Department of Commerce, and with other Government agencies.

These educational meetings are designed to inform small firms on how to qualify for defense contracts. The discussions bring out the qualification requirements for work on military contracts. Firms are advised on how to get on the bidders' lists, where to seek research and development opportunities, etc. The continuing demand for this service indicates that it is meeting a need and serving to broaden the industrial base of procurement by the Defense Department.

EFFECTS OF PUBLIC PROGRAM AND POLICY CHANGES
ON SMALL BUSINESS' SHARE OF PROCUREMENT

In the preceding section a number of program shifts within the military establishment and a number of changes in its procurement procedures were enumerated and described. How much of an impact each of these various factors may have had on small business' share of the military procurement dollar is impossible to measure. We can only consider the over-all net effect of all the factors combined.

It is surprising that, in view of all the forces at work in recent years, small business' share of military procurement should have fluctuated so little. It is safe to assume that but for the systematic attention of the Department of Defense it would be less. Federal civilian procurement from small business revealed a similar pattern of stability (making separate allowance for NASA).

Everything considered, the previous pattern of regularity in small business' ability to compete for the public procurement dollar suggests that future significant changes in its share, especially in the next five to ten years, are likely to arise from major changes in the public spending-mix as between civilian programs and military (including space) programs, rather than from major policy changes. Possible internal changes of program within those sectors, or further changes in public procurement policies designed to improve small business opportunities, will probably not have a very significant effect, over-all.

Accordingly, the following section emphasizes the future prospects of small business in the Government procurement market from the point of view of projected increases in total public purchases of goods and services from business, separately by major sector, rather than changes in the small business share.

PROSPECTS FOR SMALL BUSINESS IN THE GOVERNMENT
PROCUREMENT MARKET TO 1969 AND 1974

Total government (Federal, state, and local) procurement of goods and services from business is projected to increase from $67 billion in 1963 to about $84 billion in 1969 and over $100 billion in 1974 (all figures are in constant 1963 dollars). If small business were to maintain its share of the total, the projected increases in total procurement imply an increase in purchases from small business of about 25 per cent from 1963 to 1969, and of more than 50 per cent to 1974.

Anticipated major changes in the mix of public procurements suggest that small business will probably be able to maintain its share of the total market and possibly increase it somewhat. Two major changes are expected: first, a tremendous increase in procurement by state and local governments (see Table 17); and second, a leveling off in Federal procurement, reflecting a significant decrease in military purchases and a virtual offsetting increase in Federal civilian procurement.

These prospective developments are considered favorable to small business because the character of civilian agency

Table 17

RECENT AND PROJECTED GOVERNMENT PROCUREMENT
FROM BUSINESS

($ billions)

Year	State and Local Government Procurement from Business	Federal Procurement from Business[47]	Total Procurement
1963	25.6	41.3	66.9
1969	42.1	41.6	83.7
1974	60.9	40.8	101.7

Source: National Planning Association, National Economic Projections
to 1974, Report No. 64-3, July, 1964, p. 37.

procurement tends to result in a significantly larger share for
small business than in those of military agency procurements;
and because state and local government procurements are
believed to be largely for schools, roads, and other urban
public works projects which generate opportunities for small
business.

---

[47]The breakdown between military and civilian procurement is not
available.

CHAPTER 9   SMALL BUSINESS IN A METROPOLITAN SETTING

Small business, being in such large measure city-linked and city-oriented, has had to adapt to the changes growing out of the patterns of growth of the cities and their metropolitan areas. These changes have had various effects, some favorable, some unfavorable. The concentrations of population and purchasing power have deepened markets and offered opportunities for small business specialization in manufacturing and construction as well as trades and services. In the big city there is the opportunity for almost any specialty to achieve economies of scale. The density of business activity supports clusters of small businesses serving large businesses and one another, just as the density of the consumers' markets brings new consumers' specialties into being.

On the other hand, the same urban densities have generated integrating tendencies in the production and distribution of standardized goods and services. Just as concentrated purchasing power has created businesses rare or unknown two or three decades ago (for example, automobile and tool leasing, carry-out food shops, diaper services, vending machines), so it has tended to integrate the production and distribution of fresh milk and standard bakery products along with general merchandise retailing into fewer and larger units. Densities that support chains of large, self-service food, variety, and department stores within a single metropolitan area have made it increasingly difficult for the traditional family grocery store and other small stores to compete. More recently, the trend toward dispersion of consumer sales and services from the core of the metropolis to its neighborhoods and suburbs has disrupted the pattern of traffic flow on which the small downtown merchants and the consumers' business and industrial services thrive, creating new clusters of densities competing with the core. These recent developments will be particularly influential in the next decade. To appraise their influence, it is necessary first to outline the scope and magnitude

167

of trends in the urbanization process that will predominate over the next decade; and second, to analyze the ways in which these trends will affect small business.

THE METROPOLITAN PATTERN

Tendencies in urbanization over this coming decade will probably closely parallel what has occurred over the last five to ten years, building up their momentum.

The dominant phenomenon has been and will be the growth of major metropolitan areas in the United States. The country will continue to urbanize rapidly as rural population, which in 1960 shrank to 30 per cent of the total, will continue to shrink as people move towards the cities. The urban population in 1960 was divided about evenly between cities over and under 100,000. While most cities not in depressed areas will probably continue to grow, the major growth will occur in 212 standard metropolitan areas which contain major core cities and clusters of suburban communities and satellite cities. In 1960, these contained 113 million people or 63 per cent of the United States population. According to a set of projections made by the Rand Corporation, the 52 largest metropolitan areas, which contained 45 per cent of the population in 1960, may grow from 80 million people in 1960 to 100 million in 1970 and 124 million in 1980—and comprise close to 50 per cent of the nation's population. [1]

Even while metropolitan development is increasing, major concentrations of population will not occur at the centers but in their suburbs or exurbs, with the following characteristics. First, the extent of urban growth will be widened, as more and more rural area surrounding each metropolis is brought into the development pattern. This absorption will be hastened and eased by the extension of the interstate highway system serving the metropolitan areas and linking them with each other.

Secondly, vacant parcels in the inner suburbs of metropolitan areas will be filled by higher density garden and high-rise

---

[1] I. S. Lowry, Metropolitan Population to 1985: Trial Projections (Santa Monica, California: The Rand Corporation, 1964).

apartments, as suburban planning and zoning commissions adapt their zoning codes to what appears to be a growing pressure for outlying apartment uses.

Thirdly, despite urban renewal activity, we can expect a continuous loss, or at best, stability, of population totals for central cities. Major growth will occur outside.

In addition to the continuing trend toward metropolitanization, certain areas will probably experience more in the way of metropolitan development than others. These are the densely settled coastal bands of urbanization—the Atlantic Coast between Boston and Norfolk, the Pacific from Los Angeles to San Francisco, the urban areas of the Gulf Coast and the Great Lakes. On these coastal strips, major metropolitan groupings flow into each other, only loosely separated by remaining rural open space. Each of these "megalopolises" will contain many millions of people and many high concentrations of industrial and commercial activity. While communication between the megalopolises will be easy, the individual concentrations to a very great degree will become more and more self-contained in their social and economic activities.

Although these will be the over-all trends of population and urban concentration, certain distinct aspects of these trends require comment:

CENTRAL CITIES

In the central city areas of the metropolises, the following tendencies will be as marked in the next decade as they have been in the last.

Until the pattern of segregated housing is broken, there will be continued growth of nonwhite populations and their concentration in central areas that previously were racially mixed or all white. The increasing nonwhite population will continue to supplant the growing middle and upper income classes of the whites moving to suburban areas. Thus the central cities will take on more and more of a distinctive racial character, with the exception of certain areas described below.

As far as new construction is concerned, we can expect a continued emphasis on establishment of high-rise, high density, high income enclaves for people whose economic activities

and ties remain to the central cities, whose children have
grown, or who are single or newly married and want accessibility to their jobs and places of amusement. With the growing
enforcement of nondiscrimination clauses in housing, there
may be some mixing of the races in this type of central city
development. Some of this kind of development will be constructed through urban renewal but a great deal will be a
product of speculative construction as older, lower density
buildings, outside of the core areas but still close to downtown,
are razed to make way for these high-rise small-apartment
structures.

There will be a continuing effort at rehabilitation of some
close-in central city districts. Much of this rehabilitation will
be of the "Georgetown" [2] type where properties that have been
run down yet offer much interior space and other amenities of
accessibility are bought at relatively low prices and rehabilitated at a relatively high cost in order to bring them up to
modern standards. This will be a development primarily for
upper middle income people, because of continuing difficulties
in financing for rehabilitation and in lieu of any major breakthroughs in construction technology which would lower the cost
of construction for rehabilitated units at modern standards.

Although this activity will be common to the larger metropolises, in terms of the total urban pattern and the total urban
populations it probably will not represent a swing back to the
central city.

There are also signs that in some of the Negro ghettos, as
incomes rise a certain amount of rehabilitation takes place,
again at a fairly high cost for the upper income families.

Over the next decade there may be a certain amount of
Federally assisted rehabilitation for moderate income families
and possibly for low income families under rent supplement
programs to substitute for construction of public housing.
However, the funds that have been allocated to such activity
thus far are quite minor; and unless they increase rapidly in
the course of the next five to ten years, it may be expected
that rehabilitation will continue to be primarily for upper income families.

---

[2] An upper income section, largely of rehabilitated townhouses, in
Washington, D.C.

NEW TOWNS

A great deal has been said in the last couple of years about the possibilities of new town development in America, and there are some twenty to thirty such projects currently under construction, from Reston, near Washington, to retirement communities in New Mexico and Arizona.

The concept of the new town is not new. In contemporary terms, the new town means a large-scale development, constructed or sponsored usually by a single developer, with a mixture of housing types and some degree of self-containment through the availability of shopping facilities at both the neighborhood and "cluster of neighborhood" scales. In addition, areas are set aside for industrial development of some kind, usually the "clean" or research-oriented industries. New towns are planned from start to finish using the most modern techniques of design. There is usually a mixture of housing types in the plans. The new town is put forward by its advocates as an effort to replace the ills of suburban and central city living by a form of life which is a combination of the best of the two.

However, there are rather formidable operational, financial, and political obstacles in the way of the development of new towns. While they may eventually become a force to be reckoned with in American urban development, it is doubtful that in the next five to ten years they will replace tract suburban development as the major force in American urban growth.

TRANSPORTATION

The next five to ten years will see completion of the presently scheduled interstate highway network, particularly the urban expressway sections of this network. Completion is now scheduled for 1972. The implication of completing the highway network is very clear. By reducing travel time, it will permit a substantial extension of development from metropolitan centers into parts of the countryside that were not accessible before; and it will continue to provide linkages between metropolitan areas that will reduce the friction of distance and actually enable the expected megalopolises to grow more rapidly and easily. Thus completion of the highway system may be the single most important factor determining growth patterns of the metropolis. In the years to come, almost every major metropolitan center will have a belt route around the core of the center and another circumferential route twenty to thirty miles out, connected by radial expressways. The most desirable areas for development will be at the interchanges of these radials and the circumferential highways, both in the inner and outer systems.

There will probably be some development in mass transportation as well. San Francisco, for example, will have completed its metropolitan subway and rail transportation systems, and Boston will have completed extension to its MTA. Washington may have an inner-area subway. Mass transport systems are extremely costly, however, and Federal assistance, although growing, is still very minor compared with that for highways. Probably over the next five to ten years, mass transit growth will not significantly change the reliance on automotive transportation within and between metropolitan areas.

DEVELOPMENTS IN LOCATION OF INDUSTRY

As markets for industrial products become increasingly concentrated in these few large megalopolitan areas, industry will tend even more to locate in the general area of these markets and to be tied less and less to sources of raw materials. Thus, metropolitan areas and groups of metropolitan areas will become less specialized in the future as to their major industrial makeup and will increasingly attract a wider grouping of market-oriented industries. With the enormous effectiveness of highway transportation and the dispersion of urban population, industries will be even less tied in the future than they have been in the past to central city sites, accessible to rail lines and to concentration of workers who travel by public transportation. The kind of industrial development occurring around Route 128 in Boston, the Baltimore Beltway, and the Pennsylvania Turnpike at Philadelphia will, if anything, become even more characteristic of industrial growth in the future; that is, a grouping of plants into industrial parks close to the interchanges of high speed expressways. Individual plants which do not locate within these industrial parks will also tend to find sites near the high speed expressway lines. The advantages, of course, of the industrial parks are the economies of scale which can be afforded by provision of utilities to a large number of plants and the services such as repair and maintenance, banking, and other commercial services that can be provided more efficiently to groups of plants than to individual units. Except under massive, costly urban renewal programs, which are not now envisioned, the central cities will continue to lose their primacy as industrial areas due to physical obsolescence of aging structures and the congested industrial environments with insufficient parking and loading.

It is entirely possible that industrial subcenters will develop at the fringes of metropolitan areas that will be communities or groups of communities containing major industrial parks and heavy concentration of modern industry, somewhat as shopping center complexes are developing in the outlying areas--such places, for example, as Waltham in Massachusetts or Scarborough outside of Toronto where several industrial parks have located near the major highway systems. Outlying industrial concentration of large scale has made these once quiet suburbs now major focuses of industry not only within the metropolitan area but within the region which they serve.

THE SHOPPING CENTER

In commerce and retailing, the shopping center, which has come into its own during the postwar period, will continue and increase as the major focus of retailing activity. The wider the band of suburbanization extends, the more extensive the emphasis on shopping centers will become.

Shopping centers exist at various scales and will continue to be developed at various scales. The largest, of course, is a region-wide shopping center, of which a major metropolis may have four or five, each serving a wide segment of the metropolitan area with department stores, the specialty facilities, as well as convenience goods. In character, it is similar to what used to be confined to the downtown area of a central city.

Next in order of magnitude are various kinds of neighborhood or community shopping centers with the emphasis shifting as the scale decreases to convenience goods and groceries. The area of market reduces in scale as the scale of the shopping center decreases.

Whereas on the largest scale the regional shopping center tends to substitute for downtown, the smallest scale of neighborhood shopping center begins to resemble the function performed by a village green or town square or neighborhood grocery store as a central meeting place for people in a neighborhood or small community.

As far as office activity and financial and commercial services are concerned, the downtown areas will continue to hold their own as loci for much of the business and commercial activity of metropolitan areas. Indeed, there is some sign that these office and governmental control functions are being even more emphasized in the downtowns of central metropolitan cities.

A decentralization of office activities is beginning, however, and unless the downtowns are able to provide effective competition and retain their advantages of accessibility to a wide range of related services and facilities required for office activity, it may be that there will occur in the next five- or ten-year period a significant shift of professional and financial services as well as business headquarters to other parts of the metropolitan areas. Whether or not this type of activity isolated from downtown will be successful is something we must examine for the future. It may be that in lieu of major renewal and rehabilitation programs, downtown areas will begin to lose also their competitive characteristics for many office and service uses, particularly as industry and retailing increasingly decentralize to suburban areas along with residential development.

The office activities of downtowns will continue over the next five- to ten-year period to sustain a significant amount of retailing which serves people, particularly at lunch hours and after work. However, the office-oriented customers may be insufficient to enable the downtown retailing to survive. As is explained below, it may be that the downtowns will act as the regional shopping centers for in-town nonwhite populations who will, unless there is some major breakthrough in housing integration, continue to increase within the central city as long as they are excluded from suburban areas.

The preceding indicated something about the physical forms that the pattern of metropolitanization in the next five or ten years might assume. It is important to note, however, that

probably the most significant characteristic of metropolitanization as it affects business activity, be it large or small, is
the increasing concentration of people with middle and upper
incomes together in the metropolitan areas where they form
markets for goods and services. These markets are becoming
increasingly wealthy, demanding a wider variety of goods and
services; and by virtue of their concentration in physical areas
easily accessible by automobile and other transportation to
distribution centers for goods and services, they make for an
unparalleled opportunity for business growth.

METROPOLITANIZATION AND SMALL BUSINESS

RETAILING

The significance of shopping center construction on small
business can be seen first, perhaps, by examining how such
centers are typically brought into being. The system is quite
different from that which existed in downtown areas and in the
main streets or business strips or neighborhood shopping
areas. In the past, typically, an individual shop was housed in
an individual building: in a downtown area, a department store
or an office building with stores on the ground floor; in outlying
neighborhoods, an individual store or two or three stores together. The scale of construction was small. The scope of
activity was relatively simple and straightforward and dealt
with a limited retailing activity for which the market was
known, often intuitively.

The contemporary shopping center is typically altogether
different. An entrepreneur acquires a large parcel of land,
several acres, sometimes twenty, thirty, forty acres or more,
with enough space for the actual shopping facility, for parking,
and for eventual expansion. The entrepreneur very often uses
the services of marketing and other consultants to define his
market area, the purchasing power of the residents of that
area, and the types of goods and services that are required. A
substantial investment is required for constructing the shopping
facility and supporting facilities, such as the parking area,
which do not yield direct return but are essential to service
the center.

Either before or during the construction period, the entrepreneur typically has predetermined the types of enterprises

which will be in the shopping center. Furthermore, in order to finance the development, he must have a substantial commitment for space before the construction is completed. He tends, therefore, towards large businesses for his major space users. These may be national food chains, national department store chains, or large local businesses with triple-A credit ratings, which can make the kind of advance long-term commitments for prime space required to enable the shopping center construction to take place. Even for the supporting and smaller specialty stores, there is a tendency to prefer national chains or well-established local chains of such types as shoe stores, apparel, sportswear, that may be carefully controlled and managed. Sometimes these are franchised to local people but they are nonetheless controlled and stocked as parts of national operations with the commensurate economies of scale that come with volume purchasing and sales.

As the population continues to disperse in suburban patterns, there will be increasing opportunities for shopping centers offering a whole range of goods and services easily accessible by automobile to very large numbers of people. In this kind of a situation, where guarantees and commitments are required before actual completion of the facility and where, moreover, high rents require intensive merchandising for high volume, there is little opportunity for low-turnover stores accustomed to paying low rents for old structures, long since amortized.

However, small business can play a role in the modern shopping center. Due to the rise of incomes and the concentration of these incomes in metropolitan areas, the variety of tastes and style which emerge provide certain characteristic opportunities for small business to take advantage of the dense shopping traffic in the shopping center complexes. These are "interstitial" opportunities; or, to put it another way, individual entrepreneurs have opportunities to provide activities that complement or supplement in highly specialized ways the convenience goods stores, supermarkets, and department stores in the standardized market. The specialized markets become large enough to support merchants catering to specialized tastes.

Such retail activities are not usually the purview of national or even local chains, do not necessarily lend themselves to franchising or operation on a nation-wide scale, and require a highly personalized kind of management that can understand the market for the particular product or service. These are essentially shops where the owners and managers provide a service as well as a particular form of goods. They specialize to a degree known a few years ago only in the very largest metropolitan cities, with a range of goods and services for which there is a significant demand only in a population with a high disposable income and a large volume of discretionary purchasing power after the purchase of basic goods and services.

This kind of enterprise cannot predominate in the construction and the occupancy of shopping centers. From time to time there may be a highly specialized shopping center to serve an entire metropolitan area with specialty stores. According to a study of some eighty shopping centers throughout the country, approximately two thirds of the space taken in the facilities, ranging in size from the neighborhood variety center to the large regional center, was devoted to triple-A clients, large department stores of regional and national significance, or local chains of significant size, with about one third left for owners of individual stores. [3] Although this kind of ratio may prevail in future construction in the next five or ten years, there will be room for certain kinds of small business activity. One authority observes:

> ... still there are large numbers of small businessmen who are able to locate even in regional centers. In Baltimore, for example, in five of the largest regional centers, there are a total of 107 major and chain tenants . . . but there is also room for 156 small businesses, barber shops, clothing stores, shoe stores, jewelers, beauticians, restaurants, music shops, photography stores, sporting goods, and pet stores, to name only a few. [4]

---

[3] Thomas Lea Davidson, Some Effects of the Growth of Planned and Controlled Shopping Centers on Small Retailers, Small Business Administration, Management Research Report (1960).

[4] Dr. Sidney Cohen, in testimony before the Select Committee on Small Business, U.S. House of Representatives, 89th Cong., 1st Sess., on Small Business Problems in Urban Areas, June 8, 1965.

It is important to note that this pattern of outlying shopping center growth in metropolitan areas will be one serving primarily the white population who will be living outside of the central city. There are real questions as to where ghettoized minority populations and other center-city dwellers will shop as long as they are concentrated in central city residences. Will they, for example, do large amounts of their shopping, not only for convenience goods but for specialty items, in suburban shopping centers, patronizing white merchants and mixing with white populations, or will they shop elsewhere? What are their alternatives?

As far as convenience supermarket operations are concerned, large chain grocery operations have established themselves in the Negro ghettos to provide the same kinds of services as they do for the white population in the cities and in the shopping centers outside. But this is for staple items and not necessarily for specialty goods. It is highly possible that the downtown shopping areas will grow to depend more on the Negro population of the central city, and that specialty stores and large department stores will survive in the downtown as a function of the purchasing power of the Negro minority.

It may be, moreover, that there are particular opportunities for Negro entrepreneurs to utilize shops on the major streets of city areas outside of downtown that were once white and now are becoming more and more occupied by Negroes. A program of long-term, low interest loans to encourage Negro entrepreneurs has already been begun by the Small Business Administration and the Office of Economic Opportunity. To what extent it will be possible to increase the number of Negro small businessmen and to what extent the Negro community will patronize Negro establishments remain to be seen.

Another form of trade and service concentration of small business is the strip commercial street. These streets are main arteries, unlimited in access rather than limited, zoned for commercial activities on either side and developed in commercial and even semi-industrial uses ranging from used-car lots to pet shops, furniture stores, and trade contractors serving a wide area of the city or metropolis. Some are specialized (i.e., car lots for a mile or more as on Commonwealth Avenue in Boston); others are mixed (i.e., Georgia Avenue in Silver Spring, Maryland). Some are new (the Lee Highway in

Virginia). Others are very old and intensely developed (Spring-
field Avenue in Newark). These are not shopping centers in the
usual sense of the word, since access is not restricted and
development is often made by individual store owners. As long
as communities allow strip commercial development, it will
continue. Although aesthetically displeasing and a producer of
traffic hazards, the strip commercial street appears to be a
viable locus of small business.

There is, however, one particular kind of opportunity for
the very small merchant operation that may be of some significance over the next decade and beyond; that is the kind of shop
and store integral to large housing developments that are being
constructed, particularly high-rise housing. As inducements to
tenants, many of the new multi-unit high-rise apartment facilities have a drug store and small convenience grocery as part
of their ground floor or basement space, thus enabling the tenant
to purchase certain basic household goods within the building
complex. Rentals of this type of small store can to a degree be
subsidized by the apartment house developer if he considers it
as an inducement to tenancy. Such a store can be and often is
run by elderly couples who live in the building. This opportunity for modest earnings may become more widespread with
the expected increase in apartment units.

As new towns develop, they too will provide opportunities
for small personalized retail operations. These may appear
only slowly in the next few years and probably will not be of
great significance until there are some fundamental changes
in public policy, as noted above. One of the salient characteristics of the new towns is to be their "hominess," and
the shopping facilities that are provided in the new towns may
indeed be used as an aspect of this type of environment. Many
developers of new towns would like to have small local businesses handling the majority of the so-called "village"
shopping, close to areas of housing and even some of the larger
shopping activities of the town centers. A personalized kind
of merchandising can become a distinctly advantageous pro-
motional item for a developer of a new town. In such a case a
developer may be willing to absorb some of the costs and risks
of the usual retail construction in order to get this type of
activity in his community. The risks involved in dealing with
less than triple-A or less than chain store activities may not
appear to be so great for a new town developer in providing
such facilities as drug stores, delicatessens, shoe and apparel

stores, which in major shopping centers might be of a chain or franchise variety.

Furthermore, if legislation is eventually passed to enable the Federal Government to provide extensive credit to developers of new towns for construction of the utility and other service systems, this might be an added inducement to promoters to absorb some of the risk, thereby encouraging small businesses in the new town areas.

INDUSTRY

The growth of metropolitan and megalopolitan areas and the concentration of purchasing power which these areas encompass will make for an even greater attraction to the location of industry nearer their markets, with commensurate reduction in the importance of sites closer to sources of materials. Since most industries will also require higher levels of education and training, presence of high quality labor supply in the metropolitan areas will be an additional attraction for industrial location.

It is not clear whether developments in urbanization per se will influence the smallness or largeness of the industrial operation. There are certain things, however, which can be said as to relationships between metropolitanization and small industrial operations over the next five to ten years.

The pattern of industrial development around metropolitan areas might offer certain opportunities for small producers of components clustered around large manufacturers specializing in assembling and marketing, as in the automobile and electrical industries. As major industrial sites become developed at the nexus of highway connections and along the circumferentials, many plants may be built that specialize in materials, components, and services for larger operations located in the same metropolitan area and accessible via the highway connections. Such a pattern has already developed on Route 128 in Boston, where large electronic manufacturers have subcontracted many of their components to small companies employing 50 to 100 or 150 workers, each of which has grown up on Route 128. The small plants supply the "mother" operations and produce also for shipment to other regions.

There will be a very large and diversified specialty goods market in metropolitan areas over the next decade, and it may well be that the scope of this specialization will allow for small, almost handicraft-oriented industries to supply the goods for such specialty tastes: i.e., in very stylized "designer" items of furniture, pottery, apparel, etc. Whether they locate in the metropolitan areas or outside, such businesses will appear in response to the opportunities of the metropolitan market.

As the major construction of industrial plants takes place near the beltways and outlying expressways of metropolitan areas, there will be a shift from older, often obsolete downtown or central city structures. As a result, there will be a decline in downtown rents, as has been indicated in Boston and Philadelphia, below those of the new construction on the outskirts. This will provide a breeding ground for infant "growth" industries to become established in the in-city locations where the advantage of cheaper rent and external economies may be very strong. In Philadelphia an industrial commission has taken over an old industrial vacant building in the central area and remodeled it specifically to suit the needs of growth industries looking for low rent. Many of the electronics operations in Boston have begun in old vacant structures in the central city, and once they have become established there, they very often have moved to new plants outside. Where rental is something on the order of 50¢ to $1 a square foot, compared with $3 or $4 a square foot for new construction in the suburbs, central city space may become attractive.

Industries that do not have a great deal of fixed capital and rely mainly on supplies of cheap unskilled labor and not on external economies may shy away from location in metropolitan areas in the future, to the extent that such industries continue to exist. By the same token, the depressed areas of America, in Appalachia or Upper New England, will perhaps tend to attract more of this type of operation as time goes on. These are areas where labor costs might be lower, where communities are desperately in need of an economic base, where old obsolete plant buildings may be available or new ones may be subsidized. Such operations as manufacture of apparel or shoes could, given the availability of transportation to the market, choose locations in the depressed areas rather than in metropolitan areas.

EFFECTS OF URBAN RENEWAL AND HIGHWAY CONSTRUCTION ON SMALL BUSINESS

DISPLACEMENT EXPERIENCE

Displacement effects of urban renewal have been largely confined to central urban districts because of the nature of the program and its concern with run-down, obsolete areas. Interstate highway construction has displaced businesses in both central and in outlying areas in the process of providing expressway access to and from the downtown core. Although a substantial number of individual businesses have been affected by these programs, the detrimental impact on small business as a whole has not appeared to be very great.

According to a study by Basil C. Zimmer,[5] until 1960 or 1961 approximately 3,700 nonresidential uses were displaced annually by urban renewal, and about two to three times as many such uses were affected by highway construction and other kinds of public works. The annual total thus affected was on the order of 10,000 to 15,000 individual activities, including institutions as well as commercial, service, and manufacturing businesses.

Zimmer's study of about 300 displaced businesses in Providence, Rhode Island, (roughly half of which were removed by renewal and half by highway construction) indicated that 70 per cent of the highway-affected enterprises and approximately 60 per cent of those displaced by urban renewal found new sites to continue in operation.

Another study conducted by the School of Business Administration of the University of Connecticut in 1960 estimated that, nation-wide, about 75 per cent of the firms displaced by urban

---

[5]Basil C. Zimmer, Rebuilding Cities: The Effects of Displacement and Relocation on Small Business (Chicago: Quadrangle Books, 1964). This book is a study of the effects of displacement and relocation on small business with particular reference to the experience in Providence, Rhode Island.

renewal to that date had relocated and were successful in surviving.[6]

The urban renewal program provides assistance to business in relocating, assistance which includes reimbursement of moving costs from one site to another, as well as some help in finding new locations. The highway program does not provide this assistance, although there have been some comments to suggest that compensation to businesses for displacement by highways has sometimes been inflated to assist many of them in finding new sites.

If the above figures can be considered somewhat representative of the older cities where displacement has been the heaviest, then it would appear that some businesses have been eliminated in the course of urban renewal and highway construction, but that these represent a minority of those displaced. The displaced businesses are, to begin with, a small minority of the total business population in the cities.

For the most part, the businesses displaced and eliminated through these programs have been quite small. According to the Providence study, only 20 per cent of the 300-odd firms had over ten employees. The Connecticut report provided a succinct description of the type of business affected by renewal:

> Nearly all of the affected firms, whether they relocate successfully or not, are small businesses. Most of them are proprietorships or partnerships and many are run by elderly proprietor-managers. The majority are either in the retail or the service fields. Very few have as many as twenty-five employees, and even fewer are branches of national or regional chain operations.[7]

---

[6]William N. Kinnard, Jr., and Zenon S. Malinowski, How Urban Renewal Projects Affect Small Business, summarized in Small Business Administration, Management Research Summary (January, 1961).

[7]Ibid., p. 4.

Business uses in an area slated for urban renewal would tend not to be very strong in any case: very small stores serving the immediate, local, low-income neighborhood with convenience goods or other kinds of retail activity; retail outlets occupying relatively cheap floor space to distribute low quality goods over a larger area; manufacturing enterprises gravitating to run-down structures with low rentals. The proportion of marginal businesses displaced by highway construction may not be so high as in renewal, simply because the highway construction is no respecter of "good areas" versus "bad areas," while urban renewal is quite specifically restricted to slum and run-down neighborhoods. Nevertheless, the Providence study indicates that displacements under both kinds of clearance were predominantly very small operations.

As noted earlier, the very small convenience-goods retail shops are, with the movement of population, gradually giving way to shopping center developments or to highly specialized small retail operations. As incomes rise and the market shifts, this kind of retail activity will dwindle even further.

A conclusion of the Zimmer study was that survival in another location was much easier for the larger region-serving or community-serving activity displaced by the public works programs. The stronger the enterprise before relocation, the easier was the relocation and the more profitable the business became in the new location. It would appear that urban renewal and highway construction are again part of a number of forces which are combining to reduce the viability and the permanence of the small, traditional, neighborhood-serving retail activity in the central city.

NEW OPPORTUNITIES

The other side of the coin is whether urban renewal and highway construction create and will create in the future opportunities for small business. The opportunities growing out of highway development have been cited earlier, but the evidence on renewal is simply inconclusive. According to the Urban Renewal Administration, as of December 31, 1964, approximately 1,200 commercial buildings and approximately 400 industrial structures were completed or under construction on sites prepared by urban renewal. We have no knowledge, however, of the size or characteristics of the business and industrial activity that occupy these new buildings. There are instances of urban renewal re-use for both large and small businesses. In New Haven, for example, and in Boston, the major commercial re-uses in urban renewal areas have been large enterprises. These sites represented high costs of acquisition and construction even with the Federal write-down.

There have been, however, examples of urban renewal used for small retail and service operations. In Providence, for example, a group of local merchants about to be displaced by an urban renewal project formed a corporation which, with urban renewal assistance, was able to construct and occupy a shopping center almost entirely of local merchants, and move in before their former places of business were torn down. In Manchester, New Hampshire, and in parts of the Church Street project in New Haven, there are also examples of relatively low-cost structures that have been built and rented to groups of local merchants as part of an urban renewal program.

There is nothing inherent in the urban renewal process to prevent small business from occupying urban renewal sites, particularly when the sites serve a nearby residential or office-oriented population, or when some assistance is given by the urban renewal agency to organize and construct structures at rental levels that small firms can afford.

Until now, most urban renewal activity has dealt with residential areas and residential uses and re-uses. The residential aspects of urban renewal have, however, come under a significant amount of criticism. There may be either a reduction of clearance activity in the future or a readjustment in the nature of residential renewal. The less controversial business and industrial aspects of the program may become more prominent. The University of Connecticut study estimates that 150,000 businesses, most of them small, will be displaced by urban renewal alone during the decade of the 1960's, a much higher figure than in the past.[8] Over the next five to ten years, a larger number of downtown projects will be undertaken, primarily or exclusively for redevelopment of commercial and industrial uses.

In a typical middle-sized eastern city, the vast majority of the retail stores that would be displaced under a downtown

---

[8]See section on Retailing.

renewal program are small businesses, locally owned, serving the city as a whole and nearby industrial and residential areas. Many have been in this location for a long time. These are businesses which, without some kind of careful attention to relocation, might well be permanently eliminated under renewal. The costs of new construction would be far higher than their present occupancy costs, and suitable "temporary" locations near the downtown area during reconstruction would not exist. Special provision might be made for protection and relocation of such activities in the downtown areas where they have their market and experience. This could be done in a variety of ways: for example, by encouraging construction of new facilities in advance of displacement, or by encouraging rental of space to smaller retail firms that are unable to pay high sums through special long-term low interest loans for commercial structures that would be used to rehouse firms displaced by urban renewal projects.

CHAPTER **10** PROJECTIONS
AND
OUTLOOK

OUTLOOK FOR SMALL BUSINESS IN THE ECONOMY

The outlook for the growth of the United States economy is very bright. Both the Executive and the Congress are committed by statute and by policy to the maintenance of high levels of production, employment, and purchasing power. Within these commitments there can be variations in the rate of growth, but by any standard it may be expected that the growth of the market in the aggregate will be great.

It must be recognized that this economy is operating in a range of income, total and per capita, never before experienced in this or any other country, which suggests both great opportunities and some uncertainties as to the composition of the markets even as close as ten years ahead.[1] The Gross National Product is likely to approach $1,000 billion (at today's prices) by 1975. With the projected increase in population, GNP per capita would exceed $4,000; personal income after taxes would approach $3,000 per capita and $10,000 per household. Less than 20 per cent of consumer units would have incomes under $4,000 (still at present-day prices); almost two-thirds would have incomes over $7,500 and nearly half over $10,000. Personal consumption would rise over 50 per cent— durable goods nearly double, services by 62 per cent, and nondurables by more than one third. The volume of private investment, including residential construction, would increase about 75 per cent.

These projections imply an over-all growth rate of about 4 per cent a year. They rest on a set of explicit assumptions which have been selected as plausible in the light of the total political-economic environment of the United States as it is

[1]The statements that follow are based on projections of the National Planning Association, National Economic Projections to 1976, Report No. 65-2 (August, 1965).

Table 18

THE NATIONAL ECONOMY AT SELECTED DATES
IN BILLIONS OF 1964 DOLLARS

	Actual			Projected	
	1957	1960	1964	1970	1975
GNP	493	531	622	799	970
Personal Consumption	311	343	399	511	621
Durables	41	45	57	83	112
Nondurables	148	158	177	211	240
Services	123	141	165	217	268
Gross private investment	72	74	88	123	155
Residential construction	20	23	27	35	46
Government purchases	104	111	129	158	185

Source: National Planning Association, Report No. 65-2.

and as it can be foreseen.[2] It is not a "full employment model," which would yield somewhat higher figures; but it explicitly assumes that fiscal policies and other public decisions will be made to keep the economy operating at high levels and to avoid sharp increases in unemployment. These objectives could not be achieved if current policies and programs were to be continued unchanged over the next decade. It is not necessary to accept the assumptions or the projections literally or in their entirety in order to appreciate the magnitudes of the changes that accrue from a plausible and attainable rate of economic growth starting from the very high base already reached by the United States economy.

In addition to these magnitudes, which are powerful determinants of the "supply" of small business opportunities, the projections imply a rate of personal saving in 1970 and 1975 of about 7.5 per cent of disposable personal income. In terms of present-day prices, this would yield upwards of $50 billion of personal saving—more than half again the 1964 volume, which was a peace-time record. This would provide a very large increase in the funds potentially available for equity financing of small business.

[2] Ibid., pp. 5-11.

It is important to note that these are explicitly not fore-
casts of trends and policies of the past or present, but projections based on specified assumptions with respect to political decisions and their economic consequences.[3] The assumptions, having mainly to do with Federal, state, and local
fiscal affairs and national defense, illuminate the area of
policy discretion and decision that determines the future of
the economy. The assumptions used here are those considered
politically most plausible.

The national and sectoral projections assume an annual
rate of increase of 3 per cent in GNP per man-hour—an over-
all measure of productivity.[4] Productivity of the economy as
a whole, of course, is affected by the "product mix," that is,
the relative shares of higher-and-lower-productivity industries
in the total economy; but this changes slowly. For the product
mix at any given time, the rate of productivity is an expression
of the quality of the labor force, the quality of organization
and management of enterprise, the quality of the capital equipment, and the state of technology implied in all of these. For
present purposes, we are assuming that for the next decade
all these factors will continue to improve at about the same
rate. Under this assumption, the change in productivity for
the next five or ten years is taken as a rough measure of the
rate of change, or development, of applied technology.

The rate of productivity increase assumed in these projections is not materially different from that experienced from
1948 to 1963, and not much higher than that of 1958 to 1963.
In the light of rapid evolutions of technology, a case could be
made for assuming a higher rate of increase in productivity,
say, 3.5 per cent; and in fact an alternative NPA model in-
corporating such an assumption presents a prospect of an
even faster-growing economy. It is conservative to conclude
that at least insofar as it affects the outlook for small business, technology will continue to evolve in the next five or ten
years at about the pace of the past five years, and possibly a
little faster.

---

[3]Ibid., pp. 6-8.

[4]Ibid., pp. 9-10.

A growing population is another key element in the outlook for small business. The United States population is expected to grow at about 1.5 per cent during the next decade, a rate slightly below the recent past. 5 This growth will be reflected in the growing market for goods and services and is subsumed in the projection of GNP and other aggregate measures of the economy.

More significant are the changes in age distribution, with the increasing numbers of young and old and a stationary population in the prime working years, between the ages of thirty-five and fifty-five. The increasing numbers of the young and the old will broaden the specialized markets for goods and services especially demanded by these age groups. While the expansion of the market will increase the opportunities for integration to exploit economies of scale, the development of the demand for new products and services and the localization of markets will offer opportunities for small business. On the

Table 19

POPULATION PROJECTIONS, 1965-75

Age Group	1965 (Actual)		1970		1975	
	Number (Thousands)	Per Cent	Number (Thousands)	Per Cent	Number (Thousands)	Per Cent
All ages*	194,583	100	207,127	100	222,952	100
Under 5	20,434	11	19,828	10	23,714	11
5-14	39,475	20	41,259	20	40,727	18
15-34	53,077	27	61,676	30	71,529	32
35-54	46,476	24	46,287	22	45,990	21
55 & over	35,122	18	38,075	18	40,990	18

*Figures may not add to totals due to rounding.

Source: Department of Commerce, Bureau of the Census, Current Population Reports, Series B. (U.S. Statistical Abstract of the United States: 1966) p. 6.

---

[5] Population can be projected with a fair degree of certainty for short periods in the future. The difference between the highest and lowest among four projections for 1970 by the Bureau of the Census is less than 3 per cent and between any two adjoining projections only about 1 per cent.

other hand, the leveling off of the population between the ages of thirty-five to fifty-five will limit the increase in the number of potential entrepreneurs. The effect of the prospective population changes, therefore, will be to increase the "supply" of small business opportunities more than the "demand" and thereby to improve the quality of the opportunities.

The gradual improvement of the education of the population will provide small business with men better equipped for entrepreneurship and management. In the past, every generation has been better educated than its parents: we have come from a median eighth grade education to a median twelfth grade education in one generation. And the trend is continuing.

Table 20

PER CENT OF POPULATION IN SCHOOL

Age	1920	1940	1950	1960
17 years	35	61	68	76
18 years	22	36	40	51
19 years	14	21	25	33
20 years	8	12	18	24

Source: Bureau of the Census, Census of Population, 1960.

The increase has been particularly marked since World War II. Between 1960 and 1964 the proportion of twenty to twenty-four-year olds enrolled in school increased from 13 to 17 per cent. The current emphasis on education, backed by intensive legislative, financial, and professional support will, without doubt, accelerate the trend into the future.

Insofar as the Federal tax system acts as a restraint on the formation and growth of small business, the restraint may be expected to ease in the next decade. The National Planning Association projections used here assume specifically tax cuts by 1975 roughly comparable to the 1964 reduction.[6] The

___

[6]NPA, op. cit., p. 6.

stimulating effects of these and other fiscal decisions on the economy will result in much larger incomes, both personal and corporate, and consequently larger tax payments, even at somewhat lower rates. On the other hand, personal and corporate aftertax income would increase even more.

Disposable personal income (at constant prices) would increase by 55 per cent; retained corporate profits and capital consumption allowances (the total of retained earnings) would more than double: from about $65 billion in 1963 to about $139 billion in 1975. It is difficult to foresee the differential effect of these changes on small business. Across-the-board tax cuts will benefit larger businesses more than smaller ones, but selective cuts could be designed to give greater relief and encouragement to small business. For example, if corporate tax rates were graduated downward from a point higher than $25,000 and graduated steeply in the lower brackets, the lower rates would apply to all corporations; but they would benefit small corporations relatively more because their effective tax rates would be reduced more. If tax rates were reduced on reinvested earnings up to a specified limit, the growth of small businesses might be encouraged; again the effect would be relatively greater. However, up to now, such changes have not been publicly proposed as part of the Government's fiscal program.

The prospective growth in Federal tax revenues at a high and rising level of economic activity may serve as a drag on further economic growth unless Federal expenditures are increased substantially or Federal tax rates are reduced from time to time, or both. There will be strong political pressures for both actions, and it is almost certain that over the next decade Federal disbursements will increase sharply and Federal tax rates will be reduced measurably. State and local expenditures are certain to increase at a faster rate than Federal expenditures. Unless the much discussed proposal to shift Federal tax revenues to states and localities is adopted, unquestionably state and local tax rates will rise considerably.

Although tremendous progress has been made in increasing the understanding of fiscal policies and broadening the support for expansionist programs, we cannot be certain that the size and timing of fiscal policy actions will be adequate for the needs of vigorous and uninterrupted growth. To the degree that feasible and desirable rates of growth are not likely to be

Table 21

GOVERNMENT EXPENDITURES FOR GOODS AND SERVICES
IN BILLIONS OF 1964 DOLLARS

	Actual	Projected	
	1964	1970	1975
Federal	66	65	65
State and local	63	93	121

Source: Adapted from National Planning Association, Report No. 65-2.

achieved by exclusive reliance on fiscal policies, there will
be the need to formulate and implement appropriate monetary
policies. Both of these policy areas will have to play a positive
and constructive role; but fiscal policy is likely to be more
decisive, with monetary policy in a complementary and sup-
plementary role.

Circumstances will surely vary over time, necessitating
policy changes, but on the whole, the next decade will generally
require expansionist monetary and credit policies. These will
be necessary to assure the fullest use of the rapid increase in
savings for investment in expanded productive capacities, and
to yield a fiscal-monetary mix which will bring growth and
stability.

The adverse balance of payments situation which has faced
the United States for more than a decade could conceivably
have a significant influence on the monetary and fiscal policies
of the United States over the next several years. However, it
is more likely that the Government of the United States will
not permit balance of payments deficits to exercise any constraint on the growth of the American economy. The prospects
for improvement in our balance of payments are encouraging.
However, should adverse developments emerge, it is more
likely that a variety of selective measures will be adopted to
bring foreign payments into balance rather than resort to a
tight monetary policy. If this is the direction in which Government policy will move, then the monetary and fiscal policies

should be favorable not only to economic growth but also to small business.

The differential impacts of these developments on small business can be sketched generally. As between tax cuts and increased expenditures by the Federal Government, the former would appear to offer more opportunities and better prospects for small business than the latter. Set-asides and other preferential treatments in Federal purchase can surely help small business relative to big business, but administrative feasibility, political acceptability, and economic rationale would appear to offer little basis for hope among small businessmen that they will get a much larger share of larger Government expenditures.

As between raising state and local tax rates or, alternatively, transferring tax revenues from the Federal Government to state and local purposes, the latter would appear to be relatively more favorable to small business. The element of progressivity (tax rates graduated by ability to pay) in the Federal revenue system, as limited as it is and as eroded as it has become, is far more pronounced than in the case of state and local taxes. It can safely be concluded that relatively greater reliance on the pattern of Federal taxes and relatively less reliance on the pattern of state and local taxes would inure to the benefit of small business.

Monetary ease might not do as much differentially for small business as fiscal ease, particularly if there were substantial rate reductions in those taxes which bear most heavily on small business. However, expanded credit availability should be of particular benefit to small business. The frequent reiteration by bankers, central and otherwise, that small business has equal access to credit facilities is not entirely convincing. On a priori grounds, enlarged credit supply relative to credit demand can be safely expected to be especially beneficial to small business. Of course, to the extent that the Small Business Administration and other institutions are particularly helpful to small business in providing adequate financial resources, the benefits associated with credit ease can be further enhanced.

In general, it can be stated that those fiscal and monetary policies compatible with high and sustained levels of production, income, and employment will also tend to be of particular aid to small business. However, the margin of differential benefit to small business can be much enlarged if a variety of feasible preferences for small business are pursued in taxation, public expenditures, credit facilities, and in the selection of the fiscal-monetary policy mix.

The rising level of public expenditures will offer new opportunities for small business, even if the relative share of small business does not rise. To the extent that there is an increase in Federal purchases from business, other than those of the Defense Department and NASA, small business might enlarge its share. Greater possibilities for small business arise from the very large increase in purchases of state and local governments, provided there are policies and programs to enable small businesses to compete freely and on equal terms for this business.

Nearly half of the increase in state and local expenditures in the next decade will occur in programs other than health, education, and highways; as a result, the procurements may be varied. All told, there are more than thirty industry categories in which 5 per cent or more of output derives (directly or indirectly) from state and local government purchases, including, for example, about one fifth of new construction, one sixth of stone and clay products, about 15 per cent of lumber and paint, 12 per cent of business and institutional furniture, 18 per cent of heating, plumbing, and structural metal products, 12 per cent of electric lighting and mining, and 14 per cent of office supplies.[7]

THE OUTLOOK FOR SMALL BUSINESS
WITHIN INDUSTRY DIVISIONS

It is estimated conservatively that the business population will continue to grow for the next decade at the rate of just over 1 per cent per year—only about two-thirds as fast as the rate of growth in the past decade and more slowly than the population. The slowing down of the rate of growth reflects a

---

[7]"Interindustry Structure of the United States: A Report on the 1958 Input-Output Study," Survey of Current Business (November, 1964), p. 14.

tapering off of the extremely high rates of increase in the preceding decade in the service and "other" divisions, and the further spread of chain retailing. The rate of growth will vary widely among industry divisions, ranging from less than 1 per cent in manufacturing and retail trade to about 1.5 per cent in services and in "other divisions" (principally, finance and transportation).

The number of firms will be about 600,000 greater in 1976 than in 1966. One fourth of this increase will occur in the service industries, one fourth in retail trade, and one fourth mainly in finance and transportation. These increases, of course, are net; they represent the difference between about 5.3 million "births" and about 4.7 million "deaths" during the decade. (See Table 22.)

This is the outlook for the entire business population. What about the outlook for small business specifically? There are two clues.

First, trends in average number of employees per firm suggest that firms will be getting a little larger.[8] The postwar trend in average size has been similar for most industry divisions: a slow decline in average size in the late 1940's and early 1950's, reflecting the presence of great numbers of young, small firms born just after the War, and a gradual increase in average size since about 1954 as the birth rates and age distribution stabilized. It is projected that in 1967 the average size will be very close to that of 1947, and by 1976 it will be slightly higher. In manufacturing, average firm size projected for 1976 is larger by eight employees per firm (about 15 per cent) than the average for 1947, and most of this increase has already occurred. In all other industry divisions, differences from decade to decade, past and projected, are small. There are no grounds for expecting marked changes in the business size distributions which have remained so stable over the past several decades.

The second clue to the outlook for small business is found in the differential experience and the outlook for the sectors of small business concentration. Conclusions, sector by sector,

[8]National Planning Association, Projections of the Number of Firms by Industry and State, op. cit., p. 6.

Table 22

NONAGRICULTURAL BUSINESS FIRMS IN SELECTED INDUSTRY DIVISIONS, 1956-76

	Actual			Projected			Annual Rate of Change	
	1956	1963	1966	1970	1976	1956-66	1966-76
TOTAL	4,381.2	4,797.0	5,086.2	5,335.7	5,655.8	1.5	1.1
Construction	451.7	470.7	491.8	517.2	547.3	0.9	1.1
Manufacturing	327.3	313.0	325.4	339.5	353.4	–	0.8
Wholesale Trade	296.9	332.7	354.2	375.2	403.9	1.8	1.3
Retail Trade	1,903.2	2,038.9	2,115.5	2,189.1	2,267.1	1.1	0.7
Services	789.6	942.0	1,044.6	1,101.6	1,194.3	2.7	1.3
Other Divisions 9/	612.5	703.4	754.7	813.1	889.8	2.1	1.7

9/ Mining, finance, transportation.

Source: National Planning Association, Projections of the Number of Firms by Industry and State, Report 64-I, with adjustments for service industries.

have been given in the sector analyses in Chapters 3, 4, and 5. These conclusions also suggest that there is no reason to expect significant changes in the size distribution of the business population or its principal components, though internal shifts in size composition may be expected as small business adapts to changes in opportunities in a growing, changing economy. The services and the "other" divisions are expected to be the fastest growing, along with wholesaling. These are, in the main, sectors of small business concentration.

The number of firms in manufacturing is expected to increase, even though slowly, after a decade of ups and downs. The rate of projected increase is small and so is the number, but it is expected that by 1970 the number of firms in manufacturing will rise above the high reached in the mid-1950's before a decade of decline set in.[10] The increase in number of firms will be accompanied by an increase in the average size. This is neither an anomaly nor an inauspicious omen for the future of small manufacturing. It represents, on the one hand, the expansion of established manufacturing firms of all sizes in an expanding economy, through growth or acquisition, and on the other hand, the proliferation of new and small firms in many manufacturing sectors hospitable to them.

In retail trade the rate of increase in the number of firms is expected to be only about two-thirds as rapid in the next decade as in the one just past. This reflects the relative decline of some sectors and the further encroachment of chains on small business in some other sectors. Retailing will continue to provide about two fifths of all opportunities for small business firms.

The outlook in brief is for "small business as usual: moderately good." If the assumptions underlying the projections are proved valid by time, small business as a segment of the

---

[10] The Office of Business Economics figures include the self-employed with a fixed place of business, so that this series differs from County Business Patterns and the Census of Manufactures, which only include establishments with one employee or more. In manufacturing, the dwindling number of self-employed has resulted in a slight decline in total numbers of firms in the OBE series, while the number of establishments in both County Business Patterns and the Census of Manufactures has continued to increase.

economy will continue to offer opportunities of varying degrees of promise and profitability to a slowly increasing number of entrepreneurs. Most of the businesses formed will be short lived; a great many will achieve a modest and stable success; but only a few will grow to become large and highly profitable.

The sectoral composition of small business will change slowly as entrepreneurs respond to the shifts in demand resulting from the growth of the economy and the advance of technology. Where these create interstices of specialization within the framework of the mass-production and mass-distribution economy, there will be new opportunities for enterprising small businesses. At the very advanced stage of economic activity and technology in the United States and the rapid growth in prospect for both, there is no reason to doubt that there can be a continuing sound base for viable small business.

Concentration of big business in many crucial sectors of the economy will continue to present problems to small business. There is no expectation that concentration will diminish to a degree or in a manner that would significantly ease the impact on small business. Even apart from the effects of concentration, small business, by virtue of its smallness, will continue to labor under certain disabilities in its dealings with bigness, as competitor, customer, or supplier. If big business is also concentrated, limiting the market alternatives open to small business, the disabilities are aggravated.

One of the determining factors in the outlook for small business is the effectiveness of government in maintaining an environment conducive to the mobility and profitability of small business. Fiscal and monetary policies of government will largely determine the level at which the economy will operate. Policies with respect to antitrust laws, trade practices, and government regulation will have great influence in maintaining the competitive market. Policies with respect to research and development and patents will affect the rate and distribution of technological innovation.

Beyond these are questions of policies for positive protection and encouragement of small business per se: conspicuously, institutions and practices to obtain for small business capital and credit on terms that reflect the inherent credit-worthiness and growth prospects of individual firms; technical

assistance to help small business assimilate modern management techniques; procurement practices to give small business
at least equal access to government purchases, state and local
as well as Federal. How far these policies and practices are
carried depends on the degree of commitment to small business as an institution. Given the commitment, there is much
that can be done.

NOTES ON SOURCES

These estimates are based primarily on data compiled by the Bureau of Old-Age and Survivors' Insurance, with adjustments based on other Government sources. Data on operating businesses and on new and discontinued businesses refer to firms rather than to establishments. The firms are on an unconsolidated basis, with each corporation and corporate subsidiary counted separately. All nonfarm businesses are covered, regardless of size, including those with no employees if there is an established place of business. Professional practices are not considered business.

These data supply the best information on the total business population and on turnover over a long period of time. While information is available for the main industry divisions through 1962, more detailed industry data and data by size of business are not available for recent years.

ENTERPRISE STATISTICS: 1958

These data are derived from the 1958 Censuses of Business, Manufactures, and Mineral Industries and cover all businesses in manufacturing, minerals, public warehousing, wholesale and retail trade, and selected services. Construction, finance, insurance and real estate, transportation, communications, and public utilities are not included. The great advantage of this source is that it supplies information on size, in terms of number of employees, for companies rather than establishments. There are 135 industry classifications, and these can be related to the 1957 SIC. The grouping of detailed classifications was necessary in order to avoid unrealistic forcing of multi-industry companies into the four-digit code of the

201

primary industry of the company. Diversification is especially characteristic in manufacturing. Even with this consolidation, enterprise statistics give considerably more detailed breakdown in manufacturing than is available from the data prepared by the Office of Business Economics, and also provide separate information for single-unit and multi-unit companies. Also, because of the latter information, it is possible to determine in which categories the establishment data from the Census of Manufactures can be used to advantage.

This source affords information on firm size for only the one date. However, it is for a period well after the postwar adjustment period, and other sources indicate very considerable stability over time in the distribution of firms by size of employment.

COUNTY BUSINESS PATTERNS

This series of reports began in 1946 and has been published at three-year intervals since 1953. The reports are a by-product of employment and payroll data from Social Security tax reports, supplemented by special surveys of multi-unit companies.

They cover all nonfarm commercial and industrial activities and nonprofit organizations reported under the Federal Insurance Contributions Act. Employment data are based on the mid-March pay period. In general, businesses with no employees are not included. (However, reporting units with some payroll during the quarter are included in the smallest employee-size group even though no employees were reported for the designated pay-period.) The figures, therefore, run substantially under those from other sources on the size of the business population and on the proportion of very small units.

The unit of count is the "reporting unit." In manufacturing, each location of a company, even if there is more than one in the same county, is a separate reporting unit, which is therefore the same as an establishment in the Census of Manufactures. In the nonmanufacturing industries employers are counted once in each county for each industry in which they operate, regardless of the number of establishments. If the same employer operates in another county, his business is counted there also and appears twice in the United States total.

As a result, neither the number of businesses nor the data on size can be compared directly with other business statistics.

The reports for 1947, 1953, and 1962 have been used in this study solely to give some indication of trends in size for fairly broad industry classifications. For this purpose it is believed that they are useful. The definition of a reporting unit has been uniform throughout the period, and the general methods have remained essentially the same. The table presented excludes from the service total for each year professional services and nonprofit organizations because they are not ordinarily thought of as "businesses." Thus, increased coverage during the fifteen year period in this sector does not distort the over-all service picture.

Problems of shifts in classification are discussed in notes to the table derived from this source.

ANNUAL SURVEY OF MANUFACTURES, ACQUISITIONS AND
DISPOSALS OF MANUFACTURING FACILITIES: 1959-62

The Bureau of the Census has conducted a sample survey of manufactures regularly since 1949. The survey includes all manufacturing plants with 100 or more employees and varying proportions of medium and small establishments. The sample is selected primarily on a plant basis, but any company drawn in the sample is required to file reports for all of its manufacturing plants. The figures on acquisitions have not been inflated to universe totals, but it is believed that, because of the method of selecting the sample, the resulting understatement is slight. Acquisitions reported account for about 98 per cent of the employment estimated to be involved in changes of ownership of manufacturing facilities and for about 90 per cent of the acquisitions.

STATISTICS OF INCOME, INTERNAL REVENUE SERVICE: 1961-62

These reports are a by-product of the income tax returns of individuals engaged in business, of partnerships, and of corporations. The information available is, therefore, determined by the provisions of the tax law. In general, the data reflect operations of 1961, although returns included cover those filed for accounting periods ended July, 1961, through June 30, 1962. The returns of the great majority of sole proprietorships and most of the partnerships cover calendar year 1961. Approximately 45 per cent of the corporation returns are for the calendar year, 20 per cent for fiscal years ending between January 1 and June 30, 1962. The remainder are part year returns.

The data are based on a stratified systematic sample, selected before audit, of returns and schedules filed during the twelve-month period. In preparation for taking the sample, returns of individuals were classified by presence or absence of business receipts and size of adjusted gross income. Partnerships were classified by size of gross receipts or total income, and corporations by type of return and size of total assets. In general, it may be said that all returns were used for the largest businesses, with a decreasing sampling rate for smaller businesses where the total number of reports was much greater. Detailed information on the sampling procedure and on reliability is given in United States Business Tax Returns, 1961-1962, pp. 10-17.

PROFITABILITY RELATED TO SIZE OF BUSINESS

Statistics of the Internal Revenue Service based on business tax returns afford the only comprehensive information on business profit or income. They have some serious limitations for measuring the relative profitability of businesses of different sizes. Much less information is available for proprietorships and partnerships than for corporations and yet, in terms of the number of businesses, proprietorships and partnerships account for the great majority of businesses outside of manufacturing. However, corporations account for the major part of the business except in the service industries.

SOLE PROPRIETORSHIPS

For proprietorships no information is available on assets, and grouping by size is in terms of the amount of business receipts. The only measure of profitability possible is the percentage of firms with a net profit and the relationship of net profits to business receipts. Such data are given only for the main industry divisions.

For each industry division there is a substantial proportion of returns with total business receipts of less than $5,000 a year, even among returns showing a net profit.

Proprietorships With Business Receipts
of Less than $5,000

	All returns	Returns showing net profit
Construction	47%	47%
Manufacturing	37	33
Wholesale trade	33	29
Retail trade	22	18
Services	53	50

On the basis of the net profits which such returns yield, it is obvious that, in general, these returns do not represent "businesses" as that term is ordinarily understood. The dividing line should reasonably be at different dollar levels for the different business sectors.

CONSTRUCTION

From the amount of the average net profits for the business receipt groups under $5,000, it seems that this activity is not the major activity of the individual reporting, even though the per cent of returns with net profits compares favorably with returns showing much more business, and the ratio of net profit to business receipts is high. It is probable that most of these individuals are simply doing some carpentering, painting, or other repair work on their own while working most of the time for wages. Thus, the number of sole proprietors in this sector can reasonably be cut back to 355,000 from 679,000 and even this may not be enough of a reduction. Even with this adjustment, proprietorships account for 71 per cent of all returns in the construction industry. Net profits amount to 45.5 per cent of business receipts in the $5,000-$7,000 business-receipts group and this percentage declines steadily to 2.3 and 3.3 per cent for the two highest groups, with the decline more gradual and closely paralleling manufacturing from $20,000 on. Not until business receipts reach the levels of $100,000-$250,000 and $250,000-$500,000 does the percentage drop to a level comparable with the smallest size classes of corporations engaged in construction—6.7 and 5.4 as compared with 7.1, 6.1, and 5.1 per cent.

MANUFACTURING

In this sector the activity being reported on can hardly represent major activity below the $7,000 business receipt level. Thus, the number of proprietorships should be cut back to not over 110,000 from 194,000 and sole proprietorships would account for only 33 per cent of all manufacturing concerns instead of 47 per cent. Net profits amount to 25.4 per cent of business receipts in the $7,000-$10,000 business receipt group. Except for a rather out-of-line dip for the $20,000-$25,000 group, this percentage declines steadily to 3.8 and 2.5 per cent for the two groups with highest receipts. Some comparison can be made with manufacturing corporations in respect to the relationship between net profit and total business receipts.

For the two groups of smallest corporations, in terms of total assets (under $50,000 and $50,000-$100,000), net profit, including officers' compensation, represents 7.5 and 7.1 per cent of business receipts. These percentages are fairly comparable with those of the two groups of proprietorships having business receipts of $100,000-$250,000 and $250,000-$500,000 (7.8 and 6.9 per cent).

WHOLESALE TRADE

In this industry division wholesale trade can hardly represent the major occupation of those reporting business receipts of less than $5,000. This cuts back the number of proprietorships to approximately 219,000 from 328,000, accounting for 57 per cent of wholesale trade businesses as compared with 66 per cent when all returns are left in. Net profits amount to 37.3 per cent of business receipts for the $5,000-$7,000 group and this relationship is virtually identical for the next two size groups. After business receipts pass $15,000, the percentage declines steadily to 2.7 and 2.2 per cent for the two largest size groups. It remains substantially above the manufacturing per cent through the $50,000-$75,000 receipts group. From that point on it is lower and somewhat comparable with corporations engaged in wholesale trade.

RETAIL TRADE

It seems likely that very few of the returns showing less than $10,000 in business receipts represent full-time business activity. Housewives and others who sell greeting cards, cosmetics, and magazine subscriptions, etc., on the side, as well as businesses in operation for only a small part of the year, undoubtedly constitute a large proportion of the groups with lower receipts. Even in the $7,000-$10,000 receipts group, net profits average only $840 for the whole group and a little over $1,500 for those reporting net profit. Excluding those with under $10,000 in receipts cuts the number of proprietors back to somewhat over 1 million as against over 1.5 million, but still leaves them accounting for 69 per cent of all retail businesses. Net profits amount to a relatively low per cent of business receipts across the board and decline with increased volume of receipts from the $15,000-$20,000 level on up to the $100,000-$250,000 and $250,000-$500,000 levels, which have profit rates (5.4 and 3.6 per cent) approximately the same as retail corporations with total assets in the three lowest asset groups comprising all those with assets under $500,000 (5.2, 5.1, and 3.9 per cent).

SERVICES

It is probable that returns showing receipts of less than $4,000 hardly merit the characterization of a business, with net profits averaging $80, $560, $1,020, and $1,500 for the four low-receipts groups and $350, $800, $1,300, and $1,900, even when limited to those with a net profit. If these very small ones are eliminated, the number of proprietorships is cut from 2.1 million to 1.1 million. Even if these very small operators are omitted, sole proprietorships account for 78 per cent of the service industry businesses. For all sizes, net profits constitute a high percentage of business receipts, the highest (45.7 per cent) being that for the $4,000-$5,000 group. Beginning with the $7,000-$10,000 level through the $50,000-$75,000 there is relatively little variation and no trend. The range among these groups is only 4.5 percentage points (from 37.2 to 41.7). Above this level of receipts there is a sharp drop in the percentage, but it remains well above any of the other business sectors at the same level of receipts.

FINANCE, INSURANCE, AND REAL ESTATE

Over one third of the returns in this industry division showed business receipts less than $2,000 and 57 per cent were under $5,000. Average net income for such proprietorships indicate that they should hardly be considered as "businesses." For each of the two groups immediately above $5,000, net profits were exactly half of business receipts. For the next group, those with receipts between $10,000 and $15,000, they amounted to 53 per cent of receipts. Beyond that level of receipts the percentage dropped sharply and steadily with size.

PARTNERSHIPS

The partnership is the least frequent form of organization in each of the main industry divisions. In most divisions it also accounts for the smallest proportion of business. For this group as a whole, as with sole proprietorships, the only measure of size is in terms of the amount of business receipts, and profitability can be measured only by the relationship of net profits to business receipts, since balance sheet information is available for only 40 to 60 per cent of the returns, depending upon the industry division. The tax regulations provide that " . . . a deduction may be taken for payments to a partner for services or the use of capital where such payments are determined without regard to the income of the partnership." No data are available to indicate whether the effect of this deduction varies with size, but it seems likely that it would have the least effect on the largest firms. Within each industry division, the proportion of businesses reporting a net profit is lower than that of sole proprietorships at almost all levels of receipts. The 1960-61 report (no comparable table for 1961-62) shows that, in manufacturing, wholesale trade, and retail trade, payment to partners amounts to 17-18 per cent of net profits.

CONSTRUCTION

Only 63 per cent of the firms with business receipts under $5,000 showed a net profit. On the average, net profits amounted to only 17.9 per cent of business receipts for all firms in this size group. The per cent increased with size to 34 per cent for those with receipts between $10,000 and $15,000. From that point net profits were a continuously decreasing per cent of receipts through the group with receipts between $1 and $5 million to 4.1 per cent. The per cent was somewhat higher for those with receipts above $5 million. Almost one fourth of all partnerships in this industry reported business receipts under $15,000.

MANUFACTURING

Only 42 per cent of the firms with business receipts under $5,000 reported a net profit, resulting in an average net loss for this group as a whole. Net profits were low in relation to receipts for the next group, but amounted to 20.4 per cent for firms with receipts between $10,000 and $15,000. From that point on the trend was down, with profits amounting to only 3.2 per cent for businesses with receipts in excess of $5 million. One fifth of the partnerships in manufacturing reported business receipts under $10,000, over one third under $25,000.

WHOLESALE TRADE

In the case of wholesale trade, profits amounted to a continuously larger proportion of receipts through the $20,000-$25,000 group where they were 25.5 per cent. From that point on profitability in these terms dropped steadily with size, and net profits amounted to only 1.3 per cent of receipts for firms with receipts of $5 million or more.

RETAIL TRADE

Only 44 per cent of the partnerships in retail trade with receipts under $5,000 showed a net profit and there was a net loss for this group as a whole. At the $5,000-$10,000 receipts level, net profits were 6.5 per cent of receipts and, in general, the per cent showed a gradual increase to 11.0 per cent for the $40,000-$50,000 group. Above that level the per cent gradually declined to 2.1 per cent for the largest size group.

SERVICES

Net profits represent a much larger part of business receipts than they do for the industry divisions previously discussed and the relationship between profits and size is markedly different. The group with the smallest receipts reported almost no net profit. For the $5,000 to $10,000 group, profits were 23.6 per cent of receipts. With the next step they went up to 29.8 per cent and remained on a virtual plateau for the five size groups between $10,000 and $40,000. The per cent then increases steadily to 44.5 for partnerships with receipts of $150,000-$200,000. From that point on there is a continuous drop to 24.9 per cent for those with receipts of $5 million or more.

FINANCE, INSURANCE, AND REAL ESTATE

In this industry division 44 per cent of the partnerships report business receipts of less than $5,000 and 60 per cent less than $10,000. At the lowest level of receipts there is a net loss reported. Above that, profits form an increasing portion of receipts, reaching 35 per cent for the $25,000-$30,000 and $30,000-$40,000 groups. From this level the per cent declines to 16.8 per cent at $150,000-$200,000, but increases again.

CORPORATIONS

Over the years since data on corporate income, assets, and various items of income and expense have been available in reports of the Internal Revenue Service, interested individuals

have prepared ratios derived from these data to relate profitability, chances for expansion, or efficiency to size of the
business. The approaches have been numerous and the results
have sometimes seemed in conflict. In some cases all active
corporations have been included, in others, only those with a
net profit. In some, stockholders' equity has been used as the
basis for the rate of earnings; in others, total assets. One may
use total compiled net income or net income after tax, either
as reported or with certain adjustments.

The difference in the significance of "officers' compensa-
tions" in firms of different size is the major objection to the
use of net income as reported. The smaller corporations exist
as much to provide income in the form of managerial wages to
corporate officers as to pay dividends; and closely held corporations are free, within limits permitted by tax law and
regulations, to adjust officers' salaries in the manner which
will maximize tax advantages.

Two methods of adjustment for officers' compensation have
been used in the past.

McConnell has dealt extensively with the effect of officers'
compensation on net income or loss.[1] The smaller corporations
are usually wholly owned by one, two, or three officers who
are also full-time workers in their own concern—true of 70
per cent of nonfinancial corporations with assets under $50,000
and of 50 per cent of those with assets between $50,000 and
$250,000. He points out the fact that a portion, but not all, of
this compensation should legitimately be considered as wages
for work done. On the basis of a sample study he arrives at an
average number of full-time owner officers per firm for those
in the smallest size categories, and at an average "owner-
officer" wage in firms of comparable size, but with dispersed
ownership. From this information he arrived at a division of
officers' compensation and attributed a portion to profits.
Minor adjustments are made in the other groups with assets
under $1 million. Above that level, net income is used without
adjustment. He relates this adjusted income to stockholders'

---

[1] Joseph L. McConnell, "Corporate Earnings by Size of Firm,"
Survey of Current Business, May, 1945, pp. 6-12 and "1942 Corporate
Profits by Size of Firm," Survey of Current Business, January, 1946,
pp. 10-16.

equity rather than to total assets. This approach seems thoroughly reasonable, but a new sample study would have to be undertaken to make such an adjustment to more current data possible (his last year was 1942).

H. O. Stekler[2] makes use of a formula previously used by S. S. Alexander.[3] He assumes that, even in closely held corporations, loss firms have no incentive to overpay their officers, since they do not pay taxes, whereas the profitable firms do. He, therefore, considers the relationship between officers' compensation and assets for the loss firms to be legitimate wages, applies this to the profit firms, and attributes the difference to profits. The line of reasoning seems open to question, since it would appear that a firm may report no net income because of the amount which has been charged to officers' compensation. This is indicated, for example, by a comparison between the per cent of manufacturing corporations with net income with the per cent of sole proprietorships in this industry division showing a net profit (where this complication does not enter in), each grouped by the size of business receipts. The corporation per cent is well below the proprietorships up to a level of business receipts of $500,000 to $1 million. However, there is no reason to suppose that corporations really are less successful than sole proprietorships at the same level of business receipts. The situation is similar in wholesale and retail trade and in the service industries.

For the purposes of the present study of profitability in relation to size based on 1961-62 Corporation Income Tax returns, we have taken total assets as the base and computed two sets of percentages. The first accepts the compiled net income as reported. The second adds total officers' compensation, in the absence of a satisfactory method of splitting it, as well as interest paid, since total assets are used as the base. These have been prepared for four main industry divisions—construction, manufacturing, wholesale trade, and

---

[2]H. O. Stekler, Profitability and Size of Firm (Berkeley, California: University of California Press, 1963).

[3]S. S. Alexander, "The Effect of Size of Manufacturing Corporations on the Distribution of Rate of Return," Review of Economics & Statistics, 1949, pp. 229-235.

retail trade, although corporations account for a substantial proportion of all firms only in manufacturing and wholesale trade. In addition, computations have been prepared for selected two- and three-digit manufacturing groups. The returns of all active firms in each group are included, both those with net income and those without.

CONSTRUCTION

Using compiled net income, the group with assets under $50,000 shows a net loss. The per cent of return increases with each size group through the $500,000-$1 million group, from 1.3 per cent to 3.4 per cent, then falls off for the next three size groups. The highest per cent is that of firms with assets of $50-$100 million (8.3 per cent), but for firms with assets of $100-$250 million it is lower than for any size class above $100,000. With the addition of officers' compensation and interest to net income the picture changes radically for all size firms up through those with assets of $2.5 to $5 million, starting with a profit of almost 31 per cent and dropping steadily to 5.4 per cent for the $2.5-$5 million group. From this point on the contrast between the two sets of per cents is much less marked, as officers' compensation represents a smaller per cent of total assets.

MANUFACTURING

Again, when using unadjusted net income, those firms with assets under $50,000 show a net loss, while there is a small net income for those in the next size group. For the next two groups, but still under the asset level usually taken as marking off "small" firms ($1 million), there is a sharp increase, then a gradual one until a plateau is reached with the $10-$25 million group, interrupted by a higher per cent in the next to the highest asset group. With the addition of officers' compensation and interest to net income, the highest per cent is that of the smallest firms and declines steadily with size, at first sharply and then gradually, except for the same hump for the next-to-largest firms. The truth undoubtedly lies somewhere between these two sets of per cents. A comparison with Stekler's computation for 1955-57 for profitable firms only and with his more refined attempt at handling officers' compensation shows almost identical levels of profit for the groups with assets up to $500,000. From that level there is very little change through the $25 million group and then a decrease, except for the $100-$250 million group, which has a higher rate of income just as it did with both of our sets of figures.

McConnell's computations for 1941, based on equity rather than on total assets and using a refined method of adjustment for officers' compensation, do not indicate any clear-cut advantage for large firms. Up to $250,000 there is an increase from 21.1 to 23.3 to 25.4 per cent. Above that equity level there is a slight decrease, down to 22.3 per cent for the $10-$25 million group. Although the highest figure is shown for the $50-$100 million group (26.0), the per cent for those firms with equity over $100 million is substantially lower than that of any other group—17.5 per cent.

WHOLESALE TRADE

As with the other industry divisions, firms with assets under $50,000 show an average net loss when only compiled net income is considered. With the addition of interest and officers' compensation, income amounts to 28 per cent of total assets. The unadjusted per cent increases more or less steadily with size through the $100-$250 million group. For those with assets above this amount the per cent is lower than that of any but the two smallest size groups. The adjusted per cent falls steadily from its 28 per cent level to 7.6 per cent for firms with assets of $10-$25 million. For the three groups with assets of $25 million to $250 million it is higher, but drops for the small number with assets above that amount.

McConnell's figures for this industry division show a steady drop in profitability through the $250,000-$500,000 group, a somewhat higher level for the two groups from $500,000-$5 million, with lower levels above $5 million equity.

RETAIL TRADE

Unadjusted income in relation to assets increases steadily with the size of firm from a negative figure for firms with assets under $50,000 to almost 8 per cent for those with assets of $250 million or more. The adjusted per cent declines steadily from that of the smallest firms to 7.6 per cent for those with assets of $5-$10 million. There was some increase for firms with assets above $10 million.

It must be remembered that corporations are not typical of retail trade in general, representing only 11 per cent of all retail trade returns and only 15 per cent even when the smallest returns are eliminated (see notes on sole proprietorships).

MANUFACTURING CORPORATIONS
(TWO- AND THREE-DIGIT INDUSTRIES)

For manufacturing as a whole we had relatively consistent trends—a positive relationship to size for the unadjusted percentage and negative for the adjusted. Manufacturing embraces a wide variety of types of activity and therefore we have prepared separate figures for some of the sectors which are given detailed attention in other analysis of the place of small business in the various manufacturing industries. The industry groups covered are as follows:

Beverages, total
    Bottled and canned soft drinks, carbonated waters, and
        flavoring

Food and kindred products, total
    Meat products
    Dairy products
    Canning and preserving
    Grain mill products

Textile mill products
    Knitting mills

Apparel and other finished products made from fabrics
    Men's, youths', and boys' clothing
    Women's, misses', children's, and infants' clothing
    Hats, caps, and millinery; fur goods and other accessories
    Other fabricated textile products

Lumber and wood products, except furniture
    Logging camps, logging contractors, and sawmills and
        planing mills
    Millwork, veneer, plywood, etc.
    Wooden containers and wood products

Furniture and fixtures
    Household furniture
    Office, public building, and other furniture and fixtures

Printing, publishing, and allied industries
  Newspapers: publishing, publishing and printing
  Books
  Commercial printing, business forms, and greeting cards
  Other publishing, bookbinding, and related industries and
    service industries for the trade

Rubber and miscellaneous plastic products
  Miscellaneous plastic products

Leather and leather products
  Leather and leather products other than shoes

Stone, clay, and glass products
  Structural clay products
  Concrete, gypsum, and plaster products

Fabricated metal products
  Cutlery, hand tools, and general hardware
  Fabricated structural metal products
  Screw machine products and bolts, nuts, screws, rivets,
    and washers
  Metal stampings
  Coating, engraving, and allied services

Machinery other than electrical and transportation
  Metal working machinery and equipment

When one looks at individual sectors there is seldom a consistent trend in the adjusted profitability ratio throughout the
full range of size classes.

For the food industry as a whole there is a downward trend
with increased size through the group of firms with assets of
$25-$50 million. The rate of profit increases for the three size
groups above that level. Meat products show a generally negative, but somewhat irregular relationship to size. Neither dairy
products nor canning and preserving can be said to evidence
any real relationship between profitability and size, while the
profit rate for grain products tends to increase with size.

In the textile industry the trend is sharply downward for
businesses below $2.5 million of assets. After an interrup-
tion, the trend continues downward to the $25 million level.
Beyond that level there is no trend.

The apparel industry as a whole shows an even stronger negative relationship between profitability and size than do textiles. This is much less evident for men's and boys' clothing. In the women's and children's clothing industries only one size class ($5-$10 million) interrupts the steady downward movement of the ratio with increase in size. This is typically a small-business industry as compared with men's clothing.

APPENDIX C

TABLES

Table 1-A

BUSINESS POPULATION BY MAJOR INDUSTRY DIVISION

Average number for the years prior to 1940,
as of January 1 thereafter (thousands)

	All Industries	Contract Con- struction	Manu- facturing	Service Indus- tries	Retail Trade	Whole- sale Trade	All Other 1/
1929	3,029.0	233.8	257.0	590.9	1,327.0	148.1	472.0
1930	2,993.7	230.2	228.1	598.7	1,325.5	146.6	464.6
1931	2,916.4	218.6	195.3	592.1	1,316.7	143.9	449.7
1932	2,828.1	202.2	166.4	588.0	1,301.8	141.6	428.1
1933	2,782.1	185.4	166.8	574.9	1,291.2	141.8	422.1
1934	2,884.0	179.7	187.9	592.5	1,337.3	152.0	434.6
1935	2,991.9	180.2	205.0	615.8	1,387.2	157.0	446.5
1936	3,069.8	191.7	210.8	628.6	1,430.1	164.7	443.9
1937	3,136.3	199.0	214.3	631.3	1,469.3	170.7	451.6
1938	3,073.7	193.5	202.2	604.8	1,451.6	167.1	454.6
1939	3,222.2	199.4	221.3	615.2	1,534.6	175.6	476.1
1940	3,318.9	202.3	222.9	639.1	1,580.4	183.6	490.5
1941	3,276.0	194.2	230.4	614.6	1,560.7	190.1	486.1
1942	3,295.3	186.9	240.7	620.0	1,561.5	200.7	485.5
1943	3,030.0	164.4	242.9	579.1	1,401.4	181.8	460.4
1944	2,839.1	146.9	246.4	536.0	1,291.4	169.8	448.5
1945	2,995.4	160.1	253.1	567.6	1,356.2	186.0	472.4
1946	3,242.5	199.0	264.0	613.9	1,458.4	208.9	498.2
1947	3,651.2	268.1	302.5	686.6	1,627.0	242.8	524.4
1948	3,872.9	310.3	315.4	728.0	1,730.0	254.8	534.5
1949	3,984.2	338.9	322.5	738.6	1,782.7	260.1	541.2
1950	4,008.7	352.5	317.6	735.3	1,802.8	263.3	537.2
1951	4,067.3	377.3	322.8	733.0	1,820.9	268.6	544.6
1952	4,118.2	387.2	328.2	739.6	1,830.8	275.8	556.6
1953	4,187.7	405.3	330.7	749.9	1,846.1	283.1	572.6
1954	4,239.8	416.7	331.3	760.0	1,861.4	288.2	582.3

Table 1-A (Cont.)

BUSINESS POPULATION BY MAJOR INDUSTRY DIVISION

	All Industries	Contract Construction	Manufacturing	Service Industries	Retail Trade	Wholesale Trade	All Other 1/
1955	4,286.8	429.8	326.1	772.6	1,874.5	291.9	591.7
1956	4,381.2	451.7	327.3	789.6	1,903.2	296.9	612.5
1957	4,470.7	465.4	332.3	810.0	1,925.6	303.7	633.6
1958	4,533.0	466.0	329.0	828.0	1,955.0	309.0	647.0
1959	4,583.0	464.0	323.0	848.0	1,977.0	312.0	658.0
1960	4,658.0	476.0	323.0	872.0	1,997.0	317.0	674.0
1961	4,713.0	477.0	322.0	895.0	2,011.0	322.0	686.0
1962	4,755.0	473.0	317.0	918.0	2,022.0	327.0	698.0
1963	4,797.0	470.0	313.0	942.0	2,032.0	332.0	708.0

Projected

	All Industries	Contract Construction	Manufacturing	Service Industries	Retail Trade	Wholesale Trade	All Other 1/
1966	5,086.2	491.8	325.4	1,044.6	2,115.5	354.2	754.7
1970	5,335.7	517.2	339.5	1,101.6	2,189.1	375.2	813.1
1976	5,655.8	547.3	353.4	1,194.3	2,267.1	403.9	889.8

1/ Includes mining, finance, and transportation divisions.

Source: Historical Statistics of the United States for 1929 through
              1938.
              Business Statistics, 1963 Edition, for 1939 through 1963.
              NPA Projections of Number of Firms for 1966, 1970 and
              1976 with adjustments for service industries.
              All of above based on estimates of Office of Business
              Economics.

Table 1-B

NEW BUSINESSES, BY INDUSTRY DIVISION, 1940-62 (Thousands)

	All Industries	Contract Construction	Manu-facturing	Service Industries	Retail Trade	Wholesale Trade	All Other
1940	275.2	21.9	29.2	49.2	117.9	20.4	36.7
1941	290.0	19.9	30.9	61.7	117.4	22.6	37.4
1942	121.2	7.5	23.2	28.7	39.3	4.8	17.8
1943	146.0	8.8	25.2	28.3	49.9	7.8	25.9
1944	330.9	28.4	26.9	71.4	128.1	24.5	51.6
1945	422.7	55.8	37.2	84.5	161.4	30.2	53.6
1946	617.4	95.1	62.8	116.6	234.1	45.2	63.5
1947	460.8	73.8	39.7	90.3	179.5	29.8	47.7
1948	393.3	65.0	34.6	72.9	151.2	24.4	45.2
1949	331.1	54.2	25.8	57.5	135.5	21.1	36.8
1950	348.2	64.1	30.0	55.5	133.0	21.6	44.1
1951	327.1	53.7	28.0	53.3	122.9	20.7	48.3
1952	345.6	61.5	28.1	54.4	130.3	21.4	49.9
1953	351.6	59.8	28.2	55.8	139.7	21.1	46.9
1954	365.6	61.6	25.3	60.7	147.1	21.3	49.7
1955	408.2	68.7	29.4	67.4	161.4	22.3	59.0
1956	431.2	68.0	31.4	73.5	170.2	24.2	63.9
1957	398.0	57.0	25.0	71.0	166.0	23.0	56.0
1958	397.0	58.0	24.0	76.0	160.0	22.0	56.0
1959	422.0	67.0	27.0	82.0	161.0	23.0	62.0
1960	438.0	66.0	27.0	89.0	170.0	24.0	62.0
1961	431.0	62.0	25.0	89.0	170.0	25.0	61.0
1962 1/	430.0	60.0	25.0	91.0	168.0	25.0	61.0

1/ Based on incomplete data.

Source: Business Statistics, 1963 Edition.

Table 1-C

DISCONTINUED BUSINESSES, BY INDUSTRY DIVISION, 1940-62 (Thousands)

	All Industries	Contract Construction	Manu-facturing	Service Industries	Retail Trade	Wholesale Trade	All Other
1940	318.1	30.0	21.7	73.7	137.6	13.9	41.1
1941	270.7	27.2	20.6	56.3	116.6	12.0	38.0
1942	386.5	30.0	21.0	69.6	199.4	23.7	42.9
1943	337.0	26.3	21.8	71.4	159.9	19.8	37.8
1944	174.6	15.2	20.2	39.7	63.3	8.3	27.7
1945	175.6	16.9	26.4	38.3	59.2	7.3	27.7
1946	208.7	26.0	24.3	43.9	65.5	11.4	37.6
1947	239.2	31.6	26.8	49.0	76.5	17.7	37.6
1948	282.0	36.3	27.4	62.3	98.5	19.1	38.4
1949	306.5	40.7	30.8	60.7	115.5	18.0	41.0
1950	289.6	39.2	24.7	57.8	115.0	16.3	36.5
1951	276.2	43.9	22.7	46.6	113.0	13.5	36.4
1952	276.1	43.3	25.5	44.2	115.1	14.2	34.0
1953	299.4	48.5	27.7	45.7	124.4	16.0	37.1
1954	318.7	48.4	30.5	48.0	134.0	17.6	40.2
1955	313.8	46.8	28.2	50.4	132.7	17.3	38.3
1956	341.7	54.3	26.4	53.1	147.8	17.3	42.8
1957	335.0	57.0	29.0	53.0	137.0	17.0	43.0
1958	347.0	59.0	30.0	56.0	138.0	19.0	45.0
1959	346.0	56.0	27.0	59.0	140.0	18.0	46.0
1960	384.0	64.0	29.0	65.0	157.0	19.0	49.0
1961	389.0	65.0	30.0	65.0	159.0	21.0	50.0
1962 1/	387.0	63.0	29.0	67.0	158.0	20.0	50.0

1/ Based on incomplete data.

Source: Business Statistics, 1963 Edition.

Table 2

ENTRY AND DISCONTINUANCE RATE BY INDUSTRY DIVISION – NUMBER OF NEW BUSINESSES AND OF
BUSINESSES DISCONTINUED PER 1,000 IN OPERATION AT THE BEGINNING
OF THE YEAR – 1940–62

Year	All Industries		Construction		Manufacturing		Service Industries		Retail Trade		Wholesale Trade	
	Entry	Discontinuance	Entry	Discontinuance	Entry	Discontinuance	Entry	Discontinuance	Entry	Discontinuance	Entry	Discontinuance
1940	83	96	108	148	131	97	77	115	75	87	111	76
1941	89	83	102	140	134	89	100	92	75	75	119	63
1942	37	117	40	161	96	87	46	112	25	128	24	118
1943	48	111	54	160	104	90	49	123	36	114	43	109
1944	117	61	193	103	109	82	133	74	99	49	144	49
1945	141	59	349	106	147	104	149	67	119	44	162	39
1946	190	64	478	131	238	92	190	72	161	45	216	55
1947	126	66	275	118	131	89	132	71	110	47	123	73
1948	102	73	209	117	110	87	100	86	87	57	96	75
1949	83	77	160	120	80	96	78	82	76	65	81	69
1950	87	72	182	111	94	78	75	79	74	64	82	62
1951	80	68	142	116	87	70	73	64	67	62	77	50
1952	84	67	159	112	86	78	74	60	71	63	78	52
1953	84	71	148	120	85	84	74	61	76	67	75	57
1954	86	75	148	116	76	92	80	63	79	72	74	61

Table 2 (Cont.)

ENTRY AND DISCONTINUANCE RATE BY INDUSTRY DIVISION – NUMBER OF NEW BUSINESSES AND OF
BUSINESSES DISCONTINUED PER 1,000 IN OPERATION AT THE BEGINNING
OF THE YEAR – 1940–62

Year	All Industries		Construction		Manufacturing		Service Industries		Retail Trade		Wholesale Trade	
	Entry	Discon-tinuance	Entry	Discon-tinuance	Entry	Discon-tinuance	Entry	Discon-tinuance	Entry	Discon-tinuance	Entry	Discon-tinuance
1955	95	73	160	109	90	87	87	65	86	71	76	59
1956	98	78	151	120	96	81	93	67	89	78	82	58
1957	89	75	123	122	75	87	88	65	86	71	76	56
1958	88	77	124	127	73	91	92	68	82	71	71	62
1959	92	75	144	121	84	84	97	70	81	71	74	58
1960	94	82	139	134	84	90	102	75	85	79	76	60
1961	91	83	130	136	78	95	99	73	85	79	78	65
1962	90	81	127	133	79	93	99	73	83	78	76	61

Source: Computations based on data in Appendix Tables 1-A, 1-B, and 1-C.

Table 3-A

AVERAGE ANNUAL RATE OF GROWTH (OR DECREASE)
IN BUSINESS POPULATION BY INDUSTRY DIVISION FOR
FOUR PERIODS: 1929-39, 1947-52, 1953-59, 1960-62

Industry division	1929-39	1947-52	1953-59	1960-62
All Industries	0.6	2.2	1.5	0.9
Contract construction	-1.6	7.0	2.2	-0.4
Manufacturing	-1.5	1.5	-0.35	-1.0
Service industries	0.3	1.5	2.2	2.6
Retail trade	1.5	2.1	0.9	0.8
Wholesale trade	1.7	2.6	1.6	1.6

Source: Computations based on data in Appendix Table 1-A.

Table 3-B

AVERAGE ANNUAL TURNOVER RATE IN BUSINESS POPULATION
BY INDUSTRY DIVISION FOR THREE PERIODS: 1947-52, 1953-59,
1960-62.

	Number of New Businesses per 1,000 in operation			Number of Businesses discontinued, per 1,000 in operation		
	1947-52	1953-59	1960-62	1947-52	1953-59	1960-62
All Industries	94	90	92	71	75	82
Construction	188	143	132	116	119	134
Manufacturing	98	83	80	83	87	93
Service industries	89	87	100	74	66	74
Retail trade	81	83	84	60	72	79
Wholesale trade	90	75	77	64	59	62

Source: Computations based on data in Appendix Table 2.

Table 4

PER CENT OF FIRMS IN OPERATION AND OF PAID EMPLOYMENT BY SIZE OF FIRM
(CUMULATIVE) 1945-56

Employee-size class	1945	1946	1947	1948	1949	1951	1956
Firms							
Under 4	74.63	72.39	73.49	74.28	75.27	74.74	75.31
Under 8	87.21	85.93	86.63	87.11	87.77	87.36	86.95
Under 20	94.61	94.41	94.78	95.06	95.31	95.03	95.05
Under 50	97.85	97.84	97.99	98.11	98.22	98.09	98.13
Under 100	98.95	98.97	99.04	99.10	99.16	99.09	99.14
Under 500	99.80	99.82	99.82	99.84	99.85	99.84	99.85
Under 1,000	99.90	99.91	99.92	99.92	99.93	99.92	99.93
Under 10,000	99.99	99.99	99.99	99.99	99.99	99.99	99.99
Total	100.00	100.00	100.00	100.00	100.00	100.00	100.00
Paid Employment							
Under 4	5.1	5.8	5.9	6.1	6.5	6.3	6.5
Under 8	11.0	12.9	12.9	13.2	13.9	13.3	13.1
Under 20	18.8	22.8	22.9	23.3	24.2	23.1	23.7
Under 50	27.5	32.9	32.7	33.1	34.1	33.0	33.8
Under 100	34.2	40.5	40.0	40.4	41.4	40.3	41.2
Under 500	49.7	57.0	56.0	56.1	56.7	56.1	56.4
Under 1,000	56.4	63.4	62.3	62.4	62.7	62.1	61.9
Under 10,000	77.9	84.0	82.4	81.9	81.7	81.2	82.2
Total	100.0	100.0	100.0	100.0	100.0	100.0	100.0

Source: Survey of Current Business, September, 1959.

Table 5-A

DISTRIBUTION OF COMPANIES BY NUMBER OF EMPLOYEES, BY INDUSTRY DIVISION AND CATEGORY, 1958

Numbers in Thousands

Industry Division and Category	Total	Less than 20 Employees		20 to 249 Employees		250 or more Employees	
		Number	Per cent	Number	Per cent	Number	Per cent
All Industries	3,151.6	2,981.4	94.6	160.8	5.1	9.3	0.3
Mineral Industries	30.1	25.9	86.0	3.9	13.2	0.2	0.8
Metal mining	1.7	1.6	91.9	.1	6.8	.02	1.3
Anthracite mining	1.2	1.0	88.7	.1	10.4	.01	.9
Bituminous coal and lignite	6.2	5.3	84.9	.9	14.0	.08	1.3
Crude petroleum	9.6	8.8	92.1	.7	7.5	.04	.4
Oil and gas service	5.6	4.3	77.6	1.2	21.9	.02	.5
Nonmetallic minerals, n.e.c.	5.9	4.9	83.4	.9	15.8	.05	.8
Manufacturing	269.8	194.7	72.2	68.2	25.3	6.8	2.5
Meat packing	2.6	1.8	68.2	0.7	28.7	0.08	3.1
Prepared meats, dressed poultry	2.4	1.6	64.7	.8	32.8	.06	2.5
Dairy products	8.3	6.0	72.9	2.1	25.8	.12	1.3
Canned and frozen foods	3.0	1.6	54.7	1.2	40.6	.14	4.7
Grain mill products	2.8	2.1	74.9	.6	22.9	.06	2.2
Bakery products	5.5	3.8	69.9	1.5	27.5	.14	2.6
Sugar	.07	.007	1.0	.04	69.1	.02	29.4

Table 5-A (Cont.)

DISTRIBUTION OF COMPANIES BY NUMBER OF EMPLOYEES, BY INDUSTRY DIVISION AND CATEGORY, 1958

Numbers in Thousands

Industry Division and Category	Total	Less than 20 Employees		20 to 249 Employees		250 or more Employees	
		Number	Per cent	Number	Per cent	Number	Per cent
Manufacturing (cont.)							
Confectionery and related products	1.3	1.0	70.4	.3	24.7	.06	4.7
Alcoholic beverages	.5	.2	41.3	.2	45.1	.07	13.5
Bottled soft drinks and flavorings	4.4	3.2	71.7	1.2	27.5	.04	.8
Fats and oils	.8	.4	59.6	.3	37.6	.02	2.8
Other food products	3.5	2.9	81.9	.6	16.8	.05	1.2
Tobacco products	.4	.2	61.1	.1	30.2	.03	8.5
Broad-woven fabrics, yarn, thread, and finishing (exc. wool)	1.7	.7	41.5	.7	42.5	.28	16.0
Wool broad-woven fabrics, yarn & finishing	.6	.2	36.2	.3	53.6	.06	10.0
Knitting mills	2.6	1.1	41.2	1.4	52.5	.16	6.3
Floor covering mills	.3	.1	43.2	.1	46.8	.03	10.0
Other textile mill products	1.4	.8	61.1	.5	35.1	.05	3.7
Men's and boys' clothing	3.9	1.8	45.4	1.8	46.8	.30	7.8

Women's and children's clothing, (exc. millinery and fur goods)	12.8	5.6	44.0	7.0	54.3	.23	1.7
Millinery, fur goods and misc. apparel	4.5	3.3	73.8	1.1	25.1	.05	1.1
Fabricated textiles, n.e.c.	6.7	5.3	79.8	1.3	19.6	.04	.5
Logging, saw mills, planing mills	28.7	25.7	89.5	2.9	10.2	.10	.3
Millwork and related products	3.9	2.7	70.9	1.0	27.1	.08	2.0
Other wood products	3.8	2.9	76.1	.9	22.8	.04	1.1
Household furniture	6.2	4.1	66.1	1.9	30.6	.17	3.2
Furniture and fixtures (exc. household furniture)	3.5	2.7	77.3	.7	21.1	.05	1.6
Pulp, paper, and board	.4	.1	30.1	.2	40.1	.12	29.8
Paperboard containers and boxes	1.6	.6	43.0	.8	52.1	.08	4.8
Other paper and allied products	1.8	1.1	61.3	.6	34.7	.07	4.0
Newspapers	7.9	6.4	80.6	1.4	17.2	.17	2.1
Periodicals	2.2	1.9	83.9	.3	14.1	.04	1.9
Books	1.6	1.2	75.7	.3	21.5	.05	2.8
Miscellaneous publishing and greeting cards	1.3	1.0	82.0	.2	16.1	.02	1.8
Commercial printing & manifold business forms	17.5	14.8	84.6	2.5	14.3	.13	.6
Bookbinding and printing trade services	3.6	2.6	72.1	1.0	27.3	.02	.6
Basic chemicals, fibers, plastics & rubber	.9	.6	61.6	.3	30.2	.07	8.3
Drugs	1.2	.9	75.0	.3	21.2	.05	3.9
Cleaning and toilet goods	2.4	2.0	81.3	.4	16.5	.05	2.2
Paints and varnishes	1.4	1.0	69.7	.4	27.8	.03	2.2
Agricultural chemicals	.8	.6	73.5	.2	24.3	.02	2.1

Table 5-A (Cont.)

DISTRIBUTION OF COMPANIES BY NUMBER OF EMPLOYEES, BY INDUSTRY DIVISION AND CATEGORY, 1958

Numbers in Thousands

Industry Division and Category	Total	Less than 20 Employees		20 to 249 Employees		250 or more Employees	
		Number	Per cent	Number	Per cent	Number	Per cent
Manufacturing (cont.)							
Miscellaneous chemical products	1.7	1.4	82.3	.3	15.8	.03	1.8
Integrated petroleum extraction & refining	.06	.001	1.7	.01	19.0	.05	79.3
Petroleum refining (without extraction)	.2	.1	57.8	.06	33.3	.02	8.8
Other petroleum and coal products	.8	.6	73.6	.2	24.6	.01	1.8
Rubber products	1.0	.5	51.7	.4	39.0	.13	9.2
Plastics products, n.e.c.	2.9	2.0	67.3	.9	30.9	.05	1.7
Footwear (except rubber)	1.0	.3	28.1	.5	50.8	.21	21.1
Leather and leather products (exc. footwear)	3.1	2.0	64.5	1.0	33.1	.07	2.4
Glass products	1.1	.8	73.9	.2	21.8	.05	4.4
Hydraulic cement	.05	.003	6.0	.01	24.0	.04	70.0
Structural clay products	.8	.3	34.9	.4	57.1	.06	7.9
Ready-mixed concrete	3.0	2.2	72.5	.8	26.9	.02	.6

Concrete and plaster products (except ready-mixed concrete)	5.0	4.2	83.7	.8	15.7	.03	.6
Other nonmetallic mineral products	2.8	2.1	73.4	.7	23.7	.08	2.9
Blast furnaces and steel mills	.1	.02	18.4	.03	23.3	.07	58.3
Iron and steel foundries	1.3	.5	36.6	.7	54.6	.12	8.7
Primary steel products, n.e.c.	1.1	.6	58.2	.4	36.3	.06	5.5
Nonferrous primary metals	2.7	1.8	66.3	.8	29.9	.10	3.8
Metal cans	.06	.02	40.0	.03	46.6	.01	13.3
Cutlery, hand tools, hardware	1.9	1.2	64.7	.6	31.1	.08	4.1
Plumbing and nonelectric heating	.9	.5	61.2	.3	33.7	.04	4.9
Structural metal products	8.8	6.2	70.8	2.4	27.3	.16	1.8
Screw machine products and bolts	2.2	1.6	72.4	.6	25.6	.04	2.0
Metal stampings and services, n.e.c.	5.8	4.2	73.2	1.5	25.7	.07	1.2
Fabricated wire products	1.3	.9	67.1	.4	30.7	.03	2.2
Fabricated metal products, n.e.c.	1.9	1.2	65.0	.6	30.1	.09	4.9
Engines and turbines	.09	.04	42.2	.04	38.9	.02	18.9
Farm machinery and equipment	1.3	.9	69.5	.4	28.2	.03	2.2
Construction and like equipment	1.8	1.1	59.8	.6	34.1	.11	6.1
Metal working machinery	7.6	6.0	78.8	1.5	19.6	.12	1.5
Special industry machinery	2.9	1.9	67.0	.8	29.3	.11	3.5

Table 5-A (Cont.)

DISTRIBUTION OF COMPANIES BY NUMBER OF EMPLOYEES, BY INDUSTRY DIVISION AND CATEGORY, 1958

Numbers in Thousands

Industry Division and Category	Total	Less than 20 Employees		20 to 249 Employees		250 or more Employees	
		Number	Per cent	Number	Per cent	Number	Per cent
Manufacturing (cont.)							
General industrial machinery	3.0	2.2	72.7	.7	24.1	.10	3.2
Office machines, n.e.c.	.3	.2	54.3	.09	32.4	.04	13.3
Service industry machines	1.2	.7	63.7	.4	30.9	.06	5.4
Miscellaneous machinery (exc. electrical)	10.0	9.0	90.0	1.0	9.8	.02	.2
Radio and TV receiving equipment	2.1	1.2	55.7	.8	37.0	.16	7.3
Other electrical machinery	4.6	2.9	63.1	1.4	30.7	.29	6.2
Motor vehicles and equipment	1.9	1.2	64.5	.5	29.2	.12	6.2
Aircraft	.1	.04	42.2	.04	40.1	.03	17.5
Aircraft engines, propellers, and equipment and parts, n.e.c.	1.2	.7	58.2	.4	34.1	.09	7.6
Ships and boats	1.9	1.5	77.4	.4	19.7	.06	2.9
Other transporation equipment	.7	.4	57.1	.3	38.7	.03	4.2

Scientific instruments and mechanical measuring devices	1.1	.8	67.9	.3	26.4	.06	2.3
Optical, medical, ophthalmic goods	1.4	1.0	72.6	.4	25.1	.03	2.1
Photographic equipment	.4	.3	71.2	.1	23.5	.02	5.4
Watches and clocks	.2	.1	67.2	.05	25.3	.02	7.6
Jewelry and silverware	2.0	1.7	84.1	.3	14.9	.02	1.0
Toys and sporting goods	2.5	1.7	68.5	.7	29.1	.06	2.4
Other manufactures	9.0	6.9	76.7	2.0	22.1	.11	1.3
Ordnance and accessories	.1	.07	52.0	.04	30.4	.02	17.6
Public Warehousing	7.5	6.4	86.2	1.0	13.5	.03	.3
Wholesale Trade	213.1	190.5	89.4	22.1	10.4	.4	.2
Motor vehicles and automotive equipment	17.5	15.5	88.3	2.0	11.6	.1	.1
Drugs, chemicals, and allied products	6.2	5.5	88.4	.7	11.3	.02	.4
Groceries and related products	28.1	25.0	89.0	3.0	10.7	.1	.2
Electrical goods	7.4	6.1	82.8	1.2	16.9	.02	.3
Hardware, plumbing and heating equipment	8.2	7.0	84.9	1.2	14.6	.04	.5
Machinery and equipment and supplies	26.0	23.0	88.4	2.9	11.4	.05	.2
Lumber and construction materials	8.2	7.1	86.2	1.1	13.6	.01	.2
Other merchant wholesalers	66.2	59.3	89.6	6.9	10.2	.1	.2
Petroleum bulk stations	10.4	9.6	92.9	.7	7.0	.01	.1
Merchandise agents and brokers	25.1	23.8	94.8	1.3	5.2	.01	.1

Table 5-A (Cont.)

DISTRIBUTION OF COMPANIES BY NUMBER OF EMPLOYEES, BY INDUSTRY
DIVISION AND CATEGORY, 1958

Numbers in Thousands

Industry Division and Category	Total	Less than 20 Employees		20 to 249 Employees		250 or more Employees	
		Number	Per cent	Number	Per cent	Number	Per cent
Wholesale Trade (cont.)							
Assemblers of farm products	10.0	8.9	88.3	1.1	11.4	.02	.2
Retail Trade	1,688.3	1,641.9	97.3	45.3	2.7	1.2	.1
Building materials, hardware, farm equipment	99.4	96.1	96.6	3.3	3.3	.04	.04
Department stores	.8	--	--	.5	66.2	.3	33.9
General merchandise stores	57.4	56.4	98.2	1.0	1.8	.04	.1
Limited price variety stores	12.5	12.0	95.7	.5	3.9	.04	.4
Nonstore retailers	76.9	75.7	98.5	1.1	1.4	.05	.1
Grocery stores	247.1	243.1	98.4	3.8	1.6	.2	.1
Food stores (except groceries)	92.7	91.7	98.9	1.0	1.0	.01	*
Automotive dealers	89.2	79.9	89.6	9.3	10.4	.04	*
Gasoline service stations	202.9	202.0	99.5	1.0	.5	.02	*

Apparel and accessory stores	79.2	75.5	95.4	3.5	4.4	.2	.2
Shoe stores	15.9	15.5	97.5	.4	2.3	.03	.1
Furniture, home furnishings & equipment	95.4	92.7	97.2	2.6	2.8	.06	.1
Eating and drinking places	342.4	329.9	96.4	12.3	3.6	.2	.1
Drug and proprietary stores	51.7	44.8	96.5	1.8	3.4	.05	.1
Other retail stores	224.8	221.6	98.5	3.2	1.4	.05	*
Selected Services	942.8	921.9	97.8	20.2	2.1	.7	.1
Hotels, motels, tourist courts	83.1	79.5	95.8	3.3	4.0	.2	.2
Laundries and dry cleaning plants	65.1	59.3	91.0	5.7	8.8	.1	.2
Beauty and barber shops	213.4	212.9	99.8	.5	.2	.01	.1
Other personal services	123.1	122.4	99.4	.7	.5	.01	.1
Advertising	11.6	10.8	93.5	.7	6.0	.05	.5
Business services (exc. advertising)	96.7	93.0	96.1	3.6	3.7	.2	.2
Auto repair services and garages	120.5	119.1	98.8	1.4	1.2	.01	*
Miscellaneous repair services	143.1	142.4	99.5	.7	.5	--	--
Motion picture producers, distrib. & services	2.7	2.5	91.3	.2	7.7	.03	1.0
Motion picture theaters	10.2	9.2	89.9	1.0	9.6	.05	.5
Amusements, recreation services	73.2	70.8	96.7	2.4	3.2	.05	.1

* – Less than .05 per cent.

Source: Enterprise Statistics, 1958.

Table 5-B

PER CENT DISTRIBUTION OF SMALL COMPANIES
AMONG INDUSTRY DIVISIONS AND SELECTED CATEGORIES,[1] 1958

Industry Division and Category	Under 20 Employees	20-249 Employees	Under 250 Employees
All Industries: Number	2,981,413	160,789	3,142,202
Per cent	100.00	100.00	100.00
Mineral Industry	.87	2.47	.95
Manufacturing	6.53	42.45	8.37
Public Warehousing	.22	.63	.24
Wholesale Trade	6.39	13.76	6.76
Other merchant wholesalers	1.99	4.19	2.10
Retail Trade	55.07	28.14	53.69
Building materials, hardware, farm equipment	3.22	2.05	3.16
General merchandise stores	1.90	.63	1.83
Nonstore retailers	2.54	.68	2.44
Grocery stores	8.15	2.39	7.86
Food stores (exc. groceries)	3.08	.60	2.95
Automotive dealers	2.68	5.76	2.84
Gasoline service stations	6.77	.59	6.46
Apparel and accessory stores	2.53	2.19	2.52
Furniture, home furnishings & equipment	3.11	1.64	3.03
Eating and drinking places	11.07	7.65	10.89
Drugs and proprietary stores	1.67	1.10	1.64
Other retail stores	7.43	2.00	7.15
Selected Services	30.92	12.50	29.98
Hotels, motels, tourist courts	2.67	2.06	2.64
Laundries and dry cleaning plants	1.99	3.58	2.06
Beauty and barber shops	7.14	.32	6.79
Other personal services	4.11	.42	3.92
Business services (exc. advertising)	3.12	2.24	3.07
Auto repair services and garages	3.99	.87	3.83
Miscellaneous repair services	4.78	.40	4.55
Amusements, recreation services	2.37	1.47	2.33

[1] Only those categories are listed which include 1 per cent or over of the companies with less than 250 employees. They include almost 85 per cent of all companies of this size.

Source: Enterprise Statistics, 1958.

Table 5-C

DISTRIBUTION OF EMPLOYEES BY SIZE OF COMPANY, BY INDUSTRY
DIVISION AND CATEGORY, 1958

Numbers in Thousands

Industry Division and Category	Total	Less than 20 Employees		20 to 249 Employees		250 or more Employees	
		Number	Per cent	Number	Per cent	Number	Per cent
All Industries	30,952.0	7,224.5	23.3	8,120.1	26.2	15,607.4	50.4
Mineral Industries	574.8	114.2	19.8	199.3	34.6	261.2	45.6
Metal mining	63.8	4.1	6.4	7.8	12.2	51.9	81.3
Anthracite mining	22.4	3.0	13.4	7.1	31.8	12.2	54.5
Bituminous coal and lignite	176.2	28.7	16.3	44.1	25.0	103.5	58.7
Crude petroleum	94.9	27.0	28.4	36.5	38.5	23.3	33.0
Oil and gas services	113.0	25.7	22.7	57.8	51.1	29.4	26.0
Nonmetallic minerals	104.5	25.7	24.6	46.0	44.0	32.7	31.3
Manufacturing	17,273.0	1,129.1	6.5	4,057.3	23.5	12,085.7	70.0
Meat packing	266.7	9.7	3.6	45.1	16.9	212.0	79.5
Prepared meats and poultry	90.4	10.1	11.2	55.9	61.8	24.4	27.0
Dairy products	352.6	39.2	11.1	118.8	33.7	194.7	55.2
Canned and frozen foods	239.1	11.3	4.7	78.7	32.9	149.0	62.3
Grain mill products	141.5	13.2	9.3	35.9	25.4	92.4	65.3
Bakery products	316.4	25.5	8.1	92.3	29.1	198.4	62.8
Sugar	31.8	.04	.1	2.9	9.2	28.9	90.6
Confectionery & related products	86.8	5.4	6.2	23.1	26.6	58.3	67.1

Table 5-C (Cont.)

DISTRIBUTION OF EMPLOYEES BY SIZE OF COMPANY, BY INDUSTRY DIVISION AND CATEGORY, 1958

Numbers in Thousands

Industry Division and Category	Total	Less than 20 Employees		20 to 249 Employees		250 or more Employees	
		Number	Per cent	Number	Per cent	Number	Per cent
Manufacturing (cont.)							
Alcoholic beverages	125.1	1.5	1.2	19.1	15.3	104.5	83.5
Bottled soft drinks & flavorings	107.6	24.0	22.3	56.6	52.6	27.0	25.1
Fats and oils	40.8	3.4	8.4	14.8	36.3	22.6	55.2
Other food products	110.1	16.3	14.8	32.8	29.8	60.9	55.4
Tobacco products	104.4	2.0	1.9	8.8	8.5	93.6	89.7
Broad-woven fabrics, yarn, thread, and finishing (exc. wool)	568.8	5.1	.8	64.6	11.4	499.2	87.8
Wool broadwoven fabrics, yarn, finishing	55.3	1.5	2.6	25.6	46.3	28.2	51.0
Knitting mills	213.7	7.1	3.3	88.4	41.4	118.1	55.3
Floor covering mills	36.1	.7	1.8	7.1	19.7	28.3	78.5
Other textile mill products	73.2	4.6	6.3	31.1	42.5	37.5	51.2
Men's and boys' clothing	404.6	12.4	3.1	147.9	36.6	244.3	60.3
Women's and children's clothing (exc. millinery and fur goods)	551.8	49.2	8.9	372.9	67.6	129.7	23.5
Millinery, fur goods, misc. apparel	107.0	19.3	18.0	59.4	55.6	28.2	26.4
Fabricated textiles, n. e. c.	115.2	30.1	26.2	66.5	57.7	18.6	16.1

Logging, sawmills, & planing mills	331.1	119.3	36.0	143.6	43.4	68.2	20.6
Millwork and related products	137.2	15.1	11.0	65.9	48.0	56.2	41.0
Other wood products	87.1	16.3	18.6	49.2	56.5	21.5	24.8
Household furniture	244.0	24.9	10.2	119.4	48.9	99.7	40.9
Furniture & fixtures (exc. household)	96.8	14.8	15.3	39.7	41.0	42.3	43.7
Pulp, paper, and board	304.6	.8	.3	16.0	5.3	287.9	94.5
Paperboard containers and boxes	152.6	16.8	11.0	53.6	35.1	82.2	53.9
Other paper and allied products	105.1	7.6	7.3	41.3	39.3	56.2	53.5
Newspapers	311.8	35.2	11.3	79.9	25.6	196.7	63.1
Periodicals	76.3	9.4	12.3	17.8	23.4	49.1	64.3
Books	74.8	5.9	7.8	23.9	31.9	45.1	60.2
Miscellaneous publishing & greeting cards	40.8	4.5	10.9	12.9	31.5	23.4	57.5
Commercial printing and manifold business forms	302.7	72.3	23.9	127.5	42.1	102.9	33.9
Bookbinding and printing trade services	81.0	16.5	20.3	49.7	61.4	14.8	18.3
Basic chemicals, fibers, plastics, and rubber	516.9	3.4	.7	17.2	3.2	496.4	96.0
Drugs	115.6	4.4	3.9	15.4	13.3	95.8	82.8
Cleaning and toilet goods	110.4	9.2	8.3	21.4	19.4	79.9	72.3
Paints and varnishes	64.7	6.5	10.0	23.7	36.7	34.5	53.3
Agricultural chemicals	33.5	4.0	12.0	10.0	29.7	19.6	58.4
Miscellaneous chemical products	74.5	7.2	9.7	16.3	21.8	51.0	68.4
Integrated petroleum extracting and refining	508.2	--	--	1.7	.3	506.5	99.7
Petroleum refining (without extraction)	14.8	.7	4.7	4.3	29.0	9.8	66.3
Other petroleum and coal products	28.4	4.1	14.3	10.6	37.3	13.7	48.4

Table 5-C (Cont.)

DISTRIBUTION OF EMPLOYEES BY SIZE OF COMPANY, BY INDUSTRY DIVISION AND CATEGORY, 1958

Numbers in Thousands

Industry Division and Category	Total	Less than 20 Employees		20 to 249 Employees		250 or more Employees	
		Number	Per cent	Number	Per cent	Number	Per cent
Manufacturing (cont.)							
Rubber products	294.3	3.4	1.2	29.2	9.9	261.8	88.9
Plastics products, n.e.c.	101.7	12.2	12.0	53.5	52.6	36.1	35.5
Footwear (exc. rubber)	250.3	2.1	.8	51.9	20.7	196.4	78.5
Leather and leather products (exc. footwear)	110.4	12.1	11.0	61.9	56.1	36.5	33.1
Glass products	151.6	4.4	2.8	15.3	10.1	132.0	87.0
Hydraulic cement	38.4	.02	.1	1.7	4.4	36.7	95.5
Structural clay products	69.5	.9	1.3	30.3	43.5	38.4	55.2
Ready-mixed concrete	63.9	16.5	26.9	37.3	58.4	10.0	15.7
Concrete and plaster products (exc. ready-mixed concrete)	111.0	23.2	20.9	35.8	32.2	63.1	46.9
Other nonmetallic mineral products	173.8	12.2	7.0	41.1	23.6	120.1	69.4
Blast furnaces and steel mills	720.8	.1	.02	2.3	.3	718.4	99.6
Iron and steel foundries	158.9	4.2	2.7	54.3	34.1	100.5	63.2
Primary steel products, n.e.c.	75.1	4.2	5.6	25.1	33.6	45.8	60.9
Non-ferrous primary metals	323.7	11.5	3.6	47.5	14.7	264.7	81.8
Metal cans	107.3	.1	.1	1.8	1.7	105.3	98.2
Cutlery, hand tools, and hardware	113.4	7.2	6.3	41.7	36.8	64.5	56.9

Plumbing and non-electric heating	89.1	3.5	3.9	21.2	23.8	64.4	72.3
Structural metal products	327.7	39.0	11.9	136.2	41.6	152.6	46.6
Screw machine products and bolts	80.9	10.2	12.6	31.0	38.3	39.8	49.2
Metal stampings & metal services, n.e.c.	151.5	27.5	18.2	77.4	51.1	46.6	30.8
Fabricated wire products	59.5	5.6	9.4	27.0	45.4	26.9	45.2
Fabricated metal products, n.e.c.	136.8	5.5	4.0	37.3	27.3	94.0	68.7
Engines and turbines	88.0	.3	.3	2.4	2.7	85.3	96.9
Farm machinery and equipment	148.1	5.5	3.7	23.3	15.7	119.3	80.6
Construction and like equipment	200.5	7.5	3.7	40.0	19.9	153.1	76.4
Metalworking machinery	224.7	36.4	16.2	77.7	34.6	110.7	49.3
Special industry machinery	164.1	12.0	7.3	50.0	30.5	102.0	62.2
General industrial machinery	188.7	12.1	6.4	46.8	24.8	129.8	68.8
Office machines, n.e.c.	251.3	.9	.4	6.0	2.4	244.5	97.3
Service industry machines	98.7	4.8	4.9	23.3	23.6	70.6	71.6
Miscellaneous machinery (exc. electrical)	105.6	44.2	41.8	40.6	38.5	20.8	19.7
Radio & TV receiving equipment	571.9	7.5	1.3	57.8	10.1	506.7	88.6
Other electrical machinery	807.9	18.3	2.3	93.7	11.6	695.9	86.1
Motor vehicles and equipment	938.1	7.8	.8	32.9	3.5	897.3	95.7
Aircraft	461.9	.3	.1	2.2	.5	459.4	99.5
Aircraft engines, propellers, equipment parts, n.e.c.	390.6	4.9	1.3	26.9	6.9	358.7	91.8
Ships and boats	119.5	6.8	5.7	22.2	18.6	90.5	75.7
Other transportation equipment	67.8	2.3	3.4	18.7	27.5	46.8	69.1
Scientific instrument and mechanical measuring devices	143.7	4.4	3.1	19.2	13.3	120.2	83.6
Optical, medical, opththalmic goods	79.2	5.3	6.7	23.3	29.5	50.5	63.8
Photographic equipment	85.9	1.7	2.0	6.6	7.7	77.6	90.3
Watches and clocks	24.0	.9	3.7	3.0	12.5	20.1	83.7

Table 5-C (Cont.)

DISTRIBUTION OF EMPLOYEES BY SIZE OF COMPANY, BY INDUSTRY
DIVISION AND CATEGORY, 1958

Numbers in Thousands

Industry Division and Category	Total	Less than 20 Employees		20 to 249 Employees		250 or more Employees	
		Number	Per cent	Number	Per cent	Number	Per cent
Manufacturing (cont.)							
Jewelry and silverware	43.4	8.0	18.4	16.9	39.1	18.5	42.6
Toys and sporting goods	115.3	9.4	8.2	45.7	39.7	60.1	52.2
Other manufactures	233.4	37.6	16.1	105.5	45.2	90.3	38.7
Public Warehousing	99.9	32.6	32.6	47.0	47.0	20.3	20.4
Wholesale Trade	2,100.8	899.9	42.8	978.7	46.6	222.1	10.6
Motor vehicle and automotive equipment	173.6	85.1	49.0	80.7	46.5	7.7	4.6
Drugs, chemicals, and allied products	79.2	25.2	31.8	35.8	45.3	18.2	23.0
Groceries and related products	287.7	115.2	40.1	133.3	46.3	39.1	13.6
Electrical goods	102.1	34.3	33.5	55.1	53.9	12.8	12.6
Hardware, plumbing & heating equipment	120.1	40.6	33.8	58.2	48.5	21.2	17.7
Machinery, equipment and supplies	268.1	115.0	42.9	128.2	47.8	24.9	9.3
Lumber and construction materials	92.5	38.0	41.1	48.0	51.9	6.5	7.0

Other merchant wholesalers	639.6	274.9	42.9	297.9	46.6	66.8	10.4
Petroleum bulk stations	82.2	47.3	57.4	28.3	34.5	6.6	8.0
Merchandise agents and brokers	145.1	84.8	58.2	51.8	35.7	8.5	6.0
Assemblers of farm products	110.6	39.6	35.8	61.3	55.5	9.7	8.7
Retail Trade	8,034.1	3,745.3	46.6	1,872.5	23.3	2,416.3	30.1
Building materials, hardware, farm equipment	434.8	287.5	66.1	127.1	29.2	20.1	4.6
Department stores	989.9	--	--	52.8	5.6	937.1	94.6
General merchandise stores	142.7	75.6	53.0	46.7	32.7	20.4	14.3
Limited price variety stores	342.5	37.7	11.0	25.3	7.3	279.4	81.6
Nonstore retailers	156.6	50.0	31.9	39.4	25.2	67.1	42.9
Grocery stores	1,094.7	353.3	32.3	170.7	15.6	570.7	52.3
Food stores (except groceries)	190.8	150.2	78.7	34.6	18.1	5.9	3.1
Automotive dealers	709.6	316.5	44.6	371.9	52.4	21.1	3.0
Gasoline service stations	441.5	391.1	88.6	38.5	8.7	11.8	2.7
Apparel and accessory stores	531.3	228.6	43.0	168.3	31.7	134.4	25.3
Shoe stores	103.1	40.4	39.2	17.1	16.6	45.4	44.2
Furniture, home furnishings & equipment	380.0	243.2	64.0	106.3	28.0	30.5	8.0
Eating and drinking places	1,595.9	945.9	59.3	479.1	30.0	170.7	10.8
Drug and proprietary stores	351.7	221.6	63.0	65.7	18.7	64.4	18.3
Other retail stores	569.1	403.6	70.9	128.5	22.5	36.9	6.5
Selected Services	2,869.4	1,303.3	46.0	965.3	33.6	600.8	20.9
Hotels, motels, tourist courts	505.7	146.4	29.0	184.6	36.5	174.6	34.5
Laundries and dry cleaning plants	553.5	194.9	35.2	286.6	51.8	71.6	13.0
Beauty and barber shops	217.6	184.3	84.7	19.6	9.0	13.6	6.3
Other personal services	149.2	114.1	76.5	28.0	18.8	6.9	4.7
Advertising	110.7	26.8	24.2	35.6	32.1	48.3	43.6

Table 5-C (Cont.)

DISTRIBUTION OF EMPLOYEES BY SIZE OF COMPANY, BY INDUSTRY DIVISION AND CATEGORY, 1958

Numbers in Thousands

Industry Division and Category	Total	Less than 20 Employees		20 to 249 Employees		250 or more Employees	
		Number	Per cent	Number	Per cent	Number	Per cent
Selected Services (cont.)							
Business services (exc. advertising)	494.8	152.9	30.9	185.7	37.5	156.1	31.6
Auto repair services and garages	252.8	194.1	76.8	49.9	19.7	8.7	3.5
Miscellaneous repair services	120.7	93.6	77.5	23.5	19.5	3.5	3.0
Motion picture producers, distrib. & services	58.7	6.6	11.3	11.5	19.7	40.5	69.0
Motion picture theaters	144.3	50.7	35.1	42.7	29.6	50.9	35.3
Amusements, recreation services	261.4	138.6	53.0	97.0	37.1	25.5	9.9

Source: Enterprise Statistics, 1958. For some categories distribution of employees between smallest and largest size companies estimated on the basis of footnotes provided.

Table 6-A

CHANGE IN SIZE OF REPORTING UNITS, 1947-62 (COUNTY BUSINESS PATTERNS)

Industry	Number of Reporting Units (000's)			Average Number of Employees			Per cent Change		Per Cent of Reporting Units With Fewer Than 100 Employees			Difference Between	
	1947	1953	1962	1947	1953	1962	1947-1953	1947-1962	1947	1953	1962	1947 & 1953	1947 & 1962
All Industries	2,512.3	2,939.6	3,347.6	13.7	13.6	13.0	- 0.7	-05.1	98.2	98.3	98.3	0.1	0.1
Contract Construction Total	180.6	263.2	296.1	9.7	9.0	8.2	- 7.2	-15.5	98.9	99.0	99.2	.1	.3
General building contractors	46.1	79.5	87.3	14.1	10.3	8.4	-27.0	-40.5	98.0	98.7	99.1	.7	1.1
General contractors other than building	14.6	19.0	24.3	21.7	26.0	19.4	19.8	-11.6	95.8	95.3	96.5	- .5	.7
Special trade contractors	119.9	164.7	184.0	6.6	6.5	6.6	- 1.5	0	99.6	99.6	99.6	.0	.0
Manufacturing Total	255.2	285.7	289.7	58.5	60.6	56.6	3.6	- 3.3	90.4	90.1	90.0	- .3	- .4
Food and kindred products	35.8	36.6	38.5	37.9	38.2	41.0	.8	8.2	92.5	92.4	90.9	- .1	-1.6
Textile mill products	8.9	9.1	7.4	150.0	130.4	117.6	-13.1	-22.6	67.6	72.7	73.1	5.1	5.5
Apparel & other finished fabric products	31.6	31.4	27.0	35.0	40.4	46.4	15.1	32.6	92.6	91.1	88.8	-1.5	-3.8
Lumber and wood products	38.4	42.7	30.6	21.9	17.3	17.2	-21.0	-21.5	96.2	96.9	96.9	.7	.7
Furniture and fixtures	8.9	10.1	9.7	36.7	36.9	37.7	.3	2.7	91.6	91.9	91.4	.3	.2
Paper and allied products	4.0	4.8	5.6	114.3	107.5	104.5	- 5.3	- 8.6	74.3	72.0	74.6	-2.3	.3
Printing, publishing, and allied industries	28.9	31.9	35.0	23.8	24.5	25.8	2.9	8.4	96.0	96.0	95.7	.0	- .3
Chemicals and allied products	10.5	11.8	11.8	64.2	65.7	65.2	2.3	1.6	88.8	89.3	89.0	.5	.2
Rubber products	.9	1.2	1.4	283.0	226.8	177.2	-19.9	-37.5	71.6	73.0	74.8	1.4	3.2
Leather and leather products	5.7	5.3	4.1	70.9	73.9	85.4	4.2	20.5	83.0	80.3	76.0	-2.7	-7.0
Stone, clay & glass products	10.7	11.6	14.6	45.5	45.0	37.4	- 1.1	-17.8	90.9	90.6	92.7	- .3	1.8
Primary metal industries	5.7	6.1	6.6	211.0	215.1	178.3	1.9	-15.5	81.3	74.0	75.8	-7.3	-5.5
Fabricated metal products	15.8	20.6	24.5	62.4	54.0	43.4	-13.5	-30.5	87.6	89.3	91.0	1.7	3.4
Machinery (exc. electrical)	18.3	24.6	30.4	84.2	71.3	47.5	-15.3	-43.6	87.4	89.8	92.6	2.4	5.2

Table 6–A (Cont.)

CHANGE IN SIZE OF REPORTING UNITS 1947–62 (COUNTY BUSINESS PATTERNS)

Industry	Number of Reporting Units (000's)			Average Number of Employees			Per cent Change		Per Cent of Reporting Units With Fewer Than 100 Employees			Difference Between	
	1947	1953	1962	1947	1953	1962	1947–1953	1947–1962	1947	1953	1962	1947 & 1953	1947 & 1962
Manufacturing Total (Cont)													
Electrical machinery, equipment and supplies	4.3	5.6	9.2	208.0	198.6	152.1	− 4.5	−26.9	75.9	74.5	78.2	−1.4	2.3
Transportation equipment	4.4	5.2	6.3	327.0	374.4	243.9	14.5	−25.4	80.2	78.4	82.1	−1.8	1.9
Transportation, Communication, and Public Utilities	95.2	104.0	122.3	26.8	27.3	24.6	1.9	− 8.2	96.4	96.2	96.6	− .2	.2
Local & suburban transportation	15.9	15.7	13.7	25.1	23.7	21.9	− 5.2	−12.8	98.4	96.8	96.8	−1.6	−1.6
Trucking and warehousing	54.6	59.4	72.0	9.8	11.6	11.5	18.3	17.3	98.7	98.2	98.3	− .5	− .4
Other transportation, communication, etc.	24.7	29.0	36.1	73.6	61.5	51.2	−16.5	−30.4	91.7	91.8	93.2	.1	1.5
Wholesale Trade Total	235.5	239.1	284.0	11.5	11.9	11.4	3.5	− 0.9	98.7	98.6	98.8	− .1	1.5
Retail Trade Total	862.9	1,015.0	1,052.0	7.4	7.4	7.6	0.0	2.7	99.4	99.5	99.4	.1	.0
General merchandise	48.0	51.3	57.3	26.5	26.4	25.5	− 0.4	− 3.8	96.4	96.4	96.3	.0	.1
Food	185.3	193.5	149.9	6.1	6.8	8.4	11.5	37.7	99.6	99.3	99.1	− .3	− .1
Car dealers	38.1	51.9	45.2	11.4	12.9	13.5	13.2	18.4	99.6	99.3	99.3	− .3	− .5
Gasoline, tires	85.5	120.8	158.9	3.6	3.7	3.7	2.8	2.8	99.9	99.9	99.9	.1	− .3
Apparel and accessories	67.9	78.0	85.7	8.2	7.8	7.1	− 4.9	−14.5	100.0	99.4	99.5	− .1	.3
Furniture and equipment	43.9	56.5	63.0	6.3	6.5	5.7	3.2	− 9.6	99.2	99.7	99.8	.2	.3
Eating and drinking places	201.0	225.3	231.8	6.5	6.0	7.0	− 7.7	7.6	99.6	99.7	99.6	.1	.0
Misc. Retail stores	146.3	162.3	180.0	5.6	5.3	5.3	− 5.4	− 5.4	99.9	99.8	99.8	− .1	− .1
Services, Total	371.1	382.5	435.5	7.2	7.1	7.3	− 1.4	1.4	99.3	99.3	99.2	.0	− .1
Hotels and other lodging places	34.1	42.4	49.0	13.4	11.2	11.1	−15.4	−15.4	97.5	98.1	98.2	.6	.7
Personal services	151.1	154.2	174.1	5.8	5.6	5.1	− 3.5	−12.1	99.4	99.5	99.6	.1	.2

Industry												
Laundries & laundry services	13.6	14.0	20.3	26.0	24.3	14.5	- 7.7	-46.2	94.6	95.0	99.3	.4	2.7
Beauty and barber shops	70.6	65.9	88.0	2.5	2.4	2.8	- 4.0	12.0	100.0	100.0	100.0	.0	.0
Cleaning, dyeing, pressing, alterations, garment repair, shoe repair, hat cleaning	46.3	48.5	42.1	5.5	5.4	5.7	- 1.8	3.6	99.8	99.8	99.8	.0	.0
Business services (including accounting, etc.)	52.7	58.0	87.4	9.0	8.6	10.7	- 4.5	18.9	91.7	99.0	98.5	7.3	6.8
Auto repair and garages	60.1	47.4	64.3	3.9	3.8	4.3	- 2.6	10.2	99.8	99.9	99.9	.1	.1
Motion pictures	13.2	14.2	11.5	19.3	15.9	14.6	-17.6	-24.4	99.1	98.7	98.8	- .4	- .3
Amusements, etc.	27.9	33.5	37.0	9.2	8.2	8.8	-10.9	- 4.4	99.3	99.4	99.4	.1	.1

Source: County Business Patterns - 1947, 1953, and 1962.

For notes on the general limitations of County Business Patterns, see section on characteristics of various sources of data used in the report. In addition, shifts in industry classification have occurred within the span of time covered. Also, some groups are not individually identifiable in the 1947 tables. In some cases adjustments have been possible which give comparable figures. Changes in classification occurring between 1953 and 1962 are given in the Appendix of County Business Patterns, 1959.

The following 1958 data from the Census of Manufactures on the number of establishments show the effect of classification changes for those industries. In most cases the number of establishments affected is not large.

	Old Classification	New Classification
Food and kindred products	40,653	41,619
Textile mill products	7,735	7,675
Apparel and other finished fabrics	29,260	29,297
Lumber and wood products	37,597	37,789
Furniture and fixtures	10,517	10,160
Paper and allied products	5,338	5,271
Printing, publishing, and allied industries	35,338	35,368
Chemicals and allied products	12,200	11,309

	Old Classification	New Classification
Leather and leather products	4,374	4,534
Stone, clay and glass products	11,393	15,022
Primary metal industries	6,199	6,446
Fabricated metal products	25,194	24,782
Machinery, except electrical	31,160	29,839
Electrical machinery	6,937	8,091
Transportation equipment	6,256	6,607
Instruments and related products	3,403	3,526
Miscellaneous manufacturing	17,509	14,045

Table 6-B

NUMBER OF RETAIL TRADE REPORTING UNITS AND NUMBER OF EMPLOYEES,
1953 AND 1962, AND PER CENT CHANGE BY CLASS OF RETAIL ESTABLISHMENT

Retail Trade Class	Numbers in Thousands					
	Reporting Units			Employees		
	1953	1962	Per cent Change	1953	1962	Per cent Change
Retail Trade	1,015.0	1,052.0	+ 4	7,470.4	8,045.0	+ 8
Building Materials, etc.	72.6	72.9	--	456.3	432.3	-11
Lumber	23.2	25.2	+ 9	228.2	209.5	- 8
Hardware	38.5	36.1	- 6	199.4	169.7	-15
General Merchandise	51.3	57.3	+12	1,356.0	1,461.6	+ 8
Department stores	3.3	2.8	-15	746.0	762.0	+ 2
Variety stores	13.5	14.5	+ 7	323.7	298.3	- 8
Food	193.5	149.9	-23[1/]	1,310.5[1/]	1,252.2[1/]	- 4[1/]
Groceries	126.5	107.5	-15	857.8	1,028.8	+20
Automotive	175.5	209.5	+19	1,129.1	1,213.1	+ 7
Dealers	42.1	32.9	-22	633.6	561.3	-11
Service stations	107.1	143.8	+34	349.1	483.9	+39
Apparel	78.0	85.7	+10	606.2	610.3	+ 1
Men's	15.6	15.9	+ 2	92.4	96.9	+ 5
Women's ready-to-wear	23.1	24.3	+ 5	240.4	224.4	- 7
Shoe stores	14.5	18.8	+30	99.2	108.6	+10

Furniture, etc.	56.5	63.0	+12	367.3	360.2	– 2
Furniture and home furnishings	35.7	37.3	+ 4	238.3	225.8	– 5
Appliances	20.7	13.1	-37	128.6	80.5	-37
Eating and Drinking Places	225.3	231.8	+ 3	1,351.1	1,614.6	+20
Miscellaneous	162.3	180.0	+11	863.8	955.8	+11
Drug stores	45.5	46.3	+ 2	318.6	356.9	+12
Liquor stores	15.8	22.8	+44	42.5	66.4	+56
Farm and garden supply stores	13.5	16.8	+24	78.4	90.6	+16
Jewelry stores	14.3	13.5	– 6	70.7	61.2	-13

1/ Reflects change of classification of certain fluid milk processing establishments from Retail Trade to Manufacturing. Excluding Dairy Products Retailing, employment in Food Retailing was 1,110.8 thousand in 1953 and 1,225.5 thousand in 1962, and increase of about 10 per cent. The comparable decline in reporting units was 20 per cent.

Source: County Business Patterns, 1953 and 1962.

Table 6-C

DISTRIBUTION OF RETAIL TRADE REPORTING UNITS BY EMPLOYEE SIZE CLASS,
BY CLASS OF RETAIL ESTABLISHMENT - 1953 AND 1962
(PER CENT)

Retail Trade Class and Year		Number of Employees							
		Under 4	4-7	8-19	20-49	50-99	100-249	250-499	500 and Over
Retail Trade, Total	1953	58	24	12	4	1	0.4	0.01	0.01
	1962	58	22	14	4	1	.4	.01	.01
Building Materials, etc.	1953	49	28	17	5	0.9	.2	--	--
	1962	52	26	18	4	.5	.1	--	--
Lumber	1953	34	29	25	9	2	.4	--	--
	1962	38	29	25	7	1	.2	--	--
Hardware	1953	56	28	13	2	.5	.1	--	--
	1962	59	25	14	2	.2	.1	--	--
General Merchandise	1953	51	20	14	9	4	2	.7	.7
	1962	50	18	17	8	3	2	.8	.7
Department stores	1953	4	2	9	27	22	20	8	9
	1962	--	--	--	29	26	23	11	11
Variety stores	1953	40	19	17	14	6	3	.8	.4
	1962	38	20	22	12	5	3	.7	.3

Category	Year								
Food	1953	68	20	8	3	1	.4	.1	.1
	1962	64	18	11	4	1	.5	.2	.1
Grocery stores	1953	70	19	7	3	.8	.4	.1	.1
	1962	65	16	11	5	2	.7	.3	.2
Automotive	1953	58	23	13	5	1	.3	—	—
	1962	63	20	11	4	1	.2	—	—
Dealers	1953	18	25	35	17	4	.8	—	—
	1962	16	20	36	21	5	1	—	—
Service stations	1953	73	22	4	.7	—	—	—	—
	1962	74	20	5	.8	—	—	—	—
Apparel	1953	54	24	15	5	1	.4	.1	.1
	1962	55	24	16	5	.9	.3	.04	—
Men's	1953	59	24	13	3	.6	.3	—	—
	1962	56	25	14	4	.7	.2	—	—
Women's ready-to-wear	1953	48	24	18	7	2	.8	.2	—
	1962	50	23	18	6	1	.6	.1	—
Shoe stores	1953	53	27	14	4	1	.3	.1	—
	1962	53	28	16	3	.5	.1	—	—
Furniture, etc.	1953	54	26	15	4	.8	.3	—	—
	1962	56	24	15	3	.5	.2	—	—
Furniture & home furnishings	1953	53	27	15	4	1	.3	.1	—
	1962	53	26	17	4	.6	.2	—	—
Household appliances	1953	56	26	14	4	.7	.3	—	—
	1962	55	26	15	3	.6	.3	—	—

Table 6-C (Cont.)

DISTRIBUTION OF RETAIL TRADE REPORTING UNITS BY EMPLOYEE SIZE CLASS,
BY CLASS OF RETAIL ESTABLISHMENT - 1953 AND 1962
(PER CENT)

Retail Trade Class and Year		Number of Employees							
		Under 4	4–7	8–19	20–49	50–99	100–249	250–499	500 and Over
Eating and Drinking Places	1953	56	26	13	3	.7	.2	--	--
	1962	56	22	15	5	1	.3	--	--
Miscellaneous	1953	60	25	11	3	.5	.2	--	--
	1962	59	23	14	3	.4	.2	--	--
Drug stores	1953	44	36	15	3	.6	.2	--	--
	1962	41	32	22	4	.6	.2	--	--
Liquor stores	1953	80	16	4	.5	--	--	--	--
	1962	77	17	5	.6	--	--	--	--
Farm & garden supply	1953	56	27	13	3	.7	.2	--	--
	1962	55	27	15	3	.4	.2	--	--
Jewelry	1953	65	22	10	3	.5	.2	--	--
	1962	65	21	11	2	.4	.2	--	--

Source: County Business Patterns, 1953 and 1962.

Table 7

MANUFACTURING FACILITIES ACQUIRED BY MANUFACTURING COMPANIES, 1959-62, AND EMPLOYMENT IN ACQUIRED COMPANIES, BY INDUSTRY OF ACQUIRING COMPANY

Industry Category of Acquiring Company	Companies in Acquiring Industry 1958	Companies Acquired by Industry 1959-62	Employment of Companies Acquired	
			Total	Average per Company
Food and Kindred Products				
Meat packing	2,595	41	5,945	145
Prepared meats & dressed poultry	2,437	8	515	64
Dairy products	8,298	158	21,360	135
Canned and frozen foods	2,992	79	16,591	210
Grain mill products	2,817	53	10,158	192
Bakery products	5,452	65	8,875	137
Sugar	68	8	671	84
Confectionery & related products	1,340	20	4,583	229
Alcoholic beverages	525	40	12,157	304
Bottled soft drinks & flavorings	4,435	14	2,113	151
Fat and oils	753	15	1,690	113
Other food products	3,544	32	7,260	227
Tobacco Manufactures				
Tobacco products	350	16	4,685	293
Textile Mill Products				
Broad-woven fabrics, yarn and finishing	2,333	91	49,436	543
Knitting mills	2,577	35	7,384	211

Table 7 (Cont.)

MANUFACTURING FACILITIES ACQUIRED BY MANUFACTURING COMPANIES, 1959–62, AND
EMPLOYMENT IN ACQUIRED COMPANIES, BY INDUSTRY OF ACQUIRING COMPANY

Industry Category of Acquiring Company	Companies in Acquiring Industry 1958	Companies Acquired by Industry 1959–62	Employment of Companies Acquired	
			Total	Average per Company
Floor covering mills	250	9	2,883	320
Other textile mill products	1,352	22	3,635	165
Apparel and Related Products				
Men's and boys' clothing	3,946	32	7,299	228
Women's and children's clothing	12,810	63	22,767	361
Millinery, fur goods & misc.	11,150	11	2,415	220
Lumber and Wood Products				
Logging, saw mills & planing mills	28,678	68	18,924	278
Millwork and related products	3,868	47	7,394	157
Other wood products	3,812	17	1,852	109
Furniture and Fixtures				
Household furniture	6,205	33	4,510	137
Furniture & fixtures (exc. household)	3,504	29	4,843	167

Paper and Allied Products				
Pulp, paper, and board	409	95	32,311	340
Paperboard containers and boxes	1,568	76	21,369	281
Other paper and allied products	1,786	35	3,364	96
Printing and Publishing				
Newspapers	7,929	29	11,447	395
Periodicals	2,211	10	2,683	268
Books	1,620	8	435	54
Misc. publ. and greeting cards	1,264	8	815	102
Commercial printing and forms	17,463	30	6,401	214
Bookbinding & prtg., trade serv.	3,585	13	1,501	115
Chemicals and Allied Products				
Basic chemicals, fibers, plastics, and rubber	895	96	30,480	318
Drugs	1,218	25	7,659	306
Cleaning and toilet goods	2,443	43	6,425	149
Paints and varnishes	1,449	30	2,293	76
Agricultural chemicals	792	13	1,266	97
Misc. chemical products	1,749	17	2,613	154
Petroleum and Coal Products				
Petroleum refining	192	24	6,852	286
Other petroleum & coal products	793	16	1,526	95
Rubber and Plastics Products, n.e.c.				
Rubber products	1,009	51	9,462	186
Plastics products, n.e.c.	2,946	29	3,305	114

Table 7 (Cont.)

MANUFACTURING FACILITIES ACQUIRED BY MANUFACTURING COMPANIES, 1959–62, AND
EMPLOYMENT IN ACQUIRED COMPANIES, BY INDUSTRY OF ACQUIRING COMPANY

Industry Category of Acquiring Company	Companies in Acquiring Industry 1958	Companies Acquired by Industry 1959–62	Employment of Companies Acquired	
			Total	Average per Company
Leather and Leather Products				
Footwear (exc. rubber)	1,016	18	10,421	579
Leather & leather products (exc. footwear)	3,052	16	2,881	180
Stone, Clay, Glass Products				
Glass products	1,121	13	3,430	263
Hydraulic cement	50	8	1,794	224
Structural clay products	751	20	2,110	106
Ready-mixed concrete	2,970	15	855	57
Concrete and plaster products	4,965	51	11,279	221
Other nonmetallic min. prods.	2,802	41	9,378	229
Primary Metal Industries				
Blast furnaces and steel mills	103	36	13,451	374
Iron and steel foundries	1,336	36	10,520	292
Primary steel products, n.e.c.	1,059	32	2,770	87
Nonferrous primary metals	2,653	89	24,515	275

Fabricated Metal Products

Metal cans, cutlery, hand tools, and hardware	1,978	37	6,654	180
Plumbing, nonelectric heating)	9,684	87	12,773	147
Structural metal products)	2,194	24	2,381	99
Screw machine prods. and bolts	5,800	45	5,499	122
Metal stampings & services	1,324	13	606	47
Fabricated wire products				
Fabricated metal prods., n.e.c.	1,909	39	10,732	275

Machinery (exc. electrical)

Engines and turbines)	1,437	21	6,270	299
Farm machinery & equipment)	1,775	55	13,372	243
Construction & like equipment	7,626	40	5,170	129
Metal working machinery	2,897	62	7,895	127
Special industrial machinery	3,017	37	9,838	266
General industrial machinery	278	12	2,867	239
Office machines, n.e.c.				
Service industry machinery)	11,141	41	10,303	251
Misc. mach. (exc. electrical))				

Electrical Machinery

Radio & TV rcg. equip., commun. equipment, etc.	2,148	161	52,993	329
Other electrical machinery	4,633	162	48,953	302

Transportation Equipment

Motor vehicles & equipment	1,870	105	54,861	522
Aircraft	102	32	27,033	845

Table 7 (Cont.)

MANUFACTURING FACILITIES ACQUIRED BY MANUFACTURING COMPANIES, 1959-62, AND
EMPLOYMENT IN ACQUIRED COMPANIES, BY INDUSTRY OF ACQUIRING COMPANY

Industry Category of Acquiring Company	Companies in Acquiring Industry 1958	Companies Acquired by Industry 1959-62	Employment of Companies Acquired	
			Total	Average per Company
Aircraft engines, propellors, equipment and parts	1,236	77	17,761	231
Ships and boats	1,880	10	4,076	408
Other transportation equipment	715	22	2,903	132
Instruments and Related Products				
Scientific instruments and measuring devices	1,122	63	10,801	171
Optical, medical, & ophthalmic goods	1,417	27	2,933	109
Photographic equipment	430	20	8,214	411
Watches and clocks	198	10	1,631	163
Miscellaneous Manufacturing				
Jewelry and silverware	2,057	13	2,344	180
Toys and sporting goods	2,501	41	9,135	223
Other manufactures) Ordnance and access.)	9,117	37	6,126	166

Source: Enterprise Statistics, 1958.

Acquisitions and Disposals of Manufacturing Facilities, 1959-1962 -- 1962 Annual Survey of Manufactures.

Table 8-A

DISTRIBUTION OF BUSINESS TAX RETURNS AND OF BUSINESS RECEIPTS AMONG SOLE PROPRIETORSHIPS, PARTNERSHIPS, AND CORPORATIONS, BY INDUSTRY DIVISION-1961-62

Industry Division	Total	Sole Pro-prietorships	Partnerships	Corporations
	Number of business returns (thousands)			
All industries, except agriculture	7,728.3	5,754.6	802.5	1,171.3
Mining	65.1	35.5	15.9	13.7
Construction	824.8	678.5	62.3	84.0
Manufacturing	412.4	194.3	44.5	173.6
Transportation, commun., & sundry serv.	353.8	286.7	18.1	49.0
Wholesale and retail trade	2,585.3	1,942.8	277.6	364.9
Wholesale trade	493.5	328.1	42.0	123.4
Retail trade	2,022.9	1,563.9	228.8	230.2
Not allocable	68.8	50.7	6.8	11.3
Finance, insurance & real estate	1,009.5	461.6	207.7	340.2
Services	2,385.0	2,075.7	171.3	138.0
	Percent of business returns			
All industries, except agriculture	100	74	10	15
Mining	100	55	24	21
Construction	100	82	8	10
Manufacturing	100	47	11	42
Transportation, commun., & sundry serv.	100	81	5	14

Table 8-A (Cont.)

DISTRIBUTION OF BUSINESS TAX RETURNS AND OF BUSINESS RECEIPTS AMONG SOLE PROPRIETORSHIPS, PARTNERSHIPS, AND CORPORATIONS, BY INDUSTRY DIVISION – 1961-62

Industry Division	Total	Sole Pro-prietorships	Partnerships	Corporations
Wholesale trade	100	66	9	25
Retail trade	100	77	11	11
Finance, insurance & real estate	100	46	21	34
Services	100	87	7	6
Percent of business receipts				
All industries, except agriculture	100	14	7	79
Mining	100	9	7	84
Construction	100	25	13	63
Manufacturing	100	2	2	96
Transportation, commun., & sundry serv.	100	6	2	93
Wholesale trade	100	11	8	81
Retail trade	100	30	11	59
Finance, insurance & real estate	100	10	9	81
Services	100	41	17	42

Source: Statistics of Income – 1961-62 Business Tax Returns, Internal Revenue Service.

Table 8-A Supplement

ADJUSTED DISTRIBUTION OF BUSINESS TAX RETURNS AMONG SOLE PROPRIETORSHIPS, PARTNERSHIPS, AND CORPORATIONS, BY INDUSTRY DIVISION - 1961-62

	Total (adjusted)	Sole Proprietorships (adjusted)	Active Partnerships	Corporations
Number of business returns (thousands)				
Construction	501.7	355.4	62.3	84.0
Manufacturing	327.6	109.5	44.5	173.6
Wholesale trade	384.1	218.7	42.0	123.4
Retail trade	1,501.1	1,042.1	228.8	230.2
Services	1,406.7	1,097.4	171.3	138.0
Finance, insurance & real estate	754.9	207.0	207.7	340.2
Per cent of business returns				
Construction	100	71	12	17
Manufacturing	100	33	14	53
Wholesale trade	100	57	11	32
Retail trade	100	69	15	15
Services	100	78	12	10
Finance, insurance & real estate	100	27	28	45

Bases of reduction in number of sole proprietorships

Construction - returns with total business receipts under $5,000.

Manufacturing - total business receipts under $7,000.

Wholesale Trade - total business receipts under $5,000.

Retail Trade - total business receipts under $10,000.

Services - total business receipts under $4,000.

Finance, Insurance and Real Estate - total business receipts under $5,000.

Table 8-B

PER CENT OF BUSINESS TAX RETURNS SHOWING NET PROFIT OR INCOME, BY INDUSTRY DIVISION, TYPE OF ORGANIZATION, AND SIZE OF BUSINESS RECEIPTS - 1961-62

Size of Business Receipts	Construction Proprietorships	Construction Partnerships	Construction Corporations	Manufacturing Proprietorships	Manufacturing Partnerships	Manufacturing Corporations	Wholesale Trade Proprietorships	Wholesale Trade Partnerships	Wholesale Trade Corporations	Retail Trade Proprietorships	Retail Trade Partnerships	Retail Trade Corporations	Services Proprietorships	Services Partnerships	Services Corporations
Under $1,000	83			59			60			56			71		
$1-2,000	94			70			75			67			85		
$2-3,000	92			76			77			68			89		
$3-4,000	93	63		84	42		85	54		71	44		90	59	
$4-5,000	94		32	88		29	81		38	71		21	92		32
$5-7,000	95			86			91			72			91		
$7-10,000	93	83		88	72		91	67		76	64		92	74	
$10-15,000	94	85		92	79		92	77		78	69		93	84	
$15-20,000	91	89		90	84		88	69		83	77		94	84	
$20-25,000	90	86	35	84	82	32	93	84	49	84	78	30	95	88	44
$25-30,000	91	85		89	80		92	88		85	82		95	86	
$30-40,000	95	88	41	87	86	45	90	81	53	89	84	38	96	90	51
$40-50,000	91	89		90	86		89	87		89	88		95	92	
$50-75,000	93	87	52	90	86	54	94	88	57	91	88	49	97	92	59
$75-100,000	90	88		93	89		98	90		90	90		98	94	
$100-250,000	92	88	65	92	89	70	91	89	72	93	90	68	94	95	71
$250-500,000	94	86	76	93	89	79	91	93	82	90	91	75	86	92	75
$500-1,000,000	66	81	77	81	90	82	90	93	87	88	91	81	97	92	80
$1-5,000,000			75		89	85		90			92	87		91	73
$5-10,000,000															
$10-50,000,000	99	75	80	79	84	86	92	95	87	81	95	86	96	98	89
$50-100,000,000			83			88			87			87			91
$100-250,000,000			100			92			94			93			92
$250-500,000,000			100			92			93			83			--
$500,000,000 & Over			--			96			100			100			--

Source: Statistics of Income - Business Tax Returns--1961-62.

Table 9-A

ALL ACTIVE PROPRIETORSHIPS: NET PROFIT OR
LOSS AS PER CENT OF BUSINESS RECEIPTS, BY INDUSTRY
DIVISION AND SIZE OF BUSINESS RECEIPTS - 1961-62

Size of Business Receipts	Construction	Manufacturing	Wholesale Trade	Retail Trade	Finance, Insurance and Real Estate	Services
Under $1,000	49	-13	-14	-12	-17	16
$1-2,000	60	19	24	11	31	38
$2-3,000	58	26	27	7	36	41
$3-4,000	51	25	31	10	45	44
$4-5,000	51	30	32	11	42	46
$5-7,000	46	22	37	12	50	43
$7-10,000	35	25	37	10	50	38
$10-15,000	27	25	37	9	53	37
$15-20,000	22	21	27	9	45	42
$20-25,000	19	14	26	8	42	38
$25-30,000	15	15	23	8)		39
$30-40,000	14	13	20	8)	38	41
$40-50,000	12	13	14	7)		40
$50-75,000	10	11	13	7)	25	38
$75-100,000	9	11	9	6)		29
$100-250,000	7	8	6	5)	11)	17
$250-500,000	5	7	4	4)	)	
$500-1,000,000	2	4	3	2	5	15
$1,000,000 and over	3	3	2	1	1	10

Source: Statistics of Income - Business Tax Returns 1961-62.

Table 9-B

PROPRIETORSHIPS WITH NET PROFIT: NET PROFIT
AS PER CENT OF BUSINESS RECEIPTS, BY INDUSTRY
DIVISION AND SIZE OF BUSINESS RECEIPTS - 1961-62

Size of Business Receipts	Construction	Manufacturing	Wholesale Trade	Retail Trade	Finance, Insurance, and Real Estate	Services
Under $1,000	74	60	55	45	56	63
$1-2,000	68	51	53	37	53	55
$2-3,000	65	45	49	31	51	53
$3-4,000	58	36	44	25	55	54
$4-5,000	55	40	46	24	56	53
$5-7,000	49	32	44	23	56	50
$7-10,000	40	32	44	18	56	43
$10-15,000	29	28	42	15	56	41
$15-20,000	24	24	33	13	51	39
$20-25,000	22	20	29	12	46	40
$25-30,000	18	19	27	11	46	41
$30-40,000	15	17	23	10	42	43
$40-50,000	14	15	16	9	33	42
$50-75,000	12	13	15	8	34	39
$75-100,000	10	12	10	7	27	30
$100-250,000	8	9	7	6	14	21
$250-500,000	6	8	4	4	7	13
$500-1,000,000	5	5	3	3	5	17
$1,000,000 and over	3	3	3	2	1	12

Source: Statistics of Income - Business Tax Returns 1961-62.

Table 10

ALL ACTIVE PARTNERSHIPS: NET PROFIT OR LOSS AS PER CENT OF BUSINESS RECEIPTS, BY INDUSTRY DIVISION AND SIZE OF BUSINESS RECEIPTS – 1961–62

Size of Business Receipts	Construction	Manufacturing	Wholesale Trade	Retail Trade	Finance, Insurance, and Real Estate	Services
Under $5,000	18	-28	1/	-13	-4	1
$5–10,000	32	7	11	7	29	24
$10–15,000	34	20	22	7	31	30
$15–20,000	31	20	21	10	31	29
$20–25,000	25	19	26	10	32	30
$25–30,000	27	18	25	11	35	30
$30–40,000	23	19	24	11	35	31
$40–50,000	19	17	19	11	31	33
$50–75,000	16	15	16	9	28	36
$75–100,000	14	15	15	9	30	38
$100–150,000	12	13	11	8	18	40
$150–200,000	9	12	9	7	17	45
$200–250,000	8	9	8	7	19	36
$250–500,000	7	8	6	5	20	31
$500–1,000,000	6	7	4	4	30	29
$1–5,000,000	4	6	3	3	21	26
$5,000,000 and over	6	3	1	2	19	25

1/ Less than 0.5 per cent.
Source: Statistics of Income – Business Tax Returns 1961–62.

Table 11-A

ACTIVE CORPORATIONS: PROFITABILITY RATIOS BY ASSET SIZE FOR FOUR MAIN INDUSTRIAL GROUPS – 1961-62

Size of Total Assets	Construction			Manufacturing			Wholesale Trade			Retail Trade		
	A	B	C	A	B	C	A	B	C	A	B	C
$1-50,000	-2.3	30.6	7.1	-5.4	24.0	7.5	-2.0	27.9	6.1	-3.3	19.6	5.2
$50-100,000	1.3	18.6	6.1	1.2	19.7	7.1	3.9	20.1	5.0	2.4	16.0	5.1
$100-500,000	2.9	13.7	5.1	4.1	15.8	6.1	5.0	14.7	4.1	3.6	12.4	3.9
$500-1,000,000	3.4	10.3	4.3	6.7	13.9	5.7	4.7	11.3	2.8	4.1	9.9	2.9
$1,000-2,500,000	2.9	7.6	3.4	6.9	12.1	5.6	5.1	9.9	2.9	4.2	8.9	2.9
$2,500-5,000,000	2.4	5.4	2.8	7.8	11.6	6.0	5.7	9.3	2.8	4.4	7.7	2.8
$5,000-10,000,000	3.0	5.5	3.0	8.2	11.0	6.6	5.2	8.0	2.8	4.8	7.6	3.1
$10-25,000,000	3.5	5.8	3.7	8.5	10.7	7.2	5.4	7.6	2.6	5.8	8.2	2.9
$25-50,000,000	3.6	5.2	3.1	8.6	10.4	7.6	6.8	8.7	2.6	5.6	7.4	2.8
$50-100,000,000	8.3	10.6	10.1	8.5	10.1	7.4	7.0	8.2	1.7	6.7	8.4	3.1
$100-250,000,000	2.2	3.5	5.0	9.2	10.5	7.6	7.6	9.4	4.0	7.1	8.5	3.3
$250,000,000 and over	--	--	--	8.6	9.4	8.5	4.2	5.6	4.0	7.7	8.5	2.9

Note: In this and subsequent tables on profitability

Column A equals compiled net income as a per cent of total assets.

Column B equals compiled net income plus officers' compensation and interest paid, as a per cent of total assets.

Column C equals compiled net income plus officers' compensation, as a per cent of business receipts.

Source: Statistics of Income, Corporation Income Tax Returns 1961-62.

Table 11-B

PROFITABILITY RATIOS OF CORPORATIONS BY ASSET SIZE –
BEVERAGES (TOTAL) AND SOFT DRINKS, CARBONATED
WATERS & FLAVORING
1961-62

Size of Total Assets	Beverage Industries		Soft Drinks & Flavoring	
	A	B	A	B
$1-50,000	4.5	22.3	4.8	22.4
$50-100,000	-0.5	10.7	-0.7	10.1
$100-500,000	5.2	13.7	5.5	13.8
$500-1,000,000	12.1	17.3	15.7	21.4
$1,000-2,500,000	8.6	12.6	12.4	16.5
$2,500-5,000,000	7.5	10.7	8.4	13.9
$5-10,000,000	10.3	12.4	12.7	14.6
$10-25,000,000	10.4	12.2	7.4	9.4
$25-50,000,000	10.0	11.7	12.7	14.5
$50-100,000,000	12.1	13.7	20.2	21.7
$100-250,000,000	6.1	6.9	-	-
$250,000,000 & over	7.5	8.9	22.4	23.5

Source: For Appendix Tables 11-B to 11-M, Source Book of Statistics of Income 1961-62.

Table 11-C

PROFITABILITY RATIOS OF CORPORATIONS BY ASSET SIZE - FOOD PRODUCTS (TOTAL) AND SELECTED FOOD INDUSTRY GROUPS - 1961-62

Size of Total Assets	Food Products, Total		Meat Products		Dairy Products		Canning & Preserving		Grain Mill Products	
	A	B	A	B	A	B	A	B	A	B
$1 and under 50,000	-3.3	20.9	1.7	31.8	0.9	15.2	-5.2	8.1	-8.2	11.7
$50-100,000	1.4	15.0	-1.3	8.0	3.1	16.8	0.5	16.5	-7.6	1.9
$100-500,000	3.1	12.5	2.1	12.1	3.6	13.8	2.5	10.7	3.1	10.5
$500-1,000,000	7.3	14.2	7.7	16.3	5.9	12.5	7.5	14.3	3.5	8.9
$1,000-2,500,000	6.7	11.3	4.4	9.9	6.1	10.1	5.6	10.2	5.5	10.3
$2,500-5,000,000	6.9	10.5	6.4	10.3	6.7	9.9	6.4	10.0	8.3	12.3
$5-10,000,000	8.0	10.7	10.9	13.8	6.4	8.7	7.2	10.5	7.6	11.1
$10-25,000,000	7.9	10.3	7.7	9.2	14.1	16.0	4.4	7.2	6.3	9.2
$25-50,000,000	8.3	9.7	--	--	2.4	3.6	1.6	3.6	11.2	12.7
$50-100,000,000	10.5	12.2	2.2	4.6	6.7	8.2	14.8	18.4	13.6	15.4
$100-250,000,000	11.2	12.5	10.0	10.9	11.5	12.9	6.4	7.9	13.4	14.8
$250,000,000 & over	12.4	13.3	1.9	3.2	11.7	12.3	20.1	20.1	10.5	11.9

Table 11-D

PROFITABILITY RATIOS OF CORPORATIONS BY ASSET SIZE -
TEXTILE MILL PRODUCTS (TOTAL) AND KNITTING MILLS-
1961-62

Size of Total Assets	Textiles, Total		Knitting Mills	
	A	B	A	B
$1-50,000	-2.0	30.6	3.9	38.2
$50-100,000	4.3	25.1	1.7	23.4
$100-500,000	3.1	13.7	8.9	19.6
$500-1,000,000	5.3	11.1	5.0	11.1
$1,000-2,500,000	4.3	8.8	6.9	11.8
$2,500-5,000,000	6.5	9.7	10.5	14.0
$5-10,000,000	5.6	8.1	9.5	12.2
$10-25,000,000	5.5	7.5	7.5	9.3
$25-50,000,000	7.8	9.6	10.9	13.3
$50-100,000,000	5.4	6.9	3.5	6.8
$100-250,000,000	9.8	10.6	--	--
$250,000,000 and over	4.9	6.8	--	--

Table 11-E

PROFITABILITY RATIOS OF CORPORATIONS BY ASSET SIZE - APPAREL AND OTHER FINISHED PRODUCTS
MADE FROM FABRICS (TOTAL) AND SELECTED APPAREL INDUSTRY GROUPS - 1961-62

Size of Total Assets	Apparel, Total		Men's, Youths', and Boys' Clothing		Women's, Misses', Children's, and Infants' Clothing		Hats, Caps, Millinery, etc.		Other Fabricated Textile Products	
	A	B	A	B	A	B	A	B	A	B
$1-50,000	-5.1	32.1	-5.3	20.2	-5.1	34.1	-7.8	30.1	-2.7	35.3
$50-100,000	2.4	22.4	6.7	21.9	4.9	23.4	2.5	25.1	1.0	23.5
$100-500,000	4.6	16.4	4.5	14.7	5.0	17.1	3.1	15.6	4.3	18.0
$500-1,000,000	6.1	13.6	4.5	9.7	6.4	15.0	3.8	13.6	9.0	16.8
$1,000-2,500,000	7.7	13.7	7.2	13.5	8.6	14.6	4.8	10.5	7.4	12.7
$2,500-5,000,000	7.9	12.3	8.4	12.7	8.7	12.8	10.6	14.5	4.7	8.2
$5-10,000,000	9.5	13.4	7.2	10.9	17.4	21.2	6.6	11.4	-1.0	3.2
$10-25,000,000	5.5	8.8	5.5	9.1	9.0	11.3	3.8	6.4	-6.8	-0.6
$25-50,000,000	6.2	8.4	7.9	10.1	2.3	4.5	--	--	--	--
$50-100,000,000	8.0	9.4	8.8	10.3	--	--	--	--	6.7	7.7

Table 11-F

PROFITABILITY RATIOS OF CORPORATIONS BY ASSET SIZE – LUMBER AND WOOD PRODUCTS (TOTAL) AND SELECTED LUMBER AND WOOD INDUSTRY GROUPS – 1961-62

Size of Total Assets	Lumber & Wood Products, Total		Logging Camps, etc.		Wood Containers and Other Wood Products		Millwork, Veneer, etc.	
	A	B	A	B	A	B	A	B
$1-50,000	-10.2	12.8	-10.7	4.9	-5.1	19.2	-15.2	12.5
$50-100,000	-1.2	14.5	-3.0	10.2	0.1	14.9	-0.6	17.8
$100-500,000	1.8	11.6	-0.4	7.6	3.5	16.2	3.1	13.0
$500-1,000,000	2.1	8.2	-0.9	4.5	4.8	11.9	4.1	8.8
$1,000-2,500,000	2.8	6.6	0.9	4.3	7.0	11.3	3.4	8.4
$2,500-5,000,000	2.4	5.5	1.0	3.5	7.1	11.0	2.2	5.7
$5-10,000,000	4.4	6.7	5.2	7.0	3.4	6.5	3.7	6.3
$10-25,000,000	7.2	8.5	6.6	7.8	0.9	2.2	11.4	12.8
$25-50,000,000	6.3	7.7	6.9	8.1	4.4	6.3	5.7	6.8
$50-100,000,000	-0.2	2.4	-0.2	2.4	--	--	--	--
$100-250,000,000	2.6	4.4	1.6	3.0	--	--	3.4	5.6
$250,000,000 & over	6.2	7.0	8.0	8.1	--	--	3.6	5.5

Table 11-G

PROFITABILITY RATIOS OF CORPORATIONS BY ASSET SIZE -
FURNITURE AND FIXTURES (TOTAL), HOUSEHOLD
FURNITURE, AND OFFICE AND OTHER FURNITURE
AND FIXTURES - 1961-62

Size of Total Assets	Furniture, Total		Household Furniture		Office Furniture and Fixtures	
	A	B	A	B	A	B
$1 and under 50,000	-12.4	17.7	-15.9	12.5	- 8.0	24.5
$50-100,000	- 1.8	20.4	- 2.2	20.1	- 1.4	20.8
$100-500,000	2.7	14.1	1.7	14.7	4.4	17.8
$500-1,000,000	4.3	11.1	3.9	10.9	5.4	11.6
$1,000-2,500,000	7.9	13.3	7.3	12.8	9.4	14.5
$2,500-5,000,000	9.9	13.6	8.5	12.4	13.1	16.7
$5-10,000,000	9.0	12.2	6.3	9.5	13.0	16.3
$10-25,000,000	12.4	14.3	11.9	14.2	12.6	14.3
$25-50,000,000	10.6	11.9	13.7	15.2	8.6	9.7
$50-100,000,000	8.2	8.2	6.4	8.2	--	--

Table 11-H

PROFITABILITY RATIOS OF CORPORATIONS BY ASSET SIZE – PRINTING, PUBLISHING, AND ALLIED INDUSTRIES (TOTAL) AND SELECTED PRINTING AND PUBLISHING INDUSTRY GROUPS – 1961-62

Size of Total Assets	Printing and Publishing, Total		Newspapers		Books		Commercial Printing, etc.		Book Binding and Services to Trade	
	A	B	A	B	A	B	A	B	A	B
$1-50,000	- 2.0	33.2	4.6	35.8	- 6.1	13.6	- 1.6	38.9	1.1	30.9
$50-100,000	5.6	27.8	2.6	15.5	-10.0	5.1	6.9	32.1	10.9	35.2
$100-500,000	6.4	20.6	6.8	15.6	12.9	26.4	4.7	20.5	7.2	24.4
$500-1,000,000	9.4	17.8	12.9	19.4	12.7	23.1	8.7	17.6	7.1	14.8
$1,000-2,500,000	9.8	15.6	12.1	16.3	7.3	13.5	8.7	15.3	11.7	18.5
$2,500-5,000,000	11.6	15.7	13.1	16.1	13.2	18.0	7.8	12.0	13.3	17.1
$5-10,000,000	11.6	14.4	13.8	15.8	16.0	19.2	8.3	11.8	5.7	8.8
$10-25,000,000	11.7	13.9	14.2	16.0	8.4	10.5	10.7	13.4	14.9	17.9
$25-50,000,000	14.9	16.6	16.3	18.0	17.8	18.9	10.6	12.4	--	--
$50-100,000,000	9.9	12.0	13.1	14.3	4.1	7.9	21.5	22.1	1.9	4.4
$100-250,000,000	5.6	7.4	7.0	9.0	--	--	13.9	15.3	--	--
$250,000,000 & over	- 0.7	0.6	- 0.7	0.6	--	--	--	--	--	--

Table 11-I

PROFITABILITY RATIOS OF CORPORATIONS BY ASSET SIZE -
RUBBER AND MISCELLANEOUS PLASTICS (TOTAL) AND
MISCELLANEOUS PLASTICS PRODUCTS - 1961-62

Size of Total Assets	Rubber and Plastic Products Total		Miscellaneous Plastics	
	A	B	A	B
$1-50,000	-12.1	7.2	-14.6	6.0
$50-100,000	6.7	28.0	5.6	29.6
$100-500,000	6.0	18.9	6.0	18.1
$500-1,000,000	9.8	17.1	9.7	16.0
$1,000-2,500,000	11.0	16.3	10.0	13.7
$2,500-5,000,000	9.5	13.5	11.0	14.9
$5-10,000,000	12.4	15.3	10.1	13.1
$10-25,000,000	6.4	8.4	1.2	2.8
$25-50,000,000	2.4	4.6	3.8	6.3
$50-100,000,000	6.4	9.4	--	--
$100-250,000,000	6.8	8.4	--	--
$250,000,000 & over	11.1	11.5	--	--

Table 11-J

PROFITABILITY RATIOS OF CORPORATIONS BY ASSET SIZE -
LEATHER AND LEATHER PRODUCTS (TOTAL) AND LEATHER
GOODS OTHER THAN FOOTWEAR - 1961-62

| | Ratio of Income to Total Assets | | | |
| | Leather and Leather Products, Total | | Leather Goods Other Than Footwear | |
Size of Total Assets	A	B	A	B
$1-50,000	- 7.0	18.9	-7.6	22.9
$50-100,000	6.1	26.4	0.5	22.4
$100-500,000	1.9	13.0	3.4	14.7
$500-1,000,000	5.1	12.4	5.3	12.2
$1,000-2,500,000	5.6	11.3	5.1	10.4
$2,500-5,000,000	7.8	11.7	7.1	10.7
$5-10,000,000	5.9	8.1	0.3	2.1
$10-25,000,000	15.0	17.0	2.5	4.4
$25-50,000,000	3.9	6.2	4.1	6.4
$50-100,000,000	14.6	15.9	--	--
$100-250,000,000	3.0	4.9	--	--

Table 11-K

PROFITABILITY RATIOS OF CORPORATIONS BY ASSET SIZE -
STONE, CLAY, AND GLASS PRODUCTS (TOTAL) AND SELECTED
INDUSTRY GROUPS - 1961-62

Size of Total Assets	Stone, Clay and Glass Products, Total		Structural Clay Products		Concrete, Gypsum and Plaster	
	A	B	A	B	A	B
$1-50,000	- 5.1	11.4	-35.6	-29.9	- 4.4	12.0
$50-100,000	1.6	16.5	- 9.5	4.1	3.9	18.4
$100-500,000	4.2	13.4	3.6	10.2	3.9	13.1
$500-1,000,000	6.3	11.7	5.8	11.7	5.8	11.0
$1,000-2,500,000	4.7	9.3	3.0	7.4	2.9	9.0
$2,500-5,000,000	6.9	10.3	5.1	8.4	5.4	10.1
$5-10,000,000	10.7	11.9	9.1	11.6	8.5	10.7
$10-25,000,000	8.2	10.1	5.1	7.0	7.1	9.4
$25-50,000,000	6.2	8.1	6.1	8.3	4.6	7.4
$50-100,000,000	8.7	9.8	--	--	9.0	10.4
$100-250,000,000	14.6	15.6	9.8	10.9	12.7	13.5
$250,000,000 & over	11.2	11.9	--	--	18.8	19.2

Table 11-L

PROFITABILITY RATIOS OF CORPORATIONS BY ASSET SIZE – FABRICATED METAL PRODUCTS (TOTAL) AND SELECTED METAL INDUSTRY GROUPS – 1961-62

Size of Total Assets	Fabricated Metals, Total		Cutlery, Hand Tools, etc.		Fabricated Structural Metals		Screw Machine Products, etc.		Metal Stamping		Coating, Engraving, etc.	
	A	B	A	B	A	B	A	B	A	B	A	B
$1 and under 50,000	-3.7	28.2	-26.6	-9.8	-12.7	20.3	4.9	45.5	16.1	48.8	1.4	48.6
$50 and under 100,000	1.6	21.3	-4.4	15.1	2.1	20.4	-5.0	24.2	5.4	24.6	6.1	26.8
$100-500,000	4.7	17.7	2.9	15.5	2.8	14.3	7.0	21.5	6.5	19.8	6.8	24.8
$500-1,000,000	7.1	15.7	8.7	13.8	5.4	13.9	9.0	18.8	9.5	20.7	8.2	16.8
$1,000-2,500,000	6.9	12.5	8.3	13.7	3.8	9.1	6.0	11.1	9.6	15.6	9.2	15.2
$2,500-5,000,000	6.4	10.3	10.3	14.4	3.6	7.5	5.1	9.1	6.5	10.0	7.0	12.3
$5-10,000,000	7.7	10.4	13.6	16.3	2.6	5.3	8.5	10.7	9.6	12.1	13.6	15.6
$10-25,000,000	9.1	11.2	12.7	14.7	4.5	6.8	11.9	13.5	5.4	7.9	--	--
$25-50,000,000	6.8	8.8	9.5	10.8	0.8	3.1	4.9	6.4	11.6	13.2	--	--
$50-100,000,000	7.4	8.7	10.2	11.1	4.5	5.4	2.7	4.8	--	--	--	--
$100-250,000,000	10.5	11.7	44.1	44.8	5.7	6.9	--	--	6.5	7.7	--	--
$250,000,000 & over	8.1	9.1	--	--	--	--	--	--	--	--	--	--

Table 11-M

PROFITABILITY RATIOS OF CORPORATIONS BY ASSET SIZE -
MACHINERY (TOTAL), EXCEPT ELECTRICAL AND METAL
WORKING MACHINERY AND EQUIPMENT - 1961-62

Size of Total Assets	Machinery, Total		Metal Working Mach. & Equip.	
	A	B	A	B
$1-50,000	- 5.5	27.4	- 0.3	38.8
$50-100,000	- 0.1	20.2	- 3.8	19.8
$100-500,000	3.3	16.5	2.2	16.7
$500-1,000,000	5.8	13.9	3.9	13.5
$1,000-2,500,000	6.7	11.9	4.8	10.6
$2,500-5,000,000	7.8	11.7	6.7	10.5
$5-10,000,000	7.8	10.8	7.6	10.1
$10-25,000,000	8.3	10.4	6.5	8.4
$25-50,000,000	8.8	10.7	10.0	11.5
$50-100,000,000	9.0	10.4	9.8	11.1
$100-250,000,000	8.3	9.5	16.0	16.8
$250,000,000 & over	11.3	12.4	--	--

BIBLIOGRAPHY

BOOKS

Adams, Nate. The Structure of American Industry. New York, N.Y.: Macmillan Co., 1963.

Balderston, F. E. A Study of Cost and Organization in Thirteen Construction Firms. Cambridge, Mass.: Massachusetts Institute of Technology, 1953.

Blum, Albert A. An Annotated Bibliography of Industrial Relations and the Small Firm. Ithaca, N.Y.: New York State School of Industrial Relations at Cornell University, March, 1960.

Burlage, L. Charles. The Small Businessman and His Problems. New York, N.Y.: Vintage Press, Inc., 1958.

Calder, Grant H., et al. Small Business Counseling: An Evaluation of Techniques. Salt Lake City, Utah: University of Utah, Bureau of Economic and Business Research, 1964.

Carpenter, Walter H., and Chandler, Edward. Small Business and Pattern Bargaining. Washington, D.C.: Babson Institute Press for the Small Business Administration, July, 1961.

Christensen, Roland C. Management Success in Small and Growing Enterprises. Cambridge, Mass.: Graduate School of Business Administration, Harvard University Press, 1953.

Davidson, Thomas L., et al. Some Effects of the Growth of Planned and Controlled Shopping Centers on Small Retailers. Small Business Administration Management Research Report. Storrs, Conn.: University of Connecticut, June, 1960.

279

Dehoach, D. B. Changes in Food Retailing. Pullman, Wash.: Washington Agricultural Experiment Station, Washington State University, 1960.

Deran, Elizabeth Y. The Successful Shopkeeper: A Study of Retailer Survival in Nine Communities. Champaign, Ill.: University of Illinois, 1963.

Etcheson, Warren W., and Robb, James F. A Study of Business Terminations. Seattle, Wash.: University of Washington, 1962.

Gort, Michael. Stability and Change in Market Shares. Small Business Administration Management Research Report. Washington, D.C.: 1963.

Hall, Laura Margaret, Knapp, John, and Winsten, Christopher. Distribution in Great Britain and North America: A Study in Structure and Productivity. London, England: Oxford University Press, 1960.

Herzog, John P. The Dynamics of Large-Scale Building. Berkeley, Calif.: University of California Press, 1963.

Holdren, Robert R. Structure of the Retail Market and the Market Behavior of Retail Units. Englewood Cliffs, N.J.: Prentice-Hall, Inc., 1960.

Holloway, Robert J. Marketing Research and Market Planning for the Small Manufacturer. (Prepared for the Small Business Administration.) Minneapolis, Minn.: University of Minnesota, 1961.

International Labor Office. Services for Small-Scale Industry. Geneva, Switzerland: 1961.

Jewkes, John, Sawers, David, and Stillerman, Richard. The Sources of Invention. London, England: Macmillan Co., 1961.

Kaplan, A. D. H. Small Business: Its Place and Problems. New York, N.Y.: McGraw-Hill, 1948.

Kursh, Harry. The Franchise Boom. Englewood Cliffs, N.J.: Prentice-Hall, Inc., 1962.

Lanzilotti, Robert F. Pricing Policies and Practices of Small Manufacturers in Washington. Pullman, Wash.: Washington State University Press, 1962.

Lawyer, Kenneth. Small Business Success: Operating and Executive Characteristics. (Prepared for the Small Business Administration.) Cleveland, Ohio: Western Reserve University, 1963.

_____, et al. Study of the Origin and Operating Characteristics of Successful Metalworking Plants in Ohio. Cleveland, Ohio: Western Reserve University, 1962.

Lewis, Edwin H., and Hancock, Robert S. The Franchise System of Distribution. Minneapolis, Minn.: University of Minnesota, 1963.

Lewis, Jerry L. Identification and Evaluation of Problems and Needs of Small Manufacturing Management. Atlanta, Ga.: Engineering Experiment Station, Georgia Institute of Technology, 1961.

Lumer, Wilfred. Small Business at the Crossroads. Washington, D.C.: The Public Affairs Institute, 1956.

Maisel, Sherman. Housebuilding in Transition. Berkeley, Calif.: University of California Press, 1953.

Marting, Elizabeth (Editor). Management for the Smaller Company. New York, N.Y.: American Management Association, Inc., 1959.

Massel, Mark S. Competition and Monopoly. Washington, D.C.: The Brookings Institution, 1962.

Morgan, Howard E. Retail Market Structure and Economic Growth. (Doctoral Dissertation.) Berkeley, Calif.: University of California, 1963.

Mueller, Willard F., and Garoian, Leon. Changes in the Market Structure of Grocery Retailing. Madison, Wisc.: University of Wisconsin Press, 1961.

National Bureau of Economic Research. Business Concentration and Price Policy. Princeton, N.J.: Princeton University Press, 1955.

National Planning Association. Projections of the Number of Firms by Industry and by State for 1963, 1966, 1970 & 1976. Regional Economic Projections Series, Report No. 64-I and Statistical Appendix. Washington, D.C.: April, 1964.

National Planning Association. National Economic Projections to 1974. Report No. 64-3. Washington, D.C.: July, 1964.

New York State Department of Labor. Economic Effects of Minimum Wages: The New York Retail Trade Order of 1957-1958. Albany, N.Y.: 1964.

Omps, James Ray. Differences and Similarities Among Small Businessmen—A Survey of Four Populations. (Doctoral Dissertation.) Pittsburgh, Pa.: University of Pittsburgh, 1961.

Phillips, Joseph D. Little Business in the American Economy. Urbana, Ill.: University of Illinois Press, 1958.

Proceedings of the Pittsburgh Business Institute. Business Failure—Its Causes and Prevention. Pittsburgh, Pa.: University of Pittsburgh, 1957.

Proxmire, William. Can Small Business Survive? Chicago, Ill.: Henry Regnery Company, 1964.

Rees, Albert. Interpreting the Labor Market. Madison, Wisc.: University of Wisconsin, Industrial Relations Research Association, Publication No. 9, 1952.

Rehberg, Wallace A. and Cook, Hugh L. Cooperative Arrangements Among Small Processors. Small Business Administration Management Research Report. Washington, D.C.: June, 1963.

San Diego State College. A Study of the Problems of Small Electronics Manufacturing Companies in Southern California. Prepared for the Small Business Administration. San Diego, Calif.: San Diego State College, February, 1962.

Schwartz, David J. The Franchise System for Establishing Independent Retail Outlets. Savannah, Ga.: Georgia State College, Bureau of Business and Economic Research, Research Paper No. 14, August, 1959.

Seiden, Morton H. The Quality of Trade Credit. New York, N.Y.: National Bureau of Economic Research, Occasional Paper 87, 1964.

Seltzer, George. Small Business and Union-Wide Bargaining. Minneapolis, Minn.: University of Minnesota, 1962.

Steckler, H. O. Profitability and Size of Firm. Berkeley, Calif.: University of California Press, 1963.

Thompson, Woody. An Analysis of Environmental and Managerial Factors in the Success or Failure of Small Manufacturing Enterprise. Iowa City, Iowa: Bureau of Business and Economic Research, September, 1963.

U.S. Chamber of Commerce. Small Business: Its Role and Its Problems. Washington, D.C.: U.S. Chamber of Commerce, 1962.

Vatter, H. G. Small Enterprise and Oligopoly: A Study of the Butter, Flour, Automobile and Glass Container Industries. Corvallis, Oregon: Oregon State College Press, 1955.

Weiss, E. B. Death of the Independent Retailer. New York, N.Y.: Doyle Dane Bernbach, Inc., 1963.

Wright, Richard W. Collective Bargaining Problems of Smaller Employers. Houston, Tex.: Proceedings of Southwest Area Conference on Industrial Relations, 1957.

Yocum, James C. A Selected Bibliography of Business. (Published Literature with Information of Value to Small Business.) Columbus, Ohio: Ohio State University.

Zimmer, Basil C. Rebuilding Cities: The Effects of Displacement and Relocation on Small Business. Chicago, Ill.: Quadrangle Books, 1964.

PERIODICALS

Practical Builder (November, 1964).

"Concessionaire: Unseen Discounter," Printers' Ink, Vol. 281 (November 2, 1962).

"It's Wise to Franchise," Dun's Review and Modern Industry (March, 1962).

"Problems and Opportunities of Small Business," Iowa Business Digest, Vol. 30 (Winter, 1959).

"Problems and Opportunities of Small Business-II," Iowa Business Digest, Vol. 31 (1960).

"Small Business," Law and Contemporary Problems, Vol. XXIV (Winter, 1959).

"Task Force for Equal Opportunities," Modern Franchising (January-February, 1965).

"The Inter-Industry Structure of the United States: A Report on the 1958 Input-Output Study," Survey of Current Business, Vol. 44 (November, 1964).

Adams, Walter. "The Regulatory Commissions and Small Business," Law and Contemporary Problems, Vol. XXIV (Winter, 1959).

Adelman, Irma G. "A Stochastic Analysis of the Size Distribution of Firms," Journal of the American Statistical Association, Vol. 53 (December, 1958).

Alexander, S. S. "The Effect of Size of Manufacturing Corporations on the Distribution of Rate of Return," Review of Economics and Statistics (1949).

Brown, Leo C. "Impact of Unions in Small Plants," Monthly Labor Review (July, 1956).

Buckley, Noel. "Fortunes in Franchising," Dun's Review and Modern Industry (April, 1964).

Churchill, Betty C. "Age and Life Expectancy of Business Firms," Survey of Current Business (December, 1955).

_____. "Rise in the Business Population," Survey of Current Business (May, 1959).

_____. "Size of Business Firms," Survey of Current Business (September, 1959).

Conopa, Leonard J. "What Is Meant By Franchise Selling?," Journal of Marketing (April, 1963).

Hall, William P. "Franchising—New Scope for an Old Technique," Harvard Business Review, Vol. 42 (January-February, 1964).

Hesmer, Arnold W. "Small Manufacturing Enterprises," Harvard Business Review (November-December, 1957).

Keith, Gordon. "The Impact of Taxation on Small Business," Law and Contemporary Problems, Vol. XXIV (Winter, 1959).

Kessler, Daniel. "Discount Retailing and Leased Departments," Financial Analysts Journal, Vol. 19 (May-June, 1963).

Kinnard, William N., and Malinowski, Zenon S. "The Metal Service Industry—A Case Study of a Satellite Industry," American Machinist (1960).

Laloine, Marcel. "Small-Scale Industry in the Modern Economy," International Labor Review, Vol. LXXXIV (October, 1961).

Levenson, Harold. "Pattern Bargaining: A Case Study of the Automobile Workers," The Quarterly Journal of Economics (May, 1960).

McConnell, Joseph L. "Corporate Earnings by Size of Firm," Survey of Current Business (May, 1945).

_____. "1942 Corporate Profits by Size of Firm," Survey of Current Business (January, 1946).

Murphy, Kathryn. "Builders of New One Family Houses, 1955-1956," Construction Review (August-September, 1958).

Rosenbluth, Gideon. "The Trend in Concentration and Its Implications for Small Business," Law and Contemporary Problems, Vol. XXIV (Winter, 1959).

Sakura, Itasu, and Nakamura, Takafusa. "Size of Business in Japanese Interindustry Relations, 1951-1955," Bulletin of the Oxford University Institute of Economics and Statistics, Vol. 26 (August, 1964).

Seltzer, George. "The United Steelworkers and Unionwide Bargaining," Monthly Labor Review (February, 1961).

Stigler, George. "The Economies of Scale," Journal of Law and Economics (October, 1958).

_____. "The Division of Labor Is Limited by the Extent of the Market," Journal of Political Economy, Vol. 59 (June, 1951).

Young, A. A. "Increasing Returns and Economic Progress," The Economic Journal, Vol. 38 (December, 1928).

GOVERNMENT PUBLICATIONS

Federal Reserve System. Financing Small Business. Parts 1 and 2. Report to the Committees on Banking and Currency and the Select Committees on Small Business of the United States Congress, 85th Cong., 2nd Sess. Washington, D.C.: April 11, 1958.

Internal Revenue Service. Depreciation Guidelines and Rules. No. 456. Washington, D.C.: July, 1962.

National Science Foundation. Bibliography on the Economic and Social Implications of Scientific Research and Development. Washington, D.C.: Office of Special Studies, No. 41, July, 1959.

National Science Foundation. Proceedings, Conference on Research and Development and Its Impact on the Economy. No. 36. Washington, D.C.: May 20, 1958.

Small Business Administration. 1962 Annual Report to the President and Congress. Washington, D.C.: Government Printing Office.

_____. 1963 Annual Report to the President and Congress. Washington, D.C.: Government Printing Office.

_____. 1964 Annual Report to the President and Congress. Washington, D.C.: Government Printing Office.

_____. A Survey of Federal Government Publications of Interest to Small Business. Washington, D.C.: Government Printing Office, 1962.

_____. A Survey of University Business and Economic Research Projects, 1959-1963. Washington, D.C.: Government Printing Office, April, 1963.

_____. How Urban Renewal Projects Affect Small Business. Management Research Summary by William N. Kinnard, Jr., and Zenon S. Malinowski. Washington, D.C.: January, 1961.

_____. The Effect of Tight Money on Small Business Financing. Providence, R.I.: Management Research Report Series, June, 1963.

_____. The Financial Gap—Real or Imaginary? Denver, Colo.: University of Denver, Denver Research Institute, Management Research Report Series, 1962.

_____. Opportunities for Smaller Manufacturers. Washington, D.C.: Government Printing Office, June, 1963.

_____. Small Business and Government Research and Development. Washington, D.C.: Government Printing Office, 1962.

_____. Studies in the Factor Markets for Small Business Firms. Des Moines, Iowa: Iowa State University, Management Research Report Series, 1964.

Temporary National Economic Committee. Problems of Small Business, TNEC Monograph No. 17. Washington, D.C.: 1941.

U.S. Bureau of the Census. Annual Survey of Manufactures. Acquisitions and Disposals of Manufacturing Facilities: 1959-1962. Part 1. Washington, D.C.: Government Printing Office, 1965.

_____. Concentration Ratios In Manufacturing Industry: 1958. Parts I and II. Washington, D.C.: Government Printing Office, 1962.

U.S. Cabinet Committee on Small Business. Progress Report of the Cabinet Committee on Small Business. Washington, D.C.: August 7, 1956.

_____. Second Progress Report of the Cabinet Committee on Small Business. Washington, D.C.: December 31, 1958.

U.S. Congress, House. Select Committee on Small Business. Alleged Coercive and Discriminatory Practices Against Retail Gasoline Operators. Report No. 1423. 84th Cong., 1st Sess. Washington, D.C.: Government Printing Office, July 26, 1955.

_____. Select Committee on Small Business. Advertising Opportunities for Small Business in Television and Radio. Report No. 2576. 87th Cong., 1st Sess. Washington, D.C.: Government Printing Office, January 3, 1963.

_____. Select Committee on Small Business. Final Report of the House Select Committee on Small Business. 86th Cong. Washington, D.C.: Government Printing Office, December 27, 1960.

_____. Select Committee on Small Business. Final Report of the House Select Committee on Small Business. 87th Cong. Washington, D.C.: Government Printing Office, January 3, 1963.

_____. Select Committee on Small Business. Mergers and Superconcentration. Committee Print, 87th Cong. Washington, D.C.: Government Printing Office, November 8, 1962.

_____. Select Committee on Small Business. Small Business in the Aluminum Industry. Report No. 2232. 86th Cong., 2nd Sess. Washington, D.C.: Government Printing Office, December 22, 1960.

_____. Select Committee on Small Business. Small Business Problems in the Dairy Industry. Report No. 2231. 86th Cong., 2nd Sess. Washington, D.C.: Government Printing Office, December 22, 1960.

_____. Select Committee on Small Business. Small Business Problems in Food Distribution. Report No. 2234. 86th Cong., 2nd Sess. Washington, D.C.: Government Printing Office, December 27, 1960.

_____. Select Committee on Small Business. Small Business Problems in the Petroleum Industry. Report No. 2233. 86th Cong., 2nd Sess. Washington, D.C.: Government Printing Office, December 22, 1960.

_____. Select Committee on Small Business. Status of Small Business in Retail Trade (1948-1958). Committee Print, 86th Cong., 2nd Sess. Washington, D.C.: Government Printing Office, December 16, 1960.

U.S. Congress, Senate. Select Committee on Small Business. Eleventh Annual Report of the Senate Select Committee on Small Business. 87th Cong., 1st Sess. Washington, D.C.: Government Printing Office, February 16, 1961.

_____. Select Committee on Small Business. Twelfth Annual Report of the Senate Select Committee on Small Business. 87th Cong., 2nd Sess. Washington, D.C.: Government Printing Office, May 15, 1962.

_____. Select Committee on Small Business. Thirteenth Annual Report of the Senate Select Committee on Small Business. 88th Cong., 1st Sess. Washington, D.C.: Government Printing Office, April 2, 1963.

_____. Select Committee on Small Business. Government Competition with Business: Refrigerated Warehousing. Report No. 1948. 86th Cong., 2nd Sess. Washington, D.C.: Government Printing Office, December 30, 1960.

_____. Select Committee on Small Business. Small Business Manpower Problems. Hearings. 82nd Cong., 1st Sess. Washington, D.C.: Government Printing Office, March, 1951.

_____. Select Committee on Small Business. Small Business Participation in Defense Subcontracting. Report No. 716. 86th Cong., 1st Sess. Washington, D.C.: Government Printing Office, August 13, 1959.

_____. Select Committee on Small Business. State Taxation on Interstate Commerce. Report No. 453. 86th Cong., 1st Sess. Washington, D.C.: Government Printing Office, June 30, 1959.

_____. Select Committee on Small Business. The Impact of Suburban Shopping Centers on Independent Retailers. Report No. 1016. 86th Cong., 1st Sess. Washington, D.C.: Government Printing Office, January 5, 1960.

_____. Select Committee on Small Business. The Right to Buy. Committee Print, 86th Cong., 1st Sess. Washington, D.C.: Government Printing Office, February, 1959.

_____. Subcommittee on Antitrust and Monopoly of the Committee on the Judiciary. Distribution Problems Affecting Small Business. Part 1, "Franchising Agreements." Hearings. 89th Cong., 1st Sess. Washington, D.C.: Government Printing Office, March, 1965.

_____. Subcommittee on Patents, Trademarks, and Copyrights of the Senate Judiciary Committee. An Economic Review of the Patent System. Report No. 118. 89th Cong., 1st Sess. Washington, D.C.: Government Printing Office, March 10, 1965.

U.S. Department of Commerce. Area Redevelopment Administration. Central Business Districts and Their Metropolitan Areas; Geographic Shifts in Retail Sales, 1948-1954. Washington, D.C.: Government Printing Office, Area Trend Series 1. November, 1957.

U.S. Employment Service. Bureau of Employment Security. Unemployment Experience of Small and Large Firms. No. 195. Washington, D.C.: 1961.

White House Committee on Small Business. Progress Report to the President. Washington, D.C.: Government Printing Office, June, 1962.

_____. Small Business in the American Economy. Washington, D.C.: Government Printing Office, May, 1962.

_____. Why Help Small Business? Washington, D.C.: Government Printing Office, October, 1961.

ABOUT THE AUTHOR

Edward D. Hollander, Vice President of Robert R. Nathan Associates, Inc., has been a practicing economist in Washington for thirty years. His work has ranged over a wide field, from pioneer research in the nature of local labor markets to industrial investment in developing countries. He served as economist to the U.S. Employment Service, the War Manpower Commission, the Bureau of Labor Statistics, and the President's Council of Economic Advisors. He was for five years the "custodian" of the government's price statistics, including the Consumers Price Index. Before joining Nathan Associates in 1960, he was National Director of Americans for Democratic Action. In his present post he has done work for various agencies of the United States and several foreign governments, for leading corporations, and for trade unions. He is the author of many articles and reviews on economics.